CHRISTIAN FREEDOM IN A
PERMISSIVE SOCIETY

Books by JOHN A. T. ROBINSON
Published by THE WESTMINSTER PRESS

Christian Freedom in a Permissive Society

The New Reformation?

Christian Morals Today

Liturgy Coming to Life

Honest to God

On Being the Church in the World

JOHN A. T. ROBINSON

Christian Freedom in a Permissive Society

THE WESTMINSTER PRESS
Philadelphia

© SCM Press Ltd 1970

ISBN 0-664-24887-X

Library of Congress Catalog Card No. 75-110149

PUBLISHED BY THE WESTMINSTER PRESS®
PHILADELPHIA, PENNSYLVANIA

PRINTED IN THE UNITED STATES OF AMERICA

In memory of
JAMES A. PIKE
seeker and contender for freedom and truth
who died tragically the week this book was finished
Quaesivit arcana deserti: videt dei

(adapted from the inscription on the
Scott Polar Institute, Cambridge)

CONTENTS

INTRODUCTION

In 1960 I published a collection of essays under the title *On Being the Church in the World*. It garnered some of the things which (with one early exception) I had written 'on the side' as articles, lectures and sermons during the nineteen-fifties, when my main work lay in being a New Testament lecturer in Cambridge and the dean of a college chapel. This collection performs a similar function for the sixties, a period during which my main work has consisted of trying to combine being a radical theologian and a bishop in South London.

The selection of the pieces in this book was originally suggested by a request from the SCM Press to republish, in more permanent and substantial form, with other material, my lectures on *Christian Morals Today*, which had appeared as an SCM Broadsheet in 1964 and were now out of print. I chose the title *Christian Freedom in a Permissive Society* because, from the time that it served as a chapter heading in *Honest to God*, 'the new morality' has been, as a household phrase, equated with 'the permissive society' and all that it stands for. But my plea was in fact for a criterion of response and responsibility more rather than less searching than that of the old code morality. Most of these essays explore from one angle or another the authentic meaning of Christian freedom, both in the world and in the church.

I have nowhere attempted to define 'Christian freedom' – or, for that matter, 'the permissive society'. I think it was C. E. M. Joad, expounding Immanuel Kant (one of the greats in this field) who observed that freedom literally does not bear thinking about. Try to net it in the categories of discursive knowledge, let alone capture it in a verbal definition, and it slips through your fingers, and you end up, as deterministic philosophies do, by concluding that it does not exist. All I can do is to seek to identify it by association, by the cluster of ideas whose company it keeps. Let me try to do that first for the permissive society and then for Christian freedom.

Permissiveness – what does it suggest both to those who like and to those who dislike it? Freedom from interference or control, doing your own thing, love, laxity, licence, promiscuity – and in terms of verbs, swinging, sliding, eroding, condoning.

Christian freedom, on the other hand, has its ambience, both in the New Testament and outside it, in a very different language world – that of freedom *for* self and others and God. Its concomitants are truth, grace, love, service, responsibility, wholeness, authenticity, authority (the freedom which Jesus had that comes from going direct to source), maturity, sonship, coming of age, self-possession.

At first sight there appears no common ground (except in the highly ambiguous word 'love'). Indeed, is not the one the enemy and the opposite of the other? Yet to say this would be a serious over-simplification. For what Augustine called the lesser freedom, freedom to choose for yourself, is a precondition of the greater freedom, the freedom which comes of having chosen. And above all the antithesis suggests that Christian freedom is to be guarded by denying or going back on the permissive society. But this reaction, currently epitomized in Christopher Booker's study *The Neophiliacs*, I regard as a greater danger in the long run than anything in the permissive society itself. For the permissive society, with all its risks and puerilities, is, I believe, related to Christian freedom as adolescence is to adulthood. There is no guarantee that we shall succeed in moving forward to maturity. But we shall certainly not find it merely by deploring recent developments and going back.

A book has lately appeared by Patrick Goldring called *The Broiler-house Society*. It is a new version of the U and Non-U game. Conforming, processed, broiler-house persons are B. Non-broiler-house, 'free' persons are Non-B. One of the identity tests is who they have their morals conditioned by. These are:

B	Non-B
The Bishop of Woolwich	The Pope
The Beatles	Mrs Mary Whitehouse
Vanessa Redgrave	Cliff Richard
Edna O'Brien	Lady Dartmouth
Abortion Law Reform Association	Malcolm Muggeridge
Brigid Brophy	Sir Cyril Osborne, MP

I am flattered and honoured to be leading such a team. I am also honoured to be opposing the other team. For they are the revisionists and the reversionists (though I am sorry for Cliff Richard in this company). But the interesting thing is that, viewed from the 'right', the permissive society appears to be identical with the broiler-house society. So much for the freedom it brings! Yet simply to equate the two and still more to equate those of us in the left-hand column both with each other and with it scarcely reveals profound discernment or discrimination.

It is to explore a little deeper the differences that need to be made and the distinctiveness that attaches to the Christian perspective that this book is offered.

John A. T. Robinson

ACKNOWLEDGMENTS

The author is grateful to the following for permission to reprint previously published material:
The editor of *New Christian* for the articles on pages 82, 114, 152, 225; the editor of *The Listener* for the article on page 1; the editor of *Theology Today* for the article on page 130; the editor of *The Observer* for the article on page 241; the editor of *The Critic* for the article on page 114; the *Christian Century Foundation* for the articles on pages 225 and 232; and the Free Church of Berkeley and Morehouse-Barlow Co. for the liturgies used in Chapter 15.

1

On Being a Radical[1]

One of the interesting signs of the last few years is the way in which we are hearing again in political discussion the word 'radical'. In the period immediately after the war there was no such talk. It was a straight fight between Labour and Conservative revival. Now the situation is more subtle. It was summed up for me the other day in one of those relaxed discussions that take place after the end of a broadcast when one is off the air and can let down one's hair. The dilemma, someone said, is that one doesn't trust the integrity of the Tories and one doesn't trust the ability of Labour. And it is in such a state – whether this is fair comment or not – in which people begin casting around for a third option. Hence the talk of a 'radical' alternative.

Understandably the Liberals cash in at this point by claiming to be the residual legatees of the radical tradition. But I am not convinced that Liberalism and radicalism are so easily to be equated. I personally welcome the Liberal revival, but I do so for what I regard as radical rather than for Liberal reasons. I welcome it, not because I subscribe to the party line, but precisely because it confounds the party lines and breaks up the power blocs. And this has led me to reflect on what it really means to be a radical.

Radicalism is not a clearly defined band in the political spectrum so much as an attitude or temper of mind. True, there have been from time to time both in British and French politics specific party groups using the name Radical, located somewhere on the Liberal left. But radicalism is more of a perennial protest than a particular policy. When at certain moments of history that protest erupts, it takes

[1] A BBC broadcast, reprinted from *The Listener*, 21 February 1963.

whatever outlet is available. In 1906 it found embodiment in the programme of the Liberal Party with its curbing of the power of the Lords, old age pensions, workmen's compensation, and so on. In 1945 it was Labour, reaping the harvest of the seeds sown in 1906. But the protest cannot permanently be contained within any one party.

Radicalism represents the built-in challenge to any establishment, any institutionalism, any orthodoxy: and it is an attitude that is relevant to far more than politics. Indeed, the essence of the radical protest could be summed up in the statement of Jesus that 'the Sabbath is made for man, and not man for the Sabbath'. Persons are more important than any principles. He illustrated this by his shocking approbation of David's action in placing concern for human need, even his own, above all institutions, however secred: 'Have you not read what David did, when he was hungry, and those who were with him: how he entered the house of God and ate the bread of the Presence, which it was not lawful for him to eat nor for those who were with him, but only for the priests?'

Yet radicalism is not anarchy. It is not just being 'bolshy' or individualistic. It knows well enough that persons can be preserved, and freedom can flourish, only in a context of order. But, dissatisfied as it is simply with freedom *from*, it will always be asking: order *for* what? When the structures of order take over and persons become subservient to them, when the movement of the Spirit hardens into the institutional church, then the radical voice will begin to be heard.

What the radical stands for can perhaps be more clearly seen by comparing him with the reformist on the one hand and the revolutionary on the other.

The reformist – corresponding in political categories to the Tory reformer – continues to accept the basic proposition that man is made for the Sabbath. But, he says, the Sabbath regulations have become too rigid; we must modify them and bring them up to date. So he steals the Whig's clothes while he is bathing and lifts planks here and there from the Liberal platform. He overhauls the institution and titivates the orthodoxy; and in this way everything is enabled to go on smoothly, and the revolution is averted.

The revolutionary, on the other hand – in political terms the

Robespierres and Lenins of this world – will have nothing of the Sabbath at all. The institution is rotten, the orthodoxy stinks and enslaves. The entire structure must be changed if man is to be free.

The radical will often be found siding with the revolutionary in regarding the reformist as the real enemy. For the reformist would lull people into supposing no revolution is necessary, whereas the radical knows that for man to be made for the Sabbath is ultimately death. But equally he sees that if man is to live – rather than be subjected to a different, and perhaps deadlier, Sabbath – another revolution is required. The radical's response is to go to the roots – hence his name. It is to ask what the Sabbath is for, what human values it exists to frame, and then to try to see, at whatever cost to the institution or the orthodoxy, that it does so. Unlike the reformist, the radical is concerned constantly to subject the Sabbath to man. Yet, unlike the revolutionary, he believes in the Sabbath—for man.

This introduces another important characteristic of the radical viewpoint. Being a radical means being an 'insider', an insider to the Sabbath – as Jesus was. The revolutionary can be an 'outsider' to the structure he would see collapse: indeed, he must set himself outside it. But the radical goes to the roots of *his own* tradition. He must love it: he must weep over Jerusalem, even if he has to pronounce its doom. He must believe that the Sabbath really is valuable for man.

This means that the radical must be a man of roots. The revolutionary may be *déraciné*, but not the radical. And that is partly why in our rootless world there are so few genuine radicals. Reformism, too, requires of necessity no depth of root, merely a feel for tradition: hence it can continue to flourish where men have lost their integrity. If the Establishment can thereby be preserved, it may be expedient that one man should die for the people. For man, after all, is made for the Sabbath.

The roots of the radical, moreover, must go deep enough to provide the security from which to question, even to the fundamentals. No one can be a radical who is uncertain of his tenure – intellectually, morally, or culturally. Only the man who knows he cannot lose what the Sabbath stands for can afford to criticize it radically. Faith alone can dare to doubt – to the depths.

For the same reason a radical is necessarily a man of passion. He is jealous for the truth, the root-meaning, of what the institution has corrupted. He cannot be content to snipe from the sidelines. To be a radical means involvement, commitment. True, it means travelling light, being prepared to laugh at the institution one loves. And therefore he welcomes genuine satire and enjoys seeing the Establishment taken off. For irony is very near to faith – as it was for the Old Testament prophets. But always underneath there is a certain intensity and controlled fire. He has the salt of good humour – but the salt that savours and stings.

The radical is an 'insider' – yet always a bad party-member, an unsafe churchman. He is continually questioning the shibboleths, re-examining the orthodoxies. And he will have a disconcerting habit of finding himself closer to those whose integrity he respects than to those whose conclusions he shares.

Let me illustrate this temper of mind, not from the field of politics or religion, but of morals. For here there is a bewildering flux of orthodoxies, and many old landmarks have disappeared beneath the flood. Amid the cross-currents, the radical will find himself afloat in strange company, and yet he carries an anchor and a compass which belie the impression that he is merely drifting with the rest.

In the sphere of morals, we live in an age in which 'the Sabbath' is challenged on all sides. The law, the commandments, the standards of conventional morality, are all under fire. The established orthodoxies creak. The yoke of our fathers is too heavy to be borne.

In this situation, the reformist advocates that the Sabbath must be brought up to date. The old absolutes still remain valid : certain things are wrong, 'and nothing can make them right'. But what continue to be sins, like suicide or homosexuality, need not necessarily be crimes. Mrs Grundy can be bowed out, premium bonds and betting shops admitted, and the sanctions of fear give place to more sophisticated reasons for being moral. Yet fundamentally nothing is changed. Man is made for the Sabbath; principles take precedence over persons.

The revolutionary, on the other hand, will shed no tears for the old morality. 'Objective moral values' and their supernatural supports can happily be swept away. For the Sabbath did nothing for man anyhow, except inhibit him and burden him with feelings of guilt. Absolutes are out. Ethical relativism is the order of the day. And these modern moralities have this in common : they have taken their stand, quite correctly, against any subordination of the concrete individual personal relationship to some alien universal norm. What is right *for me* in this particular situation cannot be prescribed or deduced from some impersonal law laid up in heaven. But in the process all sense of the unconditional is lost in a sea of subjectivism, where everything goes – that is, until the Sabbath reasserts itself under the guise of Big Brother.

The radical believes with the revolutionary in 'the ethic of the situation', with nothing prescribed – *except love*, in the New Testament sense of intense personal care and concern. And this is the decisive exception. For love – utter openness to persons in all their depth and uniqueness – is the 'root' of the Sabbath. What is right is not laid down for always in 'laws which never shall be broken' : it is what love really requires of me in this particular and unrepeatable relationship. Love is the end of law precisely because it does respect persons, absolutely and unconditionally. Love alone can afford to be utterly open to the situation, or rather to the person in the situation, uniquely and for his own sake, yet without losing its direction. Really love God, really be convinced that persons matter; then, as Augustine said, you *can* do what you like.

Such an attitude to living is, as I have said, dependent upon having roots that reach very deep. For myself, I doubt if I could sustain it unless I were a Christian : for God is for me the 'depth' of love, as indeed of all reality, and it is in Christ that love is given its definition and power. But I have the utmost respect for the integrity of the radical humanist. Or perhaps it would be truer to say that, because I am a Christian, I *am* a radical humanist. For that, I believe, is the quality and direction of life to which Jesus referred when he said that the Sabbath was made for man, and when he summoned his disciples to be salt to the world.

But it would not be fair to equate the Christian outlook with the radical, to suggest that all Christians should be radicals any more than that all radicals should be Christian. For radicalism is simply *an* attitude of mind and its relevance is to some extent a matter of degree. There are some situations to which the reformist response is appropriate, others which demand the revolutionary. The radical cannot claim to have the whole truth. To remember that should help to keep him humble – for the besetting sin of the radical is self-righteousness, as complacency is of the reformist and ruthlessness of the revolutionary. Nevertheless, I believe that the radical temper is a uniquely precious element in our cultural inheritance. I have no doubt that the other two are needed – and I find myself embracing each at times. But, if I had to choose, I would rather rest my reputation, for what it is worth, on being a radical.

2

Christian Morals Today[1]

1. *Fixity and Freedom*

I tend to classify my engagements at the moment by whether they were contracted before or after the flood – the date of the flood, for archaeological purposes, being 19 March 1963.[2] For the past six months I have been in the unhappy position of working through a diary filled in large degree with commitments entered into under a very different sky. And of no engagement is this more agonizingly true than of this set of lectures. It is very definitely antediluvian. It began with an innocent letter dated nearly two years ago from your Bishop asking me to give three lectures on Christian ethics. At that time there could not have been a subject more 'cold' – unless it were the subject of 'God'! Christian ethics had long been the cinderella of theological studies, particularly in this country (though not, to its credit, in America – to which one has to go for most of the best books in English[3]). I accepted, partly because I have yet to learn how to refuse an invitation at any date you care to specify two years ahead, but also because I had a deep concern that this subject *should* be given its proper attention – even though it is not

---

[1] Lectures delivered in Liverpool Cathedral, 31 October 1963.

[2] The publication date of *Honest to God*.

[3] This, alas, still applies to the continued debate since these lectures were given: e.g., Joseph Fletcher, *Situation Ethics* and *Moral Responsibility: Situation Ethics at Work*; Harvey Cox (ed.), *The Situation Ethics Debate*; Paul Ramsey, *Deeds and Rules in Christian Ethics*; James A. Pike, *You and the New Morality*; W. Norman Pittenger, *Time for Consent?* and *Love is the Clue*; Rustum and Della Roy, *Honest Sex*; O. Sydney Barr, *The Christian New Morality*. For a good recent English contribution at a popular level, see Michael Keeling, *Morals in a Free Society* and *What is Right?*

one on which I would presume to claim any particular expertise. However, on the principle espoused by St Augustine on the Trinity, that to say something, however inadequate, is better than silence, I agreed to speak.

I need not have worried. I come before you now at a moment when silence would be golden. I would infinitely rather say nothing: indeed it is only a strong sense that keeping promises is a rather important part of Christian ethics that has prevented me begging release. For the atmosphere at the moment is still so heavily charged and so emotional – not least within the church – that almost anything one says is likely to add fuel to the flames.

The phrase 'the new morality' is bandied about in the wildest manner and has become an indiscriminate target of abuse among churchmen. It is applied to moral positions miles apart, Christian and non-Christian, and has simply come to signify invitation to sexual licence – 'the old immorality condoned', as Lord Shawcross tartly put it. And I am regarded as the author of it!

It might be worth just interjecting a historical note to restore a bit of proportion. In the first place, of course, it is not my phrase at all, but Pope Pius XII's – or rather that of the Supreme Sacred congregation of the Holy Office.[4] It had in origin nothing to do with sex, but with existentialist or 'situational' ethics. As I used it,[5] it was certainly no invitation to licence but a plea for the most searching demands of pure personal relationship as the basis of *all* moral judgements. I was not aware that I was saying in that chapter anything that would not have been familiar to anyone engaged in the teaching of New Testament ethics. In fact, despite the usual tendency of publicity to fasten only on questions of morals, this chapter provoked virtually no controversy at all for three months (witness the reviews in *The Honest to God Debate*). It was then caught up in the scandal of Mr Profumo, who was alleged to have followed my advice (though not interestingly enough on sex but on lying[6] – which

[4] 2 February 1956.
[5] *Honest to God*, chapter 6.
[6] In a letter to the *Church Times* of 14 June 1963, Mr George Goyder wrote: 'Mr Profumo can hardly be blamed if it should be found in fact that he had taken the Bishop's advice. Having read the chapter on "the New Morality" in *Honest to God* several times, I would ask your readers whether there can be any other possible construction of what the Bishop

shows how everything in English discussion gets channelled sooner
or later into one groove). Since then everybody seems to have been
ready to charge in from prepared positions, usually on the basis of
newspaper reports; and such training in Christian ethics as we have
given does not appear very notably to have equipped otherwise
responsible persons in the elementary courtesy of finding out what
a man has said before weighing into him.

But I deliberately do not want to become involved in these lectures
in the cut and thrust of current controversies. Indeed, I want to
try to undercut them. For so much of the inability to 'hear' what
the other side is saying comes from unexamined presuppositions
that go very deep, and they are reinforced psychologically by insecuri-
ties and fears which make us unreceptive and aggressive when on the
defensive. So, at the expense of being fundamental rather than
quotable, I want to try to dig down a bit, to see if we cannot establish some mutual confidence and common ground.

What I have called our 'prepared positions' look as if they rest
on widely different bases and we distrust anything that appears
to threaten or undermine them. But in ethics the 'new commandment' turns out so frequently after all to be the 'old commandment,
which you had from the beginning' (I John 2.7). Each generation
instinctively suspects the one before it or the one after it of saying
something different. It may indeed be saying it in different ways, but
if we can learn to trust each other in depth then 'fundamentalists'
and 'radicals' may come to realize that these terms represent but
different metaphors for those whose common concern is to go to the
foundations and roots. If both can accept that, then each may learn
to respect and interpret the other where they diverge.

At present, however, we seem to be drifting into a dangerous and
reactionary situation, in which liberality is in peril of being squeezed
out. What is worrying about so much of the response to new ideas

there says, other than that in the Bishop's opinion Mr Profumo may
have been right in lying to the House of Commons in order to save his
family.' It surely should not be necessary to say that to save one's family
from the hurt of knowing one has betrayed them has nothing to do
with the searching claims of Christian love. Such love demands that
we should lay ourselves open to be accepted and forgiven for what we are.
To 'save' a person one loves from the opportunities of making this response
could not be described in Christian terms as 'necessary for the sake of love'.

in the air is its undiscriminating character. There is, for instance, what Christopher Driver of *The Guardian* has called 'the Chatterley syndrome'. This just opposes everything to do with 'that book' and anything that can be lumped with it by way of cause or effect. It seems entirely incapable of appreciating that responsible people who defended it, in church and university, did so not because they were commending adultery (any more than when they defend Shakespeare or Shaw) but because of the sheer hypocrisy and injustice of a society which, while abetting on every hand the trivialization, commercialization and prostitution of sex, singled out for prosecution *the* creative artist of our generation whose whole life was a passionate protest against this.

Or again, take the undiscriminating way in which, as I said just now, the phrase 'the new morality' has overnight become a slogan – relieving those who use it of any need to distinguish between widely different views, or even to know what they are. Nothing, I judge, could be more injurious to the church than this kind of blanket thinking. For if the response of churchmen is simply undifferentiating reaction, then it will merely confirm the image which we are constantly told is a caricature. And this would be tragic in an age in which Christian *discernment* was never more necessary.

I am deeply concerned that at this juncture there shall be a real attempt at mutual understanding and communication. For I believe that the 'old' and the 'new' morality (in any sense in which I am interested in defending the latter) correspond with two starting-points, two approaches to certain perennial polarities in Christian ethics, which are not antithetical but complementary. Each begins from one point without denying the other, but each tends to suspect the other of abandoning what it holds most vital because it reaches it from the other end. Inevitably, in any genuine dialectic, one will come as a corrective to the other, and at a particular time or for particular persons one may seem the way in to the exclusion of the other. But one cannot be true simply at the expense of the other. In seeking to interpret what I believe 'the new morality' is trying to say, I hope I shall not guy or deny the old – and all I would merely ask for in return is a similar sympathy and understanding. Moreover, I would urge its detractors to credit that what motivates 'the new morality' is not an appeasing concession to the spirit of the age but an equal passion for Christian truth and integrity. For unless this is accepted and trusted there can be no advance.

In these three lectures I should like to examine three of these polarities in Christian ethics – or really it is the same polarity under three aspects. The first is that between the elements of fixity and freedom, the second that between law and love, and the third that between authority and experience.

The first of these is thrust upon our attention at once by the overall title chosen for these lectures – 'Christian Morals *Today*'. In what sense are Christian morals today different from Christian morals yesterday? Is there not an abiding Christian ethic? Indeed, can you have a new morality any more than a new gospel? The tension here is between the constant and the variable, the absolute and the relative, the eternal and the changing.

Now, neither side in the present controversy, I would submit, has any interest in denying either of these complementary elements. But to the 'old morality' it *looks* as if the advocates of the 'new' are betraying the absolutes of right and wrong and selling out to relativism. What I would seek to urge is that they have equally vital concern for the element of the unconditional but are placing it elsewhere.

The 'old morality', if we may continue to use these terms as counters, locates the unchanging element in Christian ethics in the *content* of the commands. There are certain things which are always right, and others which are always wrong. These absolute Christian standards are eternally valid, and remain unchanging in the midst of relativity and flux. And it is this body of moral teaching, grounded firmly on the laws of God and the commands of Christ, which the church exists to proclaim to every succeeding generation of men and women, whether they hear or whether they forbear.

Christian ethics, according to this view, is concerned with *applying* these standards to the changing situation. It starts from the fact that the Bible supplies a God-given 'net' or framework of conduct for human affairs. The task of moral theologians is to keep the net in repair for each generation, and to define its mesh more closely as new occasions teach new duties. There is nothing static about this conception of Christian ethics as long as it does not become ossified, and casuistry at its best has conserved fluidity with fixity in a way that compels the reluctant admiration even of those who most distrust it. But I will not expound this view further. It is the one in which most churchmen have been nurtured, whether catholic or protestant (the difference of emphasis being that the catholic tends to maintain the net by narrowing its mesh, the protestant by strengthening its cords). Rather, I should like to move on to try to interpret the opposite approach, which is in greater need of exposition.

This view starts from the other end. It does not in the least deny the need for a 'net'. No person, no society, can continue or cohere for any length of time without an accepted ethic, just as ordered life becomes impossible without a recognized legal system or a stable economy. And the Christian least of all can be disinterested in these fields. The more he loves his neighbour, the more he will be concerned that the whole *ethos* of his society – cultural, moral, legal, political and economic – is a good one, preserving personality rather than destroying it.

But he will also be the first to confess that Christ does not supply him with an ethical code, any more than he supplies him with a legal system, or a polity, or an economy. For it was not Jesus's purpose to provide any of these. Jesus's purpose was to call men to the Kingdom of God, to subject everything in their lives to the overriding, unconditional claim of God's utterly gracious yet utterly demanding rule of righteous love. And men could not acknowledge this claim without accepting the constraint of the same sacrificial, unselfregarding *agape* over all their relations with each other. It is this undeviating claim, this inescapable constraint, which provides the profoundly constant element in the distinctively Christian response in every age or clime. For it produces in Christians, however different or diversely placed, a direction, a cast, a style of life, which is recognizably and gloriously the same. Yet *what* precisely they must do to embody this claim will differ with every century, group and individual.

The elements of fixity and freedom are still there, but the mixture is different; and it allows those who start from the second end to treat freely what, for those starting from the other end, seems most fixed. And this not unnaturally is disconcerting. To those for whom the element of constancy in Christian ethics is content-centred, changes in what the Church teaches in different generations or cultures must inevitably appear as a threat – or as a mark of imperfection. Ideally it always ought to be the same for all men everywhere. If this is not, it is a sign of unhappy division or of moral decline. And the answer in either case is a reiterated affirmation of the abiding, unchanging values.

But realism, if nothing else, requires us to admit that the situation is not so simple. The *content* of Christian morals has over the centuries changed considerably. And I believe that Christians should not have too troubled a conscience about the fact that *what* their brethren have believed to be right and wrong in different situations has differed, and still differs, widely.

We can see this most clearly in the field of economics and politics. There is no one Christian social ethic, and even a short remove in space or time reveals how limited is the reference even of the greatest moral theology. I yield to no one in my admiration for Dr Emil Brunner's contribution to Christian ethical thinking, yet in his *Justice and Social Order* an Englishman cannot help seeing peeping out from time to time the presuppositions of a conservative, somewhat complacent *petit-bourgeois* Swiss society (and no doubt he would regard our meagre contribution to ethics, if ever he reads it, as equally insular). Or how subtly dated now seem the social ethics of the Christendom Group of the 1930s, or even of William Temple. This is not to detract in the least from their work. It is simply to recognize that there is no such thing as *a* Christian ethic. The raw material of an ethic is provided by the ethos of a society or a century or a group. Times change and even Christians change with them. And, as we are increasingly aware in our complex technocratic society, our moral judgements have to take into account all kinds of purely technical assessments in which Christians have no peculiar or unchanging wisdom.

As long as we allow for this relativistic factor in all ethical judgements and are not afraid to face it as Christians, then we shall not be unduly disturbed by our divergent moralities. Of course, a sizable part of these differences must always be put down to slowness, stupidity and sin – and the blindness of Christians to such issues as slavery, war and race is, in retrospect, frightening. Nevertheless, the changes and differences are, I think, far more to be attributed not to moral enlightenment (if any) but to the fact that the non-moral factors are constantly shifting, so that what were not moral issues become so, and *vice versa*. A problem is redefined or its scale is altered until a difference in degree becomes a difference in kind. A change in biological or psychological knowledge may modify our understanding of the responsibility involved, or a shift in the structure of society may cause the same behaviour (such as gambling or drink) to have very different social consequences.

As examples of this process one could cite the obvious differences and changes in our ethic of war – recent non-moral factors rendering obsolescent, I should judge, most of the straight pacifist and anti-pacifist debate, as well as the classical doctrine of the just war. Or take the matter of capital punishment. Even within my brief ministry, the whole temper of the church's pronouncement has changed, and I cannot believe that this is due simply to the fact that bishops were more enlightened in 1962 than they were in 1948. Our understanding of punishment has been subtly modified by non-theological factors, so that we can see the enormity of some of the things we do, as previously men came to see the enormity of burning witches. The church's attitude to homosexuality has undergone the same transition – and one day perhaps the Government will catch up on both these issues.[7]

Again, our changed moral attitude to suicide is another obvious example – though the 1959 report, published by the Church Information Office, *Ought Suicide to be a Crime?*, will, I trust, appear in retrospect like the 1930 Lambeth Conference findings on birth-control: only the first tentative steps of the Church of England into the twentieth century. For it sees suicide, I believe, in less than realistic terms, primarily as sin of the individual against society rather than the other way round, and it resorts to the frightening category of 'normal' as opposed to compulsive suicide.

As yet a further example, I should like to see the whole question ventilated as to whether the church is in any way permanently wedded to the 'marital offence' as the sole ground of divorce. If a marriage-relationship is dead, is it not more honest to say so, rather than drive one party into adultery to prove it? I am glad Canon T. R. Milford raises this in his recent pamphlet, *Talking of Sex*,[8] and

[7] It has.
[8] *Frontier Pamphlet*, No. 1. See also D. A. Rhymes, *No New Morality*, pp. 6of.

I am convinced the churches will live to regret the statement issued in opposition to Mr Leo Abse's Matrimonial Causes Bill (1963), which would have permitted divorce after seven years' continuous separation even if no 'offence' had been committed.[9]

I cite these issues as examples of how the Christian ethic is not an unchanging body of fixed teaching. But though many would admit this in the field of social ethics (while regarding it perhaps as a weakness), they would vociferously repudiate such a conclusion in the field of personal ethics. Here there are some things that are always wrong and nothing can make them right. But where do we draw the line even here? The power of modern drugs, for instance, to keep old people artificially alive has posed some odd problems to the most fundamental commandment underlying the Hippocratic oath.

I would, of course, be the first to agree that there are a whole class of actions – like stealing, lying, killing, committing adultery – which are so fundamentally destructive of human relationships that no differences of century or society can change their character. But this does not, of course, mean that stealing or lying can in certain circumstances never be right. All Christians would admit that they could be. And the church has traditionally said that some killing – in a just war, for instance, or in capital punishment – is right. Moreover, one has to define what is killing (as in the illustration I have just given from terminal illness) or what is adultery. There are, for instance, grave moral factors to be weighed in A.I.D. (artificial insemination donor) but I for one could never say unequivocally that it is simply adultery and therefore always wrong.

The truth is that in theology, as in every other science, there is a gradual progression from 'pure' to 'applied'. The closer one keeps to the 'pure' centre the more confidently one can talk of 'timeless' truths, but the more specific the application the more variable the conclusions. In Christian ethics the only pure statement is the command to love: every other injunction depends on it and is an

[9] Since this was first written there has been an extraordinary shift. The Report of the Archbishops' Commission, *Putting Asunder: a Divorce Law for Contemporary Society*, recommended the death of the marriage relationship as the sole ground of divorce. With modifications, accepted by the church, this has now been translated into law. It is a good instance of how an established church can still lead public opinion.

explication or application of it. There are some things of which one may say that it is so inconceivable that they could ever be an expression of love – like cruelty to children or rape – that one could say without much fear of contradiction that for Christians they are always wrong. But they are so persistently wrong *for that reason*. There is not a whole list of things which are 'sins' *per se*. That is not to say that there are not working rules which for practical purposes one can lay down as guides to Christian conduct – the catechetical passages in the New Testament epistles give plentiful examples. But in the last resort – St Paul makes it as clear as Jesus – these various commandments are comprehended under the one command of love and based upon it. Apart from this there are no unbreakable rules.

Now let us recognize that we should all like to escape this conclusion. Life would be very much simpler if as a Christian one could say that certain things are in all conditions and for all persons always and absolutely wrong (though it's odd, as Alasdair MacIntyre has remarked,[10] how the unbreakable rules propounded by Christians always turn out to be about sex and not about war). But if I am to retain my integrity as a New Testament scholar I cannot say this. For the Christian ethic does not consist of these sorts of invariable propositions. Of course, we all need rules – the church needs rules – and from the very first there has been a tendency, to which I shall return in the next lecture, to turn the teaching of Jesus into a set of rules, a fixed code of conduct, valid for all Christians at all times. But Christ does not supply such a code, any more than he wrote a book.

Yet having insisted on this, one must at once go on to say that Christians wrote books and, within the New Testament, both in the Epistles and Gospels, we find blocks of ethical material, constructing out of the teaching and example of Christ patterns of conduct for the life of the church. And the form critics of the New Testament have reminded us that all the teaching of Jesus comes to us through the net, as it were, of the earliest Christian communities. There is nothing surprising or disturbing about this – what we learn of Christ in every age comes to us through the net of the teaching church. But what comes to us also judges that net, and enables us to recognize that what may be the embodiment of the divine com-

---

[10] 'God and the Theologians', *Encounter*, September 1963, p. 10.

mand in one generation can be its distortion in the next. This process, indeed, of judgement and supersession, is one which we can see going on right through the Bible, in the Old Testament as well as the New. Each society needs its own moral net. And the church of the old covenant helped to provide a series of these for the societies in which it lived, refining it successively in what we know as the Deuteronomic laws, the Priestly Code and the Rabbinic *torah*. And at once we see the process starting again in the Epistles of the New Testament. Because the implications of the Gospel are so immediate for the relationships between master and slave, male and female, Jew and Gentile, the early Christians are impelled without delay to start constructing a code for governing their connections 'in the Lord'.

But it is essential to recognize that these are human constructions, arrived at under the purifying and correcting guidance of the living Word and Spirit of God. Jesus does not hesitate to question the legislation even of Moses himself or to refer to the ethical constructions of Judaism as 'the traditions of men'. Similarly, for our moral guidance on slavery, the place of women in society, or the Jewish problem, the codes of the first century are only of limited value – while the church's first effort at canon law (Acts 15.22-9), emanating from the council of Jerusalem, was a dead letter almost as soon as the ink was dry (a thought that revives me occasionally in Convocation!).

A moral net there must be in any society. Christians must be to the fore in every age in helping to construct it, criticize it, and keep it in repair. But there is no one ethical system that can claim to be Christian. For that is not where the constancy resides. The old morality rightly calls us to remember the eternal foundation in which all human life is grounded: 'I the Lord do not change; therefore you, O sons of Jacob, are not consumed.' (Malachi 3.6). It becomes brittle and unbending (and therefore weak precisely where it thinks it is strong) when it transfers the constancy of the foundation to the permanence of the superstructure.

My plea is that Christians must not fear flux or be alarmed at the relativity of all ethics to the ethos of their day. We assume too readily that God is in the rocks but not in the rapids. We identify him instinctively with what is permanent and see ourselves commissioned to stand for the changeless in a welter of chaos not of his making. But that is a Greek assumption, not a biblical one. We are not here as Christians with changeless principles to apply to an alien process. God is *in* the history, addressing us and claiming us through it. And what he says will not always be the same as he said to our fathers. Yet if we are his sheep, we shall recognize his voice. For Jesus Christ is the same, yesterday and today and for ever. And yet the Jesus we serve is the Christ come and coming in the flesh. He wills to become incarnate in, the contemporary of, every generation; and this means that the Christ of today is not simply the Christ of yesterday. We must embrace the relativities and not fear them. For the assurance we are given is not of a fixity impervious to change, but of a faithfulness promising purchase over it.

2. Law and Love

I began my first lecture by saying that my intention in these three talks was to make an attempt at interpretation between the 'new morality' and the 'old' in what threatens to be a disruptive debate. My contention was that each side must try to understand and respect the other as having an equally genuine concern for the fundamentals on which Christian morality rests. For as I see it, they represent complementary rather than contradictory attempts to do justice to the great polarities which lie at the heart of the Christian ethic. Each tends to start at the opposite end from the other, and each for a particular individual, or even perhaps for a whole generation or culture, may be the way in. But we cannot afford to allow a sterile antagonism to develop between them: for each needs the emphasis that the other would cherish.

I began by examining the tension that must always exist in Christian ethics between the fixed and the free, the constant and the changing, the absolute and the relative. I suggested that what the new morality is saying to us – and I believe it needs urgently to be said at a time of unprecedentedly rapid social change – is that we need not fear flux: God is in the rapids as much as in the rocks, and as Christians we are free to swim and not merely to cling.

I want now to look at another aspect of the same polarity, the tension between law and love. No Christian can ever set these in bare opposition or fix on one to the exclusion of the other as the sole focus of his ethic. Nevertheless, there is a real danger, as recent sparring has shown, of one side supposing that the other *is* denying what it has no intention of denying – because it begins from a different point. And, before we know where we are, the charges of legalism and antinomianism[11] are being flung around. Phrases like 'the Cambridge antinomians' and 'South Bank religion', with both of which brushes I have the misfortune to be tarred, are further evidence of the slogan-thinking with which the press has fed us this year.

But let us try to see what both sides are saying, coolly and charitably. The old morality (if we must use these labels) starts from the position, which no one could deny, that the Old Testament comes before the New. In that sense law has a priority over love. Love builds on law, and it comes to fulfil it, not to destroy it: the second mile of love presupposes the first mile of law. And still for each man, as for the Jew, law is the tutor which brings him to Christ; and even when he is 'no longer under law but under grace' (Rom. 6.14), he is still 'under the law of Christ' (I Cor. 9.21). St Paul continued to insist that 'the law is in itself holy, and the commandment is holy and just and good' (Rom. 7.12) and repudiated with vehemence the charge of antinomianism. The Christian can never say that he is beyond or outside the sphere of law. He needs it for himself, he needs it for his children, and he certainly cannot dispense with it for his society.

I hope that is a reasonably fair statement of the case, and there is certainly nothing in it that I would want to dispute or deny.[12] I would ask only that the opposite emphasis, the other way into the same complex of Christian truth, should be heard with equal understanding, and not simply dismissed for the 'damage' it can do.

This other way in starts from facts which equally the old morality would not wish to deny. It insists that the Christian *is* under grace and not under law. It insists that the law is but a tutor, and not

[11] '*Antinomian:* one who maintains that the moral law is not binding on Christians' (*The Concise Oxford Dictionary*).
[12] See further G. A. F. Knight, *Law and Grace*, and A. R. Vidler, *Christ's Strange Work*.

the master. It insists on the priority of love in every sense except the temporal – for on this one command is made by Jesus to hang all the law and the prophets (Matt. 22.40). The second mile in fact changes the basis of the first *as law*. Love is the end, the *telos*, of the law not merely in the sense that it fulfils it (which it does), but in the sense that it abolishes it as the foundation of the Christian's relationship whether with God or man. Of that the Epistle to the Galatians can leave us in no possible doubt: it is the *magna charta* of the freedom with which Christ has set us free. Moreover, any ethic which is genuinely Christian will always be open to the charge of destroying the law and the temple. Jesus faced this charge; Stephen faced it; Paul faced it. Antinomianism is always a false accusation, but I should immediately suspect there was something sub-Christian about an ethic which did not provoke it. I am honoured that my university is now associated with it!

With all this, as I said, I imagine no Christian would want to disagree. All that the so-called 'new morality' is concerned to do (and, of course, it is nothing new at all) is to start from this emphasis, without denying the other. The heat in fact is generated on both sides by the denial of the denials – which really is rather absurd, though it may be unavoidable. For, in fact, each side, in order to safeguard the element which it feels is being threatened, can easily be led into statements which destroy the proper tension. Inevitably one will be provoked into utterance by distortions or one-sidednesses which it detects in the other, and this will lead to counter-charges. But rather than get caught up in this, let me try to say simply what those of us who are dubbed antinomians are seeking to get accepted. And since one of the charges is that we are primarily impelled by the pressures of the contemporary situation and by the impossibility of 'selling' the old medicine because it is unpalatable, I should like to base what I have to say firmly on the compulsions, as I see them, of the New Testament. I believe that the Holy Spirit *is* speaking to the churches through the deadness for so many today of the old morality. But he is speaking as always, if it is really he, by taking the things of Christ and showing them to us. What he is showing us is what we have heard from the beginning. There is fundamentally nothing new here, though as always, when we feel its power, it is fresh and explosive.

I suppose that what we want to see accepted as a starting-point is that the Christian ethic can never honestly be presented as law plus love or law qualified by love, *however much safer that would be*. There is no question that law has its place, but that place is at the boundaries, and not at the centre. This was the revolution which Jesus represented for the Pharisees. His teaching was not a reform of legalism but its death. As Professor Paul Ramsey puts it in his *Basic Christian Ethics*,[13]

> A faithful Jew stayed as close as possible to the observance of the law even when he had to depart from it. Jesus stayed as close as possible to the fulfilment of human need, no matter how wide of the . . . law this led him.

And this, of course, as the Scribes well saw, is terribly dangerous doctrine. It needs its checks and balances : it cries aloud for letters to the church press ! And to these 'the new morality' says : 'Fine – as long as no attempt is made to substitute law again for love as the centre and basis of it all.' But that is what precisely it sees happening, in exhortations, however earnest, to return to 'the Law of God' as the foundation of the moral life.

But this is what the New Testament refuses to allow us to do. As Professor C. F. D. Moule has recently insisted, writing on 'The New Testament and Moral Decisions',[14] the ten commandments are not the basis of Christian morals, on which an ethic of love goes on to build. Of course, the commandment of love does not contradict or relieve men of the obligations of the old : it summarizes them and immeasurably deepens them. In fact, in the Sermon on the Mount Jesus takes several of them, pointing through them and beyond to the unconditional claim of God upon man and of person upon person they were framed to safeguard. But in the process he destroys them *as law*. As St Paul said subsequently, 'Against such things there is no law' (Gal. 5.23) – nor, he might have added, for them either.

Jesus's treatment of the fourth commandment, for instance, effectively subjected it to the concern for which it stood, in a way that undercut it as law altogether. 'The sabbath was made for man, not

[13] P. 56.
[14] *The Expository Times*, September 1963, pp. 370f.

man for the sabbath' (Mark 2.27). It was no longer a case of starting from the law and reforming it to make it more loving. As Paul Ramsey comments again,[15]

> Jewish ethics was a legalism modified by humanitarianism, which meant also a humanitarianism *limited* by legalism.

Jesus's ethic was unconditional neighbour-love, and weighed against that the law was not less important, but nothing. Against the counter-claim of 'doing good', the Sabbath regulation, as regulation, was null : law and love were simply incommensurable. But, in terms of the real purpose of the Sabbath rest, Jesus claimed that his actions were not its negation but in the profoundest sense its fulfilment :

> Ought not this woman, a daughter of Abraham whom Satan bound for eighteen years, to be loosed from this bond on the Sabbath day? (Luke 13.16).

Not in the case of every commandment might there be such a clash of practice, but the principle was the same. More often it was a matter of simply 'going beyond' – though so far beyond that one was soon quite outside the sphere of law. Equal retribution – an eye for an eye and a tooth for a tooth – can be translated into law; but turning the other cheek can never be. Murder and adultery can be codified as crimes; but to make anger and lust indistinguishable from them is not only bad law : it is to destroy the basis on which law operates. Equally, to say that all divorce involves adultery is not a new law : indeed, it is palpably untrue as law, and merely confuses perfectly valid legal distinctions. Rather, it is to say to the Jew, who regarded adultery heinously (at any rate by a woman) but divorce lightly, that all divorce is morally (though not legally) adultery. If you divorce your wife because you do not like her face, you are making her, morally, an adultress. And this perhaps explains the famous Matthean exception, 'except for the reason of forni-cation' (Matt. 5.32). For as she has already committed fornication, you cannot, technically, *make her* an adultress : she has already made herself one. This clause may be a rather heavy-handed addition to clear Jesus of what would otherwise be a logical contradiction.

[15] *Op. cit.*, pp. 56f.

But the clause is also a reminder that this particular injunction in the Sermon on the Mount has been treated by the old morality entirely differently from any other.[16] To go no further afield, Jesus makes two closely parallel statements about adultery – first, that all *lust* is the moral equivalent of adultery, and, secondly, that all *divorce* is the moral equivalent of adultery. No one has thought to treat the former as legislation; but the latter has been erected into a law (of the church if not of the state) according to which divorce is always and in every circumstance wrong (or, if Matthew's exception is allowed, in all circumstances but one).

Now it is important to recognize a distinction at this point. Clearly, both a Christian society and Christians on behalf of the society they live in must have rules and laws about divorce. There is nothing wrong in that. They are bound, as I said in my last lecture, to construct a moral net. And within the pages of the New Testament we see that happening in the Christian community (at this stage, of course, only for its own members). The web is very embryonic, and we are not in a position now to reconstruct it. It is interesting to note, however, that at three points at least the rulings for which we have evidence certainly would not have passed the Convocations of Canterbury and York!

If, as is usually assumed, Matthew's exception (whatever may have been its original intention) reflects the discipline at least of his church, then divorce was presumably definitely permitted to Christians on grounds of adultery. But the official mind of the Church of England is different. Again, St Paul allows Christians on conversion to divorce their pagan partners if these will not live with them (I Cor. 7.12-16) – hardly a permission to commend itself today either to church or state. (In fact, Paul's permissiveness must be contrasted with the regulations in the Old Israel where under Ezra the Lord's people were *compelled* to divorce their pagan spouses (Ezra 10).) And, finally, the practice of cohabitation in celibacy of which we get such a fascinating keyhole glimpse in I Cor. 7.36-38, so far from being a better thing than marriage, as St Paul asserts, would today be regarded as a cause of scandal – certainly in a vicarage!

All this is but a way of saying that while the church, like the

[16] Cf. H. Oppenheimer, *Law and Love*, pp. 72f.; D. A. Rhymes, *op. cit.*, pp. 56–71.

state, must have its rules, they are certainly not timeless. Indeed, even today the main branches of Christendom, Roman, Orthodox, Anglican and Protestant, all have different divorce disciplines. Nevertheless, some law there must be, and we should not be surprised to see the teaching of Jesus formed within the New Testament into material for that sort of code, both for catechetical and disciplinary purposes.

What is quite different is to regard the teaching of Jesus itself as a code, to see it as laying down for all Christians at all times, or indeed for any Christians at any time, what they should do. It is the encroachment of this view upon the thinking of the church that 'the new morality' would see as more dangerous *in the long run* than the hazards of its opposite. Not that it underrates the hazards of its opposite, and I certainly appreciate the harm done by irresponsible talk (though most of it, I believe, has in fact come from irresponsible and alarmist reporting). The deeper one's concern for persons, the more effectively one wants to see love buttressed by law. But if law usurps the place of love because it is safer, that safety is the safety of death.

I said earlier that Jesus's purpose was not to provide an ethical code but to proclaim the Kingdom. And this is the point to which I believe we must constantly return if we are to evaluate his moral teaching aright. For in his sayings we find a concentration upon the vertical of the divine imperative which would otherwise be inexplicable. This is not, I am convinced, as Albert Schweitzer thought, for a reason external to the ethic itself – because Jesus reckoned the horizontal line of history to be so short as to be negligible. Rather, it is because the claim of the Kingdom, of men's 'ultimate' relation to God, was the 'one thing' with which at all costs they must come to terms if they were to find life. To that all else was secondary. And this explains why Jesus did not concern himself, as any moralist must, to adjust or reconcile the conflicting claims which any real-life situation raises: 'Who made me a judge or divider over you?' (Luke 12.14). His concern, rather, was to uncover with piercing clarity what the unconditional claim of the divine *agape* meant when translated into love of neighbour. Consequently, his illustrations always isolate the single neighbour, confronting a man in this sharply focused instance with the total demand of love, *as though no other claims existed.* To quote Paul Ramsey again,

> Not only all prudential calculation of consequences likely to fall upon the agent himself, but likewise all sober regard for the future performance of his responsibility for family and friends, duties towards oneself and *fixed* duties to others, both alike were jettisoned from view.[17]
>
> We may scarcely be able to perform it in regard to a single . . . neighbour. It was never intended to be performed as a new law for the adjudication of neighbour-claims in a settled society. Nevertheless, 'we are able to be transformed by it'.[18]

Regarded as a code of conduct, prescribing what one should do in any situation, the Sermon on the Mount is quite impracticable. It tears the individual loose from any horizontal nexus. In any given precept it rules out of consideration all other interests, all other values, all other people. It never weighs conflicting responsibilities or helps a man to balance his commitments. It simply says, 'Give to him who asks you', with never a thought for the stewardship of money. It commends the widow who throws 'all her livelihood' into the treasury without asking who is to support her henceforth. It does not take into account – it does not reckon to take into account – the fact that there is always more than one neighbour to be considered, always more than one claim upon one. For instance, while I was preparing the material for this lecture, someone asked to borrow one of the chief books I was consulting. 'From him that would borrow turn not away.' Your claim or his? I did not in fact lend it to him.

Even the complete waiver of one's *own* rights is seldom a simple matter affecting oneself alone. As Brunner puts it, 'If, as a good Christian', an industrial worker 'is willing to endure the injustice of his position – so far as *he* is concerned – for the sake of others he ought not to do so'.[19] And even more, what of other people's

---

[17] *Op. cit.*, p. 39.
[18] *Op. cit.*, p. 43. The last phrase is cited from M. Dibelius, *The Sermon on the Mount*, p. 135.
[19] *The Divine Imperative*, p. 431.

rights? What should the Good Samaritan have done if he had arrived on the scene while the robbers were still at work? Should he have tried to beat them off – or should he himself have passed by on the other side? Or, to quote Professor John Knox,

> Jesus said: 'If any man smite you on one cheek turn the other also'; here the situation is relatively simple – you and your enemy. But Jesus did not say: 'If any man smite one of your friends, lead him to another friend that he may smite *him* also.' Not only is it clear that Jesus could have made no such statement, but also that he would have felt that the involvement of the interests of others . . . transformed the whole moral situation and placed our obligations with respect to it in a radically different light.[20]

What 'A' does in that situation Jesus simply does not say, though from the parable of the two debtors,

> it is evident that love which for itself claims nothing may yet for the sake of another claim everything, that anyone who unhesitatingly and times without number renounces 'what is due' when he himself alone bears the brunt of such a decision may nevertheless turn full circle and insist with utter severity upon full payment of what is due to others.[21]

But the point is that the moral teaching of Jesus is not to be judged by its adequacy as a code. As such it is entirely inadequate. It says nothing whatever, for instance, about how a man is to pursue what after all occupies most of our waking hours (when we are not being slapped in the face or asked for our coat), namely, our everyday work, or how one is to be a good citizen and a positive and useful member of society.

It is worth noting that, in contrast, the earliest summaries of the Church's ethical teaching *are* concerned with precisely such things. They are practical injunctions on the basic Christian virtues in a pagan world – about how Christians are to get on with their

[20] *The Christian Answer* (ed. H. P. van Dusen), p. 173; quoted P. Ramsey, *op. cit.*, pp. 170f. See further J. Knox, *The Ethics of Jesus in the Teaching of the Church*.

[21] P. Ramsey, *op. cit.*, p. 171.

work and support others, the responsibilities of wives, children, slaves
and masters, the Christian's reputation in a non-Christian society,
his duties towards the government authorities, etc.[22] Many of the
injunctions (for instance, about not returning evil for evil, loving
one's enemies, etc.) are in fact clearly dependent on Jesus's teaching.
But the maxims of the Christian catechesis are, as Dodd points
out,[23] in contrast with the Sermon on the Mount, practical rules
for day to day living. No one has suggested they are impracticable,
though they are clearly only possible 'in the Lord'.

Now it is significant that we do not at once feel that the ethics
of the Epistles are a great let-down after the ethics of the Gospels,
that there is a disastrous drop in spiritual temperature, such as
we often sense in the sub-apostolic age. There is nothing more
astringent than the moral tone of I Peter. But if the Sermon on the
Mount were intended to be a perfectionist ethic which Christians
were to fulfil literally at that level or not at all, then the ethics of
the Epistles, prescribing for Christians very much involved in the
compromises of the world, would appear an intolerable accommodation.

I think this comparison and contrast helps us to see more clearly
what the sayings of the Sermon on the Mount are meant to be.
They are, as it were, the *parables* of the Kingdom in its moral
claims, flashlight pictures of the uncompromising demand which
the Kingdom must make upon anyone who would respond to it.
As Dodd puts it,

> The ethical teaching of the Gospels . . . is not so much detailed
> guidance for conduct in this or that situation as a disclosure of
> the absolute standards which alone are relevant when the King-
> dom of God is upon us. These standards, however, are not defined
> in general and abstract propositions, but in dramatic pictures of
> action in concrete situations; and they are intended to appeal to
> the conscience by way of the imagination.[24]

The Sermon on the Mount does not say in advance, 'This is what
in every circumstance or in any circumstance you must do', but,

[22] Cf. C. H. Dodd, *Gospel and Law*, pp. 18–22.
[23] *Op. cit.*, pp. 51f.
[24] *Op. cit.*, pp. 60f.

'This is the kind of thing which at any moment, if you are open to the absolute unconditional will of God, the Kingdom, or love, can demand of you'. It is 'relevant' not because it solves our moral problems (that is the kind of relevance we are always asking for), but because 'it transforms us' (and that is the kind of relevance we don't ask for, but which in the end is what changes us and the world). In other words, Jesus's purpose was not to order the fruit, but to 'make the tree good' (Matt. 12.33).

Brunner, I think, put the matter very well when he wrote, now over thirty years ago:

The Commandments – both of the Decalogue and of the Sermon on the Mount – are God-given paradigms of love. . . . Each of these commandments does two things: it makes the one Command concrete, and it also abstracts from the concrete reality. It stands, so to speak, in the centre between the infinitely varied reality of life and the unity of the divine will of love. It shows us what love would mean in this or that more or less 'special' but still general case, and it commands us to do this very thing. Then is this the beginning of casuistry? No. It is of the utmost importance to note how unsystematic, how 'casual', are all the commandments which are scattered through the New Testament. Here and there a plunge is made into human life and something is 'lifted out' in order to make the meaning of love clearer. But the matter which has been singled out is not held fast as such; it is allowed to slip back again. Care is taken to avoid the possibility of even *apparently* dividing life up into various 'cases' or 'instances' which, as such, could be prejudged in a legalistic manner. None of the commandments in the Sermon on the Mount are to be understood as laws, so that those who hear them can go away feeling, 'Now I know what I have to do!' If it were possible to read the Sermon on the Mount in this legalistic way the absolute and binding character of the Divine Command would be weakened, the sense of responsibility for decision would be broken, the electrical charge of the moral moment would be released.[25]

That is the note which 'the new morality' is concerned shall not

[25] *The Divine Imperative*, pp. 135f.

be muffled if the distinctively Christian contribution is to be heard. It is not, I believe, an irresponsible or an immoral witness. And to insist on this at the centre is not to doubt the necessity of law in its place. The plea for the priority of love fully recognizes the obligation upon Christians in each generation to help fashion and frame the moral net which will best preserve the body and soul of *their society*. We have seen the Christians of the first century seeking to relate the command of *agape* to their bewildering new environments, Jewish and Gentile, in the Graeco-Roman world. From their obedience we can indeed learn what the Spirit may be saying to the churches of the twentieth century. But we shall not do it by treating their formulations (any more than those of the Old Testament) as a permanent code – nor by attempting to solve the perplexities of our generation with 'the Bible says'.

For, not only do 'new occasions teach new duties', but 'time makes ancient good uncouth'. This is most obvious in the case of social ethics – if only because the early Christians were simply responsible *to* power, whereas we are also responsible *for* power – and what power! But it is true also at the most personal level. Take, for instance, the much debated problem as to the *limits* of pre-marital sex for engaged couples (and I deliberately put it in this way). You can only find things of very dubious relevance in the Old Testament – where the social context was so utterly different and offences against women were primarily offences against property.[26] Jesus really said nothing about it (his only recorded utterances are about adultery or prostitutes). And to settle what is a responsible and searching question by a sweeping reference to 'fornication and all uncleanness' (Eph. 5.3) is to invite the recent comment of an atheist that these questions are too serious to be discussed at the religious level. For *porneia*, as its derivation implies, always has associations in the New Testament with promiscuity, if not with prostitution. It 'describes the relationship in which one of the parties can be purchased as a thing is purchased and discarded as a thing is discarded and where there is neither union of, nor respect for, personality'.[27] To assume that this applies to all

---

[26] See on this whole question the excellent discussion in W. G. Cole, *Sex and Love in the Bible*, chapter 7.

[27] W. Barclay, *Flesh and Spirit*, p. 24.

relationships between engaged couples is to prejudge the moral issue in an utterly insensitive and irresponsible way.

This is not in the least to suggest, as proponents of the 'old morality' have been quick to do, that advocates of the 'new' treat this matter laxly or lightly. Some, indeed, to whom this label has been attached have done so, and I would want strongly to dissociate myself from them. I believe the nexus between bed and board, between sex and the sharing of life at every level, must be pressed as strongly as ever by those who really care for persons as persons. But these are the kind of terms in which I believe this question has to be sorted out for young people – as, for instance, Hugh Montefiore does in his admirable and conservative essay in *God, Sex and War*.[28] And, of course, I recognize to the full that all of us, especially young people, have to have working rules. But my point is that when these are questioned, as they are being questioned, the Christian is driven back to base them not on law ('Fornication is always wrong') but on love, on what a deep concern for persons as whole persons, in their entire social context, really requires.

Finally, the account I have given of Jesus's moral teaching will, I hope, help to dispel what is surely one of the most superficial charges against 'the new morality', namely, that it is individualistic. The 'paradigms of love' do indeed frequently strip the individual down to the bare relationship between him and God and the single neighbour. But that is not because Jesus or anyone else thinks that a system of ethics can be based on such deliberate abstraction. Moral decisions are inextricably corporate and social – and even more so for the Christian, since, as Professor Moule has reminded us in that same article in *The Expository Times*,[29] the normal 'organ of perception through which the Holy Spirit may be expected to speak with distinctively moral guidance is the *Christian worshipping community listening critically*'. Moreover, most of those who are concerned with the emphases now labelled 'the new morality' have come to them through engagement in the problems of *social* ethics. This is particularly true of Professor Joseph Fletcher,[30] whom I

[28] 'Personal Relations before Marriage' (ed. D. M. MacKinnon), pp. 61–98.
[29] September 1963, pp. 372f.
[30] Cf. e.g. his *Morals and Medicine*.

quoted extensively in *Honest to God*. Indeed, I would humbly suggest that those who suppose we are advocating an individualistic love ethic which has no place for law or justice might refer to the essay on 'Power' in my earlier book, *On Being the Church in the World*.[31]

The 'new morality' is not in the least interested in jettisoning law, or in weakening what in *Honest to God*[32] I called 'the dykes of love in a loveless world'. But it also believes it has something to say which is not an incitement to immorality or to individualism, and for which it craves a quiet, unemotional and honest hearing.

3. *Authority and Experience*

In the two previous lectures I tried to show how the differences between the 'old morality' and the 'new' which have been so blown up and distended of late are in fact differences of 'way in' to certain abiding realities in Christian ethics which *all* Christians have an equal interest in holding in their proper, creative tension. However it may look, neither side wishes to destroy that tension, and I believe that the precipitate reactions and hasty accusations are the result largely of misunderstanding and anxiety. I hope I have shown that in the case of the polarity between the fixed and the free in Christian morals and of that between law and love. I now want to look at what is really but a further aspect of the same duality – the tension between authority and experience.

Another way of putting this would be to state it as the difference between the transcendent and the immanent in Christian ethics, or between the deductive approach and the inductive. As before, there should be no suggestion on either side that one pole is being emphasized to the exclusion of the other. But each side starts from the opposite end and the apparent difference can be great and disconcerting.

The so-called 'old morality' begins from the deductive, the transcendent and the authoritative. It stresses the revealed character of the Christian moral standard, grounded as it is in the sanctions of Sinai and 'the clear teaching of our Lord'. It starts from Christian

[31] Revised ed. (Pelican Books), pp. 53–71.
[32] P. 110.

principles which are valid 'without respect of persons', and then applies them to particular situations and persons. Each case must be considered on its own merits and classical deductive morality takes this very seriously. It is unfortunate that 'casuistry' should have got such a bad name, because it suggests that the principle can only be made to fit the case by a certain stretching and manipulation. That is not so, and the morality of authority seeks to do full justice to the facts of experience. But, as its teaching for instance on divorce illustrates, the principles come first: persons, with all the compassion in the world, have to be brought under them. There is nothing necessarily authoritarian about this approach – that is a sub-Christian distortion of it. But, because it misses any clear-cut authority in the other approach, it easily detects in this loss a betrayal of the revealed, transcendental character of Christian morals.

But there is no such intention from the other side to betray this dimension. It simply starts from the other way in. It begins from the fact that, like all modern sciences, theology – and moral theology in particular—is to be understood as an inductive discipline. It proceeds empirically, from the particular to the general. It starts from persons rather than principles, from experienced relationships rather than revealed commandments. But it does not disclaim authority. Indeed, modern science has a high authority. Its authority, however, is of a different kind.

In the same way it is not opposed to revelation. On the contrary, it would claim that it authenticates itself as revelation in the distinctively Christian manner disclosed in the Incarnation. There the divine is known not deductively but inductively. It enters through the stable door of ordinary human history and everyday experience. Jesus wills to come among men claiming the authority simply of 'the Son of Man', carrying no celestial credentials or heavenly certificates. It was only in man and as man that his contemporaries could see the Son of God. The process of revelation was an inductive one, implying a gradual opening of blind eyes. And yet Jesus spoke with authority, as never man did. It was not an external, 'heteronomous' authority, which relied on authentication from other sources: it was 'not as the scribes', who pointed away from themselves to the 'authorities'. But neither was it the authority of the autonomous man, who speaks and acts in his own right. 'I can do nothing on my own authority', Jesus insisted; 'if I bear witness to myself, my testimony is not true' (John 5.30f.). Rather, it was what Tillich describes as the authority of 'theonomy', of the divine light shining through his words and his works, authenticating him and his mission. It was an authority which his contemporaries were quick to sense: 'He taught them as one who had authority' (Mark 1.22). 'What is this? A new teaching! With authority he commands even the unclean spirits and they obey him' (Mark 1.27). And it is significant how a modern exponent of Jesus's words seems to have caught the ear of a generation tired of authorities by dwelling on their intrinsic, almost mystical, authority. I refer to Werner Pelz's *God is no More.*

In the great debate about authority in John 10 Jesus refers to this self-authenticating quality of his words and actions to those who recognize his voice: 'My deeds done in my Father's name are my credentials, but because you are not sheep of my flock you do not believe. My own sheep listen to my voice; I know them and they follow me' (John 10.27, NEB). And three chapters later St John lays bare the character of this authority in the unforgettable scene when 'Jesus, well aware that the Father had entrusted everything to him, and that he had come from God and was going back to God, rose from table, laid aside his garments, and taking a towel, tied it round him' (John 13.3ff.). 'You call me "Master and Lord",' he says, 'and rightly so, for that is what I am', but the sole authority he would exercise is that of *agape*, of 'the man for others'. Again, when New Testament critics have seen in the parable of the Sheep and the Goats (despite its single unsupported source in Matthew) the unmistakable authenticity of the Master,[33] it is because they recognize in it this same note – silencing every other consideration – that the one thing that finally counts is treating persons as persons with unconditional seriousness. This is the authority of him who was Lord of the Sabbath, because he dared to say that the Sabbath was made for man.

This is the end from which the 'new morality' begins. And I suspect it is probably the way in for Christian ethics today. For

[33] Cf. the references in my article 'The "Parable" of the Sheep and the Goats', *Twelve New Testament Studies*, p. 76.

I believe that an ethic will have authority for most of our generation only as it *is* empirical and starts firmly from the data of actual personal relationships as they now are. In testimony, let me quote a recent contributor to *New Society*. Writing on 5 September 1963, under the title 'Moral Education in Chaos', Mr James Hemming said this:

> One element of the moral change of the recent era is that the morality of obedience to external absolutes is being replaced by the morality of involvement and discovery. . . . We are faced today not by problems of application in terms of absolutes but by problems of searching out a satisfactory moral basis for personal life and for society. The search itself is the moral education. It is a search in which all young people are ready to join, as anyone who has worked with adolescent groups is well aware.

And earlier in the same article he had said:

> The debate is not primarily one of science versus religion but of discovering common ground. At a time when theologians are rejecting outmoded God concepts, scientists are penetrating so far into the nature of things that the mystery of existence becomes more baffling than ever. Indeed, Christian orthodoxy is now beginning to look like an oversimplification of something infinitely more mysterious and complex than our fathers supposed. What could be more evocative and exciting than participating in this debate?

What are we to make as Christians of this frank plea for a morality of involvement and discovery? I believe we should welcome it. Indeed, I would go further and accept what he says later:

> Both scientific and religious viewpoints are, today, humanisms. But neither is only a humanism because each accepts that existence itself is shrouded in mystery. Each may wish to put something different into that mystery. One group may put a personal God there; the other a question mark; but each will agree that the ground of man's being is humanism within a mystery. This is the new starting-point. It provides a vast unifying common ground in terms of human involvement and purpose.

I agree with him – not necessarily with where he ends (I do not know whether he could call himself a Christian),[34] but with where he begins. I believe Christians must walk this road with humility, and with reverence before the mystery, learning obedience, like their Master, through the suffering of experience – with no sense that they have the answers all the time. There is nothing more patronizing or repugnant to modern man than the slightest suggestion of intellectual or moral slumming. Christians cannot say, 'Yes, we will join you in your search – but, of course, though you don't know it, we know in advance that certain things are always wrong.' If they think they know this, then they had much better wait for the others at the end of the road. One of the most immoral forms of Christology is that to which the Alexandrian Fathers were prone, which supposed that Jesus, though he may have appeared to learn obedience through the ordinary processes of experience, could at any moment, as it were, switch on his divine consciousness. Nothing short of complete incarnation and total identification is a tolerable interpretation of the New Testament evidence. Similarly, if Christians are differently placed from their non-Christian neighbours it is not because they are provided with the answers from outside or beyond the moral struggle. It is because in and through the involvement they believe they have also the mind of Christ and the participation of the Spirit.

To accept the inductive point of departure is not for the Christian to be reduced simply to an ethic of discovery or to a self-contained humanism. For he believes that in the search is not only the moral education but the revelation. The Word of the Lord is there – yet not as proposition but as presence. The Christian goes in trusting that God is always in the situation before him and that if and as he genuinely gives himself in love he will find God – for God is love – and if he serves people, with no thought for them but as persons, he will discover himself ministering to Christ. This trust is not the clear-cut confidence of a deductive ethic. Inevitably it *appears* less authoritative than that of 'the old morality'. But for some of us it may be the only assurance we have, and I am not

[34] He has since elaborated his own position in his book *Individual Morality*, in which he argues for a 'passionate, life affirming humanism' with a religious fervour and openness.

convinced the New Testament necessarily promises more. It is more tentative. Yet it carries a conviction of its own, the authority of honesty and integrity. Men respect Christians whom they genuinely believe to be men of like passions with themselves, and yet in whom they can discern, however dimly, the likeness of *the* Son of Man. At any rate I know there is nowhere else where I can be. I certainly have no temptation to strike a posture or to be there just to 'get alongside people'.

On some moral issues, it would seem, Christians from both camps would readily accept that this is the position in which they find themselves. In the fearful problems of modern war, for instance, the advocates of 'the old morality' would not appear to be marked out from their brethren by any noticeable deductive certainty. Unless they are absolute pacifists, abjuring all use of power, they recognize as much as anyone that there are no unbreakable rules which decide for them in this sphere. It means going in and wrestling through the problems posed by the terrible responsibility inherent in this power. Some will see the best way to prevent the holocaust to lie along the road of unilateral renunciation, others along the road of multilateral control. I am convinced that through this agony the Spirit is deepening our education and increasing our sensibilities – and probably bringing us closer together. But I certainly see no sign of authoritative pronouncements such as Christians claim to be able to make with confidence in other fields.

Or consider again the question of capital punishment, on which I touched in my first lecture. On the whole, it would be true to say in the past that the 'old morality' stood solidly behind the death penalty. I have had many letters quoting as decisive Exodus 21.12: 'Whoever strikes a man so that he dies shall be put to death.' (They do not go on to quote the parallel command five verses later: 'Whosoever curses his father or mother shall be put to death'!) But what advance – if I may dare to use the word – we have made in the recent decades has almost all been forced upon us from the empirical end. It is not texts that have been quoted but figures – figures that show the futility of the penalty as a deterrent, its psychological and individual effects on society, the results of its abolition in other countries, the miscarriages of justice, etc. Our moral, psychological and social sensibilities have been quickened by a greater knowledge.

And no one seriously thinks that for Christians to be persuaded by facts to agree with what many humanists have been saying before them is to abandon belief in an ethic of revelation or to open the flood-gates to moral relativism.

The same is true of our attitude to homosexuality.[35] The notion, until recently almost universal, is now surely dying, that a responsible Christian could settle the issue by quoting texts like I Cor. 6.9, which declares outright (in the unfortunate translation of the RSV) that 'homosexuals' cannot 'inherit the Kingdom of God'. Admittedly the sheer quantity of one's letters would suggest that such ideas were far from dead – especially the letters written in blue biro on ruled paper with the more pungent words in capitals underlined three times! But in so far as there has been a shift in responsible opinion (and it is indicated by the overwhelming mass of official church support for the recommendation of the 1957 Wolfenden Report that 'homosexual behaviour between consenting adults in private should no longer be a criminal offence'[36]), it is again due to pressure from the empirical side. We have come to a much greater awareness of the facts, particularly about the causes of homosexuality and about the truly appalling social consequences of our present law (for blackmail, for suicide, and for the denial to a sizable minority of our population of any deep, free or secure personal relationships). And no one again (apart from certain organs of the national press) is seriously suggesting that those pressing for a new morality here are abetting corruption.

But somehow in heterosexual relations the situation is quite different. The slightest suggestion ·that it may be necessary to start from the other end and leave the deductive certainties (however much they may have long since failed to contain the flood) is greeted as an open invitation to immorality. But this reaction really is not good enough; and how any responsible churchman could

---

[35] See further, since this was written, W. N. Pittenger, *Time for Consent?*
[36] It was backed by the Archbishops of Canterbury and York, the Church Assembly, the Church of England Moral Welfare Council, the Roman Catholic Advisory Committee on Prostitution and Homosexual Offences, the Methodist Conference, and leaders of the Church of Scotland and the Free Churches. It was opposed by the General Assembly of the Church of Scotland and by the Salvation Army. It has since, of course, been translated into law.

have read such an invitation out of the chapter in my book – if he really *had* read it – passes my belief. Of course, the inductive approach is more dangerous. The ends are not prescribed, the answers are not settled beforehand. But this is only to say that a real *decision* is involved in any responsible moral choice.

Let me illustrate the difference of approach by reference again to the question of sex-relations before marriage. The deductive approach starts from the institution of marriage, and makes this the decisive factor. Inside marriage sex is all right, outside it it is wrong. There is a clear-cut line, and the issue for the individual is decided in advance. But in fact, even for the deductive approach, the matter is not as simple as this. For, clearly, just because it is inside marriage a sex relationship is not necessarily right. Indeed, I imagine any marriage guidance counsellor would agree that there is probably as much exploitation of sex, physical and emotional, inside marriage as outside it. But the traditional morality in fact applies a double standard. It says that within marriage one cannot presume to prescribe. What is exploitation and what is not depends upon the particular personal relationship, and it would be impertient to say from the outside that certain things were always right and others always wrong. In other words, within marriage it adopts the criteria of the inductive approach. But outside marriage these criteria are irrelevant. Right and wrong can be laid down in advance and from without: nothing in the quality of the personal relationship or situation of the individuals concerned can affect the way the decision goes.

If then one starts from this point of view, it is the marriage line which is decisive – so much so that it leads to different criteria of judgement either side of it. But the inductive point of view starts from the primacy of persons and personal relationships. It insists, to quote Howard Root's eminently sane and, I should have thought, unexceptionable lecture on 'Ethical Problems of Sex' in *God, Sex and War*,[37] that 'marriage, like the Sabbath, was made for man, not man for marriage'. But one has only to say this to be suspected of advocating laxity and immorality. In fact, it is to plead for a much more searching and demanding criterion of ethical judgement, both inside and outside marriage, than the simple application

[37] *Op cit.*, p. 45.

of an external rule. The ground on which the decision must be based is what deep Christian love for the other person as a whole person (as opposed to exploitation and enjoyment, even if mutual) really demands,[38] – and that within the total social context. Now one of the factors, indeed a major factor, in this decision is the unity I referred to before between bed and board. Outside marriage sex is bound to be the expression of less than an unreserved sharing and commitment of one person to another. It certainly cannot be guaranteed as such within marriage, but in both cases this is the moral criterion. The decisive thing in the moral judgement is not the line itself, but the presence or absence of love at the deepest level. The inductive approach rests upon the fact that at this ultimate level, in the sight of God (and here is where the Christian finds himself constrained by the distinctive revelation of *agape* in the face of Jesus Christ), persons matter more, imponderably more, than any principles. And therefore principles can never *dictate* to persons, however much they may help them (and often, indeed, save them) in their moral choices.

Exactly the same criterion will apply, on this view, to divorce. The factors to be taken into account – the wreck of the personal relationship, the children, the third parties involved, the vows, the weakening of the marriage nexus in society, etc. – all these are part of the agonizing calculation to be made. But ultimately, when love's account has been done, it must be *this* that is decisive, not something prescribed from without in advance, which robs the calculation of any point.

The difference, again, between the deductive and inductive approaches may be illustrated by the way in which changes in empirical fact are allowed to affect moral decisions. It would be widely agreed that in some areas of choice, for instance, in issues of defence or economics, purely technical changes can greatly affect not merely the application of principles but the whole direction of a Christian's moral judgement. Even in the realm of sex, the world population explosion has had this effect. It has placed the issue of birth control in an entirely new context – so much so that many would now regard the official Roman Catholic line, with its frus-

[38] Cf. the admirable discussion of this by D. A. Rhymes, *op. cit.*, pp. 23–37; and (from as far back as 1892) V. Soloviev, *The Meaning of Love*.

trating effect on United Nations' action to feed the hungry, as positively immoral.

But in sex ethics in general, Christians seem to *fear* changes of fact, as weakening the moral foundations. This in turn provokes non-Christians into embracing them as *providing* moral foundations, which, of course, they can never do: for no 'is' can of itself supply an 'ought'. Thus, we have the familiar sterile antithesis. On the one hand there are those who say that no social or physical changes can make any essential difference to moral judgements: the principles remain the same and unaffected. On the other hand, we have those (often indiscriminately identified with the 'new morality') who say that trends in our society, or the strength of sex impulses, or the widening gap between physical maturity and educational independence, are themselves reasons for changing our morals. The effect of both attitudes is to restrict the area of personal responsibility for decision. In the former case, the moral judgement is already settled beforehand: the individual has simply to choose whether to accept it. In the latter case, the issue has ceased to be debated at the moral level: the individual has merely to decide with which impulses, trends or conventions to go along.

My concern is that Christians, in love as in war, should *have* the terrible freedom with which God has endowed us, and should exercise it responsibly. They must decide *for themselves* – though this certainly does not mean that they must decide *on their own*. They should not be loaded with the burden of decision alone. Nevertheless, the church cannot take it *from* them. Nor can it honestly in the long run rely on non-moral factors to shield them from their freedom. But there has been a tendency, especially in the matter of pre-marital sex, not only to prescribe the answers, but to use hitherto unchanging facts to underwrite the anwers in such a way as to ground the decision on something less than conviction, on fear rather than freedom. In particular, there has been a heavy reliance on the risks of conception, infection and detection. And Christians could find themselves coming to have a vested interest in maintaining these conditions because they cannot trust the freedom. Would we really like to see a 100 per cent sure contraceptive available at clinics – or would we rather compel young people to chastity or to chance? Are we really determined to remove from promiscuity the risk of V.D. – as we perhaps might by making it a notifiable disease and by screening immigrants? Do we really want the furtiveness taken out of pre-marital sex – or do we prefer to keep it that way? In other words, where do we put our trust for keeping people moral? We have got to recognize that the facts – the medical facts and the social facts – may change, and change rapidly. I can only say that in the case of my own children I would much rather give them the built-in moral values to use the freedom creatively for themselves than shelter them from it. Of course, we must protect the young – but the chief target here would seem to be those who exploit their emotions and commercialize sex in a way that treats them as so much less than persons.

I am concerned that the young, like others, should genuinely be free – to decide responsibly for themselves what love at its deepest really requires *of them*. But there could hardly be anything further from that than 'free love' – which is usually neither 'love' nor 'free'.

Consider, for instance, this conversation from the film, *Room at the Top*: 'I *do* love you,' she protests; 'I would do anything for you.' 'Sure,' he retorts, 'you would do anything – except the one thing any girl would do for the man she loves.' So she succumbs – the victim of emotional blackmail.

That is not love. It is much more fear than love – fear of losing him if she doesn't. Under that sort of fear, persons are not free. And thousands of young people today are simply being played upon in this matter of sex. They cannot afford not to go along with the rest. 'Dread of being a social outcast is the main reason why teenagers have sexual intercourse before marriage', writes a girl student in *Sixth Form Opinion*.

I want a morality which frees people from that. But I know we shall not get it by simply saying 'Thou shalt not!' a bit louder. Young people today ask, 'Why?' They want a basis for morality that makes sense in terms of personal relationships. They want *honesty* in sex, as in everything else. And that is what chastity is – inside marriage or out of it. It is not just abstinence. It is honesty in sex: having physical relationships that *truthfully express* the degree of personal commitment that is there underneath.

I believe that most young people are genuinely looking for a morality that cuts deeper, is more searching and less superficial than the ready-made rules of their parents – rules honoured more in the breach than in the observance. As Sir Edward Boyle has said, 'Never has there been more serious discussion of the human love relationship than is going on today.' 'I believe young people can be brought to realize that a close personal relationship can be either the most life-enhancing and joyous, or alternatively, the most destructive thing on earth.' And in all this they desperately need help, not condemnation.

I referred earlier to the description of Christianity as 'humanism within a mystery'. It may not be adequate as a definition, but as a signpost, as a pointer to the way in, particularly for our genera-tion, I think it has much to be said for it. That, after all, is where the first disciples started, and it is an approach that makes sense to our scientifically trained world – moving from experience to authority, through the immanent to the transcendent. The Christian in treading this way with the rest of his contemporaries is not abandoning the authoritative or the transcendent. Rather, he has the double trust, born of his doctrines of Creation and of the Incarnation, that, since man is made in the image of God, a true humanism *must* lead through to the divine, and, since in the man Christ Jesus he has *the* image of the invisible God, he knows what a genuinely human existence is.

The trouble is that the traditional deductive morality so often appears to be *anti-humanist*. I am sure it is not necessarily so, but this is how it looks. The point is made by Dr Peter L. Berger, the American sociologist, in his book, *The Precarious Vision*:

A simple definition of a humanist ethic might be one which orientates its conceptions and imperatives towards men rather than institutions. Thus, a humanist ethic, such as is generally accepted in Western democracies, would hold that political institutions exist for the welfare of men. Recent history has given us ample opportunity to observe the consequences of a contrary ethic that maintains that men exist for the welfare of the state. It is one of the ironies of history (and one of the consequences of the Babylonian captivity of the Christian faith in religious forms) that Christian ethical thought has frequently found itself in the anti-humanist camp. We would suggest, from our understanding of society and of the Christian faith, that a Christian ethic will always be humanist in the sense just given.[39]

I cannot think that the old morality would disagree, but the insensitiveness with which its exponents sometimes seem to dismiss the priority of persons over principles often causes one to wince. Time and again one is made to sense that the deepest springs of compassion, the most perceptive awareness of human beings and their needs, come from the non-Christian creative artists of our time, not from its churchmen and theologians. One thinks, for instance of a film like A *Taste of Honey*, or indeed *West Side Story*. To hear such things dismissed from the pulpit, as I did the other day, as 'kitchen sink', is to understand why so many of the most sensitive men and women of our day have already voted with their feet and left our pews. They feel they must work out their own salvation, and find their own ethic – many of them with deep moral seriousness.

My plea to church people in these lectures has been to consider whether in what is dubbed the 'new morality' there may not be struggling to be born an equally honest attempt *under the Spirit* to 'perceive and know what things we ought to do'. We know we have not got it all buttoned up – and never shall have. But we are sustained by the faith that the authority is given in the experience and that through the immanent, if we are sufficiently open, we must be met by the transcendent. We cannot pretend to have the answers in advance, but, if we have the humility, we may be content to rest in the conviction with which St Paul closes the most prolonged and delicate moral discussion in the whole New Testament: 'And I *think* that I have the Spirit of God' (I Cor. 7.40).

4. *Starting from the Other End*

As an appendix to these lectures I add some material from the lectures I gave in America in May 1964, at Hartford Seminary and Cornell University, under the title 'The New Reformation?' When they came to be published the following year in England the

[39] op. cit., p. 199.

'hysterical morass' (as the *Times Literary Supplement* called it) was still such that I was advised by persons whose judgement I respected that if this section were included nothing else in the book would be 'heard'! Since it was not central to the argument, but exemplified a principle I had already illustrated from other fields, I reluctantly agreed to suppress it. Its tameness now is a measure of how in the interval the mood has changed, and I hope matured.

The principle I was arguing for[40] is that the church must be prepared to start its thinking today from two ends at once, with no guarantee that the results will meet neatly in the middle. These are: (1) the end of the traditional Christian teaching, where the questions (as in the Catechism) are the church's questions to which it waits to have its own answers returned, and (2) the end where the world asks the questions, sets the agenda, and provides the size and shape of the lump which the church must leaven. Unless, I argued, the church was prepared to start from this other end as well, none of its answers, however good, would be adequate. I illustrated this from the field of doctrine, liturgy and the structures of the church. I wanted also to include morals. For the lectures I had given as *Christian Morals Today* were, I recognized, one-sided, or rather one-ended. They were addressed to a predominantly Christian audience (though much bigger and much younger than I expected) and, in the prevailing atmosphere of explosive controversy, they leant over backwards to start where the presuppositions of that audience lay. Hence I judged subsequently that something 'from the other end' was necessary to correct the balance. So this was what I said.

In the sphere of morals, as elsewhere, we have got to begin from opposite ends at once, with no assurance of an easy synthesis. Clearly we have every obligation to reinterpret the Christian moral teaching as intelligently as we can, and to say what it means today. This is a far-reaching task, and I certainly do not underestimate its importance. If it is not done, and we simply have to make do with the 'old morality', then we shall deserve not to be heeded.

But there is another task, starting not from where the church is but where the world is, on which we have hardly begun, and

---

[40] *The New Reformation?*, chapter 4, 'Living in the Overlap'.

which most churchmen, I suspect, would scarcely even recognize as a Christian undertaking. Indeed, for an ecclesiastic openly to raise the issue will doubtless be hailed as irresponsible and widely misrepresented.

Up till now in the Anglo-Saxon world we have been able to persuade ourselves that it is the church that supplies the rules under which the moral game is played. It is 'Christian standards' that have been the norm from which the nation has departed. The church has provided the ring, even if it has not succeeded in holding it. And the ring has been that inherited from the 'religious', and largely pre-scientific, society of medieval and reformation Europe. The question has hardly been asked how Christ could be Lord of 'religionless' secular society, in which the church, so far from dictating the terms, is called to the role of a servant within a a structure not of her own devising. In the period of the new Reformation, with the final end of Christendom – that is, of a culture dominated by churchmen – this is likely to be the normal role of the church. Indeed, one can say that it *is* the normal role of the church, and that any other is untypical if not aberrant. As Albert van den Heuvel puts it :

> The slave nature of the church must mean that we let the world impose on us the structures in which we can serve rather than that we impose our structures upon the world – and the latter is in fact what we have done. We impose our structures on all people – even on the pagans, if we still can. Instead of taking the *morphe tou doulou*, the form of the slave, we have mostly taken *one* structure which once was relevant and which once served – and have made it ultimate and final.[41]

As an example of this in the field of morals, let me risk taking again the controversial question of the relation of sex to marriage. I am reluctant to do so because by selecting it I could merely add to the impression that this is *the* issue that churchmen think important. In fact, I have to agree with Mr Colin MacInnes[42] that one of the biggest barriers between the church and the world is 'the almost indecent obsession that the churches have with sex'. They

[41] *The Humiliation of the Church*, p. 56f.
[42] *New Society*, 29 August 1963.

'harp and nag on this theme to such an extent that they give the impression of a hostility to the animal part of our natures which most normal human creatures . . . will not reject at any price'. (It is only fair to say that our society as a whole is just as adolescent and a good deal more hypocritical in this obsessiveness.) There are many other issues fraught with far more destructive possibilities for personality and personal relationship. Nor do I pick on this because I am interested in concentrating on individual as opposed to social ethics. Indeed, I do not think this is an issue primarily of personal morals. As Harvey Cox observes:

> It is strange how even people who see most clearly that crime, illegitimacy, narcotic addiction, and poverty are largely structural problems still interpret the increase in premarital sexual experience as a breakdown in personal morals.[43]

I select this issue simply because it is a prime example of the Church starting from a position of its own which it regards as absolute and unalterable, in a way that it has long ceased to do in fields like those of economics or war.

In the matter of the relation of sex to marriage, churchmen constantly speak as if there were *one* position which is Christian and which it is their task to make as compelling as they can for those 'outside'. Indeed, starting from the church's end in society as it still is, I would agree that there is a real priority to spell out in intelligible contemporary terms what underlies the traditional insistence on the exclusive unity of bed and board, and to show how it makes sense not only in terms of prescriptive rules but in terms of the deepest concern of Christian love. This I tried to do in my earlier lectures. Indeed, to do anything else within this structure would rightly be regarded as irresponsible. For I believe that as things are, and have been, this is what Christian love and Christian law point to as their fulfilment. I am not convinced that sex can be whole and deep and free outside the total sharing and full responsibility of person for person which marriage represents.

But I am very conscious of the fact that the structure is changing rapidly. And it would be disastrous for the church to find itself committed to the position that it is only over such a society that

[43] *The Secular City*, p. 213.

Christ can be Lord or only within its assumptions about the place of sex that an individual can be a Christian. For the people of God have in fact found themselves in situations where the connection between sex and marriage has been very differently regarded. Let me give some obvious examples.

1. For much of the Old Testament period polygamy was accepted as a form of relationship through which a faithful response to Yahweh could quite properly be made. Indeed, it is remarkable (particularly in contrast to the treatment given to the monarchy) that there is no subsequent decrying of polygamy in the Prophets or depreciation of it in the Histories. The change to monogamy came through a social rather than a religious revolution.

2. In the Law books of the Old Testament, most of the regulations governing sexual behaviour spring not from any profound understanding of the intimate relationship between sex and personality but from the fact that women were an important and inviolable form of property[44] – an overtone still to be caught in the argument, recently repeated by a high ecclesiastic of the Church of England, that no man wants second-hand goods !

3. To jump to more recent times (and passing over the darkest ages of the church's association of sexuality with sin), we find a typical Reformation estimate of the relation between sex and marriage in the Preface to the 1662 Marriage service of *The Book of Common Prayer*: 'Secondly, (matrimony) was ordained for a remedy against sin, and to avoid fornication; that such persons as have not the gift of continency might marry'. It is a measure of the change that no responsible Christian minister or counsellor today could urge wedlock on this ground: in fact, he would certainly regard it as a thoroughly bad reason for two persons to embark on the high responsibility of marriage.

One could give many other examples in church history of different estimates of the place of sex in life and its relationship to marriage. Even without bringing in societies which have entirely different sexual structures from our own (and of course this is a very pressing problem in the younger churches), the idea that the church is committed to one unchanging pattern, which is *the* Christian one, is clearly very questionable. I believe the church must learn to live

[44] On all these questions see W. G. Cole, *Sex and Love in the Bible.*

with this idea – or in the period of the second Reformation it will be dismissed as part of the 'medieval' world, *and nothing it says on anything else will carry much conviction if it is out of touch here.* For we are surely on the brink of a society which is moving (through many casualties) to a very different conception of the place of sex and its relation to marriage from that which has prevailed in the largely pre-scientific cultures in which the Christian church has so far happened to live. It will not necessarily be a happier society, let alone a better one. And its forms will certainly not be dictated by the church. But, for good or for ill, it is the society which the church of the new Reformation will have to baptize into Christ – if it is not simply to retire behind its own pallisade.

Let us extrapolate beyond the present confused transition. Sooner or later (and today it is usually sooner rather than later) we are likely to reach a situation when parenthood will be completely voluntary. Indeed, instead of taking *ad hoc* steps to prevent conception, we may reach the opposite position, where immunity is the norm, except when and as men and women deliberately choose to have children. Moreover, I find it difficult to believe that we cannot remove the scourge of V.D. as we have already, virtually, removed the scourge of T.B. Indeed, if it was a killer, I suspect we should already be on the way to doing so. Furthermore, with the fears of conception and infection lifted, the stigma of detection, which induces furtiveness, insecurity and guilt, and condemns the possibility of deep, free, and therefore truly loving, relationships outside a certain area of society's approval, is likely to disappear rapidly.

If we accept this situation as the given context of our thinking – and no moralizing about its desirablity will in itself change it – then many things will look rather different. The case for drawing a firm line at *one point* (namely, the danger point of technical virginity[45]) in the degree of sexuality in a relationship loses much

[45] Harvey Cox draws attention to the obsessive preoccupation which has narrowed down the meaning of the word 'intercourse' to the crossing of this one line: 'A pert young graduate of a denominational college assured me recently that although she had necked to orgasm every week-end for two years, she had never "gone all the way". Her "pre-marital chastity" was intact. Or was it? Only, I submit, by the most technical definition of what is meant by preserving virginity' (*op. cit.*, p. 210).

of its force – as does the inhibition against lesser forms of sexual expression for fear of escalating and 'going too far'. All close human relationships have some element of sexuality in them. We confine the overt acknowledgment of this to certain conventional channels, suppressing or repressing the rest. But the conventions constantly shift, as for instance, in our attitudes to decency in dress, to dancing, or to freedom of association between the sexes. We could well move towards a society in which sexual expression in any degree which is honest to the relationship – in which the outward genuinely represents the inward[46] – becomes a perfectly natural part of normal relationships. Within this situation, marriage will continue to mean the life-long and exclusive commitment of two persons to each other with all they have and are, and acceptance of the responsibility for children. It will preclude other relations, whether sexual or not, which threaten the precedence of that total mutual commitment.

There is no necessary reason why the morals of such a society should be lax. Indeed, they might be more penetrating and, in the proper sense of that abused word, puritan.[47] Morality could increasingly come to be judged by the inherent quality of the relationship, by its maturity, freedom and responsibility, rather than (as so often at present) by its degree of sexuality. Of course, there will continue to be sex relations (however far they go or do not go) which are dishonest, unchaste and immoral, because they do not express a real love, a genuine intimacy, but are casual, exploitive or merely lustful. And, within marriage, there will be relationships with others and with the partner that cut at its root and destroy its basis. But the requirement for divorce could well be a much more searching demonstration that this had happened beyond repair – that there was no marriage left. Adultery as a ground for it would then have to show that the person concerned really had gone over to another (in the full sense of the word's derivation) and not simply that a single specific act of sexuality had been established.

Any new placing of sex in society is likely to be fraught with just as much tension as the traditional restrictions have produced.

[46] For an excellent statement of this from a Christian point of view, see Rustum and Della Roy, *Honest Sex*.
[47] See the valuable analysis of puritanism in Christopher Driver, *A Future for the Free Churches?*, chapter 2.

And 'living in the overlap' will make intolerable emotional demands on those whose patterns of behaviour have been shaped by a different structure. I am not recommending it. I am simply saying that the Christian has to face squarely, and without jeremiads, the implications of a change that is already well advanced, and to begin his moral thinking, like his doctrinal thinking, from this end *as well as* from that of bringing up to date the traditional moral theology. It should surely not be impossible for him to contribute creatively in a situation where quality rather than quantity of sexuality is the criterion, where a relationship is assessed by its integrity rather than by the number of lines it crosses. The Christian, holding all relationships, including those of *eros*, within the *agape* defined and vindicated for him in Christ, will continue to witness to the most selfless test of what such integrity means.

An instructive parallel with the old Reformation lies in the field of usury.[48] The church started, legitimately enough, from the position that usury, except under strictly controlled conditions, was exploitive and destructive of persons and their freedom. But with the scientific use of money pioneered by the capitalist revolution interest became potentially creative and liberating, making possible a vast increase in human freedom. While preserving the values and insights embodied in its old stance, the church was challenged to begin its thinking also from the other end.[49] The Calvinists made a notable effort to do this. But the main body of Christendom stuck to modifying its medieval witness, with increasing lack of relevance and conviction. In consequence, the church failed to formulate a new social ethic, and the Reformed contribution was dissolved in the acids of eighteenth- and nineteenth-century economic individualism. The result was that when the capitalist system itself became more destructive of personal relationships and freedom than ever the mediaeval money-lender was, the church had no ground on which to take a stand. In sex, the ring was held and a relevant bourgeois morality was developed, thanks largely to Luther and the Puritans. But there is every indication that it will not survive

[48] See, subsequently, the article by John T. Noonan, Jr., 'Authority, Usury and Contraception', in the American Roman Catholic journal *Cross Currents*, 16.1 (Winter 1966), pp. 55–79.
[49] Cf. R. H. Tawney, *Religion and the Rise of Capitalism*.

the transition to the 'secular city' any more successfully than the mediaeval doctrine of usury was able to be transplanted in the culture of the mercantile town.

Can a Christian ethic be worked out for the coming new society that starts from very different presuppositions from those of the church's choosing in the period during which she was able to impose? It is the same question that was put to her by the Renaissance in terms of cosmology.[50] The first Reformation depended on her having the humility to be able to start from the end of the telescope as well as from that of the Bible. The second will depend on a similar readiness for the role of the servant in a scientific revolution that is bound to affect the basis of personal relationships, biologically and psychologically, far more intimately and catastrophically.[51]

[50] Cf. Arthur Koestler, *The Sleepwalkers*.

[51] Cf., as an indication of the distance we have travelled even since these words were written, G. Rattray Taylor, *The Biological Time Bomb*.

3

Abortion[1]

1. *The Responsibility of Freedom*[2]

A recent article by a Roman Catholic journalist[3] on the contraceptive dilemma before his church contained these words:

> Even the day-to-day operations of the pill are too little known. The possibility that it works by some sort of instantaneous abortion, as some believe the ultra-uterine coil works, has not yet been foreclosed. The vision of a Pope solving a birth control problem by unwittingly endorsing abortion is enough to keep many a theologian awake at nights.

Suppose some methods of birth control, whether drugs now under investigation or intra-uterine devices, do work by contranidation, preventing the establishment of the fertilized ovum on the wall of the womb, rather than by contraception, does it matter? Is this technically abortion? And if so is it for this reason 'out'?

Part of the trouble is that the very word 'abortion' is such a loaded one, legally and morally. This is hardly surprising when under English law any attempt at abortion, successful or unsuccessful, by another agent or by the woman herself, still in theory renders the person convicted liable to imprisonment for life. And morally it has acquired the overtones of child-murder. Hence the problem has until recently tended to be pushed under the carpet by politicians and churchmen alike. Yet the statistics of misery –

[1] Both these pieces were written before the Abortion Act of 1968. I have left them, despite a little overlapping, as they stood.
[2] *Medical World*, January 1966.
[3] John Leo, 'Rethinking Birth Control', *Christianity and Crisis*, 26 July 1965.

not to mention the farcical unenforceability of the law – make it, now that the death penalty is abolished and the Wolfenden Report in sight of implementation, one of the most urgent causes of social reform.

The question revolves around the prevention or suspension of pregnancy. And the first thing to recognize is that the line between these two is arbitrary. For, like all biological processes, pregnancy is a continuum. When can it really be said to have set in (so that it can be 'interrupted' rather than prevented)? 'Was it the moment when the spermatozoon penetrated the ovum? Or the moment, some time later, when the nuclei fused to give the full set of chromosomes? Or a few hours later still, when the cell first divided, thus showing that it had the capability of growth?'[4] Or can indeed a a woman properly be said to be pregnant until the fertilized ovum becomes attached to the uterus wall rather than lost by spontaneous ejection – the destiny, it has been estimated, of at least a third and possibly a half of all such?

What would otherwise be a cool scientific discussion has been overheated by the introduction into this question of the theological category of the 'soul'. At what point does the 'soul' enter – so that thenceforth one is dealing not with a purely biological organism but with an immortal person? For many centuries there was no unanimity on this. Augustine, for instance, accepted the traditional view found in Aristotle that a rational soul was not present in the foetus for a considerable time – forty days in the case of the male and eighty in that of the female(!). This has since been abandoned by the Roman Catholic Church in favour of the theory of 'immediate animation' – so that from the moment of union of male and female cells we have to do with a person with an absolute right to life (in contrast with animals who have no souls and therefore no rights). This right is unconditional. It cannot be affected by the fact that the life may have been initiated by criminal assault, be likely to be hopelessly deformed, or even be in danger of killing the mother (the last was the ruling of Pope Pius XI as recently as 1949).

This theory, which has brought such heat to the argument, must, I believe, be rejected on at least four counts.

[4] Glanville Williams. Introduction to Alice Jenkins's *Law for the Rich*, p. 17.

1. Any theory that has to the ordinary conscience such grotesque, and even monstrous, consequences, is surely wrong somewhere. One may appreciate the values it is trying to safeguard but revolt at the price it asks for them.

2. There is the fact that it is quite incapable of proof or disproof. To say that a human foetus at any particular moment of time has or has not a 'soul' is to make a statement on which no empirical evidence can be adduced for or against. On the verification principle, therefore, it must be questioned whether it is even a meaningful statement. If a Hindu chooses to believe that an unborn cow has a soul (and therefore must be accorded the same treatment), no one can show him to be wrong.

3. In this form, moreover, the theory embodies an unbiblical conception, to which the Christian theologian has no particular attachment. The view that each individual possesses an immortal soul is a Greek, not a biblical one. It is indeed a Hellenized equivalent of the Hebraic insistence that each person is called to a unique life in relationship to God which transcends the purely physical or temporal. On that every Christian would be agreed. But the biblical tradition is committed to no notion of the union of any kind of immortal entity or substance with the foetus.

4. Finally, as Dr Glanville Williams points out,[5] no one consistently believes in the theory or subscribes emotionally to the view that a fertilized ovum is a person.

We do not regard a miscarriage, when it occurs naturally, as the death of a human being – even as an accidental death. This attitude is reflected in the law. A foetus that is spontaneously aborted before the end of the seventh month can be burned in the back garden or put into a hospital incinerator. No statutory notice of birth need be given. There are no obsequies. Even the Catholics, who now generally maintain that this foetus has a soul, do not perform a funeral service. . . .

In the light of these facts, it seems safe to assert that when an embryo or foetus is spontaneously aborted we do not customarily regard it as a person. By what freak of logic, then, can we assert

---

[5] *Op. cit.*, pp. 16f.

that if the abortion is deliberately induced the foetus becomes a person?

With the theory upon which the traditional morality and legality rest so questionable, what should we do? Basically, there would seem to me two possible approaches. We can reject the theory, but continue to start from the position it is concerned to sanction. Or we can begin again from another end altogether.

In the former case, we shall say that the act of interrupting a pregnancy at any stage is in itself wrong and if justified at all can only be permitted in the most carefully defined conditions and with the most stringent safeguards. This is the reformist position. There may be – and most people would say there are – instances where abortion, though an evil, is the lesser of two.

The main objection to this approach, however desirable as far as it goes, is that it will do very little to change the real scandal and misery of the situation. Estimates of the number of illegal abortions in Britain vary between 10,000 and 100,000 a year, and they cause incalculable damage to health and happiness. In the vast majority of these cases it would be impossible to indicate 'grave risk of serious injury to the patient's physical or mental health', however widely that was interpreted. Those determined on an abortion would continue to get one. And the more formidable the safeguards – e.g., two medical opinions rather than one – the more people would be inclined to by-pass the whole process. And with pills rather than surgery round the corner, evasion would be far easier, though hardly less dangerous in unauthorized hands. The law would either be flouted as at present or whittled away into contempt.

For political reasons in the broadest sense it is no doubt necessary to begin from the reformist position – just as the Homicide Act had to precede the total abolition of capital punishment. But as a permanent resting place I believe that the one will be found as unsatisfactory as the other. Meanwhile, I should wish to urge that we lose no time in beginning our thinking also from the other end.

The reformist approach seeks to translate into acceptable legislation a modification of a morality which it does not submit to any radical reappraisal. This morality starts from the view that there are certain acts which are right or wrong in themselves, though it may be necessary to adjust to 'cases' (or, in other words, to persons). Abortion, on these premises, is always wrong, but it may be permissible for humane reasons as the lesser of two evils.

This is the kind of morality to which I believe the teaching of Jesus came as a radical challenge. That there are certain things in themselves laid down as right and wrong without respect of persons was the basis of the Jewish legalism with which he found himself at odds. As Professor Paul Ramsey puts it:

> A faithful Jew stayed as close as possible to observance of the law even when he had to depart from it. Judaism varied the rules so as to care for human need. Jesus stayed as close as possible to the fulfilment of human need, no matter how wide of the ... law this led him.[6]

I suggest that this provides the clue for a fresh starting-point. The basic fact from which we must begin is not that interposition to the biological processes of pregnancy is of itself sinful or criminal. It is that concern for persons as persons and for their freedom and maturity as responsible human beings matters more than anything else. And never was this so important to stress as today. For one of the aspects of the modern world is the vastly increased freedom available to man over sex as over the rest of nature. For the first time parenthood is within sight of becoming completely voluntary. This is a great freedom, bringing with it corresponding responsibility. What we do about sex becomes more and more a matter of personal choice and not simply of natural processes beyond our control. It is in this setting – this new setting – that the whole interrelated issue of the prevention and suspension of pregnancy must be seen.

There is no need in this context to argue the case for the prevention of pregnancy responsibly undertaken. Nothing suggests that the availability of contraception has led to less responsibility in parenthood – rather the opposite. Prevention, here as everywhere, is altogether better than cure. No one is arguing that abortion is in any way to be preferred to contraception. The sole question is whether termination is acceptable if prevention has failed – a question

---

[6] *Basic Christian Ethics*, p. 56. I have reversed the order of the last two sentences.

that must in time become rarer as the use and efficiency of contraceptives increase. Should a mechanical – or a human – failure compel enforced parenthood? Abortion is resorted to, in the vast majority of cases, by married women who cannot face the prospect of more children and by those who would otherwise have illegitimate ones. In the acute crisis of over-population in which the human race is already engulfed, can it be right to force parents to bear children they do not want? Or can it be right to insist that they be reduced to the physical or psychological condition in which the termination of pregnancy may be classed as 'therapeutic'?

Indeed, I would like to question the very phrase 'therapeutic abortion'. Abortion of itself is not a therapy for anything – except presumably for a purely gynaecological disorder. Psychologically it may set up as much as it removes. So much of the mental agony for which abortion may appear the only 'cure' is in fact brought on by the desperation, the shame, the furtiveness, the isolation, to which the woman is driven by the present attitude of our society and its laws. The real therapy is to remove these conditions, so that the decision can be made openly and with the freedom that comes from a knowledge that there is, from the beginning, a genuine option.

In the last resort, the right to decide must rest not with a doctor, or a judge, or any third party, but with the mother herself. This is in no way to prejudge the moral issue. She still has the responsibility for choice – supported by all the pastoral concern and clinical advice that can be made available to her. And this last point needs to be stressed. For in the emotional turmoil of an unwanted pregnancy she is likely to be in no state to take this decision alone – which is precisely what she is so often forced to do by our present law. Every woman who feels she cannot tolerate pregnancy should have complete freedom of professional advice, and this advice should be helpful, sympathetic and willing in principle to include termination. But, as in the field of homosexuality, any really creative and constructive approach depends first on removing the overhanging threat of criminal proceedings.

But whatever the provision for supportive help the decision must in the final analysis be with the woman concerned. No one else can take it for her or take it from her, if she is to be a genuinely free moral agent. It is a terrible freedom to have, and for others to share:

for another potential human life is involved. But it is not a uniquely different problem. It is part of the burden and responsibility of our creativity, of our power to have or not to have children. The difference in our day is that we are increasingly called upon to exercise that choice rather than have it taken for us by nature or society.

The mother may decide to let nature take its course, despite all she intended – and the odds are surely that this will leave fewer scars unless the counter-indications are overwhelming. In any case, what may be right for one may be psychologically disastrous for another; and, as St Paul says, 'anything which does not arise from conviction is sin' (Rom. 14.23). The function of society with its laws is not to foreclose the decision, as it tries to now – with such ignominious failure and glaring inequality between rich and poor. Its function is to provide the ring-fence within which the individual can be truly responsible, and then to defend this freedom, like other freedoms, against abuse and exploitation.

2. *Beyond Law Reform*[7]

This has been a remarkable year. Abortion is no longer under the carpet of church or state. Not only have two Bills, Lord Silkin's and Mr David Steel's, made progress in the Lords and Commons which a year ago no one would have deemed possible, but the Church of England has issued two reports: *Abortion: an Ethical Discussion* and *Putting Asunder: a Divorce Law for Contemporary Society*, that reveal a remarkable movement at work, which has come to further expression this week in the refreshing British Council of Churches' Report, *Sex and Morality*.

And in my small way I myself have been propelled quite a distance. A year ago I was hardly involved in the subject of abortion reform and as ignorant as most. In the field of law reform I had concentrated, like many others, on capital punishment and homosexuality. Then last autumn I was asked for an article for an issue of *Medical World* being planned on abortion. Thinking it was a neglected subject on which churchmen, including myself, tended to bury their heads in the sand, I timorously agreed. By the time the

[7] Lecture to the Annual General Meeting of the Abortion Law Reform Association, 22 October 1966. Reprinted in *Twentieth Century*, First Quarter, 1967.

article appeared in January, however, the entire scene had changed.

It has been a year in which the issues of law reform have really come to a head. And the fight is only just joined. There is still much to be seen through. For nothing creative can seriously be done this side of law reform. But we are, I think, near enough the top of the hump to look beyond it. For we have to realize that even the most liberal law we can conceivably get at this moment will scarcely touch the hard core of the problem. Of the (up to) 100,000 abortions each year in this country and the million-plus in the United States not more than a small proportion could, or should, in good faith be legalized even under a bill as wide as Mr Steel's. For, in order substantially to alleviate the toll, both mental and physical, of illegal terminations, the law would have to be stretched to the point of being discredited. A law that requires evidence, before it becomes applicable, of 'serious risk to life or grave injury to health' or of 'severe overstrain'[8] will either drive people to this, or be twisted, or one suspects, in a vast number of cases, continue to be ignored. *Of course* we must go through this stage; but I guess that it will be as impossible to rest there as it was with the Homicide Act in the abolition of capital punishment. However, my concern this evening is not with the next stage in law reform – that is premature – but beyond it altogether to fundamental realities and long-term goals, which it is never too soon to consider.

Let me first make clear the position from which I speak. This is certainly not in any official capacity as a bishop of the established church. It is as a concerned Christian man – and, in this field, very much a layman. And by a Christian standpoint I do not mean, as many people instinctively suppose, a dogmatic moral orthodoxy which brings a packet of pre-determined absolutes to 'apply' to a given situation, with a view to laying down what is right and what is wrong. In fact, I do not start – and I do not think the Christian gospel starts – from 'ought' at all, with the object of moulding to it what 'is'. Rather, the Christian starts alongside everyone else, with what 'is', and then looks at it and through it and out of it with the eyes of *agape* – love as he knows this defined in Christ. Indeed, I believe that he more than anyone else must start from what 'is' in a non-moralistic, non-judgemental way and go on staying

[8] In the event it was fortunately a good deal more liberally phrased.

with it till he sees what love really indicates in this situation. This is not just passive acceptance of what is, let alone acquiescence in it. It is active identification, incarnation (to use the Christian technical term), involving what the Rumanian novelist Petru Dumitriu, the author of *Incognito*, calls 'vanquishing lethargy by love'.

First, then, I should like to start from and to stay with certain facts, certain realities of the situation, which simply are, however we might wish them otherwise.

1. A person determined on having an abortion will get it somehow. This is just a hard fact to be respected, which one is not required to condone or condemn. One cannot legislate abortion out of existence any more than one can legislate alcohol out of existence by prohibition. I am not, I hasten to add, putting them on a par in any other way! But they belong to a class of things which in the last resort all who really want will get, be the law what it may. These also include prostitution, gambling, homosexual relations, divorce, suicide and, probably, euthanasia. In other words, we must face the fact that prohibition in these fields cannot finally be enforced. This is no argument for not having any laws, let alone for retaining bad ones. Law, as I shall go on to say, has a real place here in protecting society and the individual. But there is bound to be an area, however reduced by intelligent and liberal legislation, in which there is much activity which though not legal is nevertheless licit, in the sense that it is allowed by society for fear of finding something worse.

Abortion is a good example of this uneasy and unhappy compromise. Not only is the present law manifestly unenforcible, with glaring inequality between rich and poor, but there is a great deal of evidence of police toleration and not merely of police failure as in other crime. There are few prosecutions. If there were more, there would be an outcry. There was an article in the American women's magazine *Ladies' Home Journal* for May of this year which provided evidence in Los Angeles of a deliberate policy of tolerating good, though illegal, abortionists in order to drive out the bad, rather than force everyone into the backstreets. Others will know better than I what is the *de facto* balance in this country. Some of you will remember an article in *The Guardian* of two years ago (7 April 1964) describing a student abortion service in London University which was so thinly veiled as to be incredible unless a *modus vivendi* is in fact operating. And the new law, if passed, though it will ease the situation, is certainly not going to remove it. This seems to me the first fact of life with which we have got to live.

2. There is the new scientific setting within which the discussion of abortion must now take place. Until very recently (and indeed in most people's minds still) abortion has come into the same bracket as child-murder, infanticide, exposure. The very word has moral and emotional overtones which immediately sets it in a different universe of discourse from 'the medical termination of pregnancy'. But today its continuity is not so much with these emotionally loaded terms as with the now almost clinical discussion of contraception. Indeed contraception is being seen to be such a continuous process that at what stage one intercepts it is, except to those who introduce dogmatic considerations like the entry of a 'soul', a matter of relative indifference. It is increasingly possible, especially in the field of intra-uterine devices, that contraceptives may in fact work by interception. Is this technically abortion? And if so, so what? To draw attention to this does not settle, or even raise, the moral issue. But I believe it is bound profoundly to affect the ambience of the discussion. And, as I shall say, I suspect that we are merely at the beginning of what is likely to become a fundamentally new situation in which scientific advances may alter the whole perspective.

3. There is the new and still scarcely imaginable fact of the population explosion. It raises in a new context the old question: 'Should any people be *forced* to have children they do not want?' And, knowing as we do more and more of the effects on the genuinely unwanted (as opposed to unplanned) child, have we the moral right, especially in the light of the coming crisis, to insist on its birth? This choice comes at a time when we can no longer slough off the problem by leaving the matter in the hands of nature or the lap of the gods. Children are not a gift of the Lord which cannot be denied: births are not made in heaven. In fact, even in the biblical myth, the onus is laid squarely on *man* both to subdue the earth and to be fruitful and multiply; and in neither case is he to do this without responsibility or limit. The difference today is that he has the means and the knowledge to be fully answerable. We can no longer put down unwanted births to processes we have but limited powers to

control or reverse. To refuse to control or reverse them is a deliberate act of freedom, carrying with it a formidable burden of responsibility.

4. This last consideration is especially relevant in cases involving substantial risk of the child being born with serious physical or mental abnormality. It will be even more pressing if, as we cannot doubt, the progress of medical science gradually eliminates the factor of pre-natal ignorance and uncertainty. At the moment there is a very considerable chance of aborting foetuses that would have turned out perfectly normal. But if ever we approach a position of virtual certainty, could society compel a woman, as the Church of England report on Abortion thinks it should, to mother a baby which it as good as knows is going to be deformed? This seems to me a very heavy responsibility, especially in view of the pathetically inadequate provision made by the statutory services for such children and their parents. This reflects the fact that most of us as individuals and as a community would prefer not to absorb in this direction energies, time and money which we could be putting to many other things. Have we the moral right to force the unfortunate parents to do so? This is quite different from society saying that these children ought not to be born. And if the parents take a free and responsible decision that they should be born, then society has a clear duty to afford them every support.

So far I have merely tried to set out certain realities which provide the context for our moral decisions. Some of these realities have changed and will change, with considerable effect on the issues to be decided. And the first thing, as I said, that love does is to listen, to stick with the realities and not to hive off from them into moralizing judgements.

Now may I set out similarly four long-term concerns and goals of love in this field?

1. *Maximize knowledge.* This may sound a harmless and uncontroversial thing to say. Yet it is potentially very threatening to established attitudes. So much traditional morality is in fact buttressed by ignorance and fear. Many are deterred from abortion because it is difficult or dangerous. Do we really want it made easier, not, in the first instance, to obtain (for that involves a moral issue) but simply to effect? Even suppose we thought it in most cases wrong, should

we welcome medical research to make it simpler?

Let me, as a layman, speculate on developments that may or may not have the likelihood of fulfilment in the foreseeable future. It would seem to me possible, not to say probable, that we shall look back on the present procedures of surgical abortion as unbelievably crude and messy. It may not be long before the kind of research that has produced the contraceptive pill leads to a similar pill capable of effecting a fairly simple suspension of chemical conditions essential to the continued hospitality of the foetus by the uterus. Indeed, research in this direction could equally bring invaluable knowledge enabling us to *prevent* many unwanted miscarriages that bring such distress to childless couples. It is obvious that in this situation any law prohibiting abortion would be far more easily circumvented even than it is at present by surgery.

A recent article in the *New Statesman* (27 May 1966) on 'New Advances in Contraception' closed with these words:

> There seems little doubt that the future of contraception lies in the development of a female Pill which is aspirin-cheap, fully effective, and so innocuous that it can be safely sold from the shelves of the supermarkets.

That prospect may be enough to cause many a flutter. What if it should refer to a similar pill for abortion? I imagine everyone would agree that the situation would be radically changed. The moral issue in fact remains exactly the same: the decision whether to take the pill is still there. Nothing is prejudged. Yet the knowledge transforms.

Nevertheless I am still convinced that love says 'yes' to that knowledge. For it has no interest in keeping people moral by ignorance or fear.

2. *Maximize freedom.* This is only another way of saying that love has equally no interest in keeping people moral by act of Parliament. But this is precisely what we are constantly trying to do. For we fear freedom. Yet real love can only desire people to be as truly free as they possibly can be and not to have what should be *their* moral decision taken for them by others. This, of course, is a counsel of perfection – but Christian love is always aimed *in this direction* rather than the opposite. Nor does this in the least mean that love is

against law or sees no function for it. Love is concerned to maximize the use of freedom and at the same time to protect persons (whether the self or others) from its abuse and exploitation. This applies in all fields of social ethics, whether the activity is desirable or undesirable. A man must be free to choose it or not: otherwise he will not be a moral being. But the law must be prepared to protect him or his fellows from the abuse of this choice. Thus *The Guardian* wisely wrote recently (20 May 1966):

> Everyone has a right to play the pools; but no one is entitled to exploit to his own profit the weakness which makes a man a compulsive gambler.

What, then, in abortion is the place of the law? Hitherto, and equally under any new legislation we may get, the place of the law has been to *make* the decision: it is ultimately the judge who decides, with or without the consultation of doctors. I believe, rather, that the place of law is to *safeguard* the decision, to enhance and protect the freedom to decide, which must lie ultimately, if it is to be a moral decision, with the woman herself. By enhancing and protecting the freedom I would wish to include a number of things. It should include making it possible for the woman concerned to take as informed, guided and supported a decision as society can contrive to enable her to make. It is perfectly proper that society should try to protect people from ill-considered, panicky, pressurized or potentially dangerous decisions. It can properly make it difficult for people to shrug off the effects of their irresponsibility. It can reasonably refuse abortion simply 'on demand' and it can erect dissuasives of various kinds. Certainly it must safeguard the consciences of doctors who refuse to be party to it. But in the last resort I believe it must place the decision where it belongs, if it is to be moral and not forced. And it must do everything it responsibly can to enlarge that freedom quantitatively and, still more, qualitatively. Abortion by consent, as I believe divorce by consent, or euthanasia by consent, however safeguarded, is ultimately the only basis for a moral, even if morally wrong, decision.

3. *Abolish abortion as a crime.* This follows from what I have just said about genuinely making abortion a free decision. Again, this is not in any way to prejudge its morality. In this I see a parallel with

suicide. Indeed, abortion is, I believe, much more comparable with suicide than with murder, with which it has traditionally been bracketed. The motives which so often lead to it are the same. Moreover, the *de facto*, if not *de jure*, position is not all that different. Attempted suicide, unlike aiding and abetting a suicide, is no longer a crime. And, in practice (if only because it is so difficult to prove) an attempt at abortion, successful or unsuccessful, by the woman herself is not prosecuted, even though it is still in theory punishable by life-imprisonment. Proceedings are confined to those procuring abortions for others. But suppose in the end the normal method of abortion is a self-administered pill. It is possible, and indeed highly desirable, until it is proved harmless, that prosecutions should occur for the unauthorized distribution of such a drug. But is it conceivable that the act of taking the drug itself should long continue to be a criminal offence? Such questions are the proper concern of social medicine, as of morality. But unless there is exploitation of others or danger to health should the criminal judge be involved?

It is difficult to predict how in fact we shall get to the stage beyond law reform. I am inclined to think it is more likely to come about by scientific changes such as I have sketched than by any considered decision of society that abortion, like homosexual acts in private, *ought* not to be a crime. But whichever way it comes, I believe that, with all proper safeguards, it is a goal of love in this field.

4. *Abolish abortion.* Not prohibit abortion, but abolish abortion. At this point there is a real difference from gambling, drink, prostitution and the rest. No one *wants* an abortion for its own sake. It only exists *faute de mieux*. And the way to abolish abortion is to make the first line of defence really effective. And this, too, is a revolution to which love says 'yes'. This means making contraception 100 per cent efficient and – more hazardously – fully available. *Of course* this carries with it the risk of encouraging immorality. But, again, it is impossible to make people *moral* by threat of the consequences. And to use unwanted babies' lives as the threat seems to me a curious buttress of morality. Certainly I could never wish to keep my daughters moral by such a means. I have no desire whatever to encourage them to sexual intercourse outside marriage, but if that were their choice I should be grateful for them to be able to go to an advice clinic. I salute those who have started them, and would

want to press upon society and the churches the priority of seeing that the expensive resources of time and training are made available so that this work can continue to mean advice of the whole person.

Again, one does not know what the future will bring. It is not inconceivable that we may find ourselves entering an age when, by immunization or other means, it will be possible normally to be sterile unless and until one chooses to be fertile – so that the 'birth pill' will then properly be so called. Once society had adjusted to such a situation there is no reason why it should be more immoral – any more than there is reason to suppose that contraception has already increased immorality: it has merely increased freedom. But such a situation does have within it the possibility of abolishing abortion. It is on the cards that abortion, like child exposure, will come to be seen as a horror of an uncivilized age. But before that there are many attitudes to change and battles to be won. In that delightful Danish book *The A.B.Z. of Love* there occurs the sentence in the article on 'Homosexuality':

It is Danish legislation on the question that is to blame. . . . No more than thirty years ago people were put in prison for having homosexual relationships with another adult.

That certainly puts us Anglo-Saxons in our place. Is it possible that in the next generation someone will be able to say of England and the United States: 'No more than thirty years ago people were put in prison for abortion'?

It may perhaps have seemed to some that in this lecture I have been so permissive about abortion as to imply that I regard it quite neutrally, or even as a good thing. I would therefore end by saying unequivocally that I regard it as an evil thing, as a scourge to be removed from any civilized society. For there is nothing creative about it at all. It is destructive of personal life, and I see no point in arguing exactly where this may be said to begin. It is not in itself therapeutic, except of a purely gynaecological disorder. It is much more likely to bring on adverse physical or psychological conse-quences. Unlike contraception, it does not make for love. Indeed, as a widespread phenomenon it undermines the relationships as well as the health of a society. Countries that have dropped all barriers to it have on the whole not liked what they have seen, and have drawn back.

The question, as I see it, is: How do we abolish abortion? The answers I have given are: maximize knowledge; maximize freedom; abolish abortion as a criminal offence. These are precisely the opposite of those given by prohibitionists. The tragedy is that most moralists are by instinct prohibitionists, and they tend to think that those who are anti-prohibitionist are enemies of morality. This seriously undermines the forces of reform, playing straight into the hands of those who want to sweep the whole thing underground or keep it there for their own profit. I welcome what has happened in the past year: it is a great step in the right direction. But the final step – *beyond* law reform – is likely to be as divisive as any so far. It will expose the roots, and therefore the real radicals.

4

Obscenity and Maturity

Censorship is, I believe, the next goal for liberal reform in 'the civilized society'. The phrase is that of Roy Jenkins, now Britain's Chancellor of the Exchequer, formerly her most distinguished Home Secretary for many a year. He was reviewing, against the background of jeremiads about increased permissiveness, some of the notable achievements of Britain in legislative reform over the past decade. For in that period, particularly in the latter half of it, some quite fundamental changes of law have taken place in the field of personal ethics – on suicide, capital punishment, homosexuality, abortion and divorce. There is plenty of room still for improvement and tidying up in all these areas, and there are other issues rising rapidly above the horizon, especially those connected with advances in medicine on the frontiers of life and death and with the inroads of technology on personal privacy. But meanwhile there is a surviving feature of the previous landscape which now sticks out like a sore thumb – literary censorship.

But first let us remember how fortunate we are. In English and North American society 'censorship' means one thing, the censorship of obscenity. But these are about the only major areas of the world in which this is true. Elsewhere political censorship, in one vile form or another, so preoccupies attention that other types are scarcely worth fighting. I was talking to a Polish girl when writing this article. She could not understand my concern.

And we should not ourselves dismiss the need for eternal vigilance on the political front. It was an eye-opener to those of us in the West European democratic tradition to realize the lack of freedom in French television to cover the student rebellion of 1968. Over a year later, despite amnesty for students and workers, nothing has been done, at the time of writing, to reinstate the commentators, reporters and research assistants who were fired from the state radio and TV corporation, O.R.T.F., because of their protest strike.

But more subtly, of course, all our societies, and not least American society, are shot through with invisible forms of censorship, mostly to prevent voices being heard or facts being exposed. And the slanting, the selection, the pulping and the pre-digesting of what comes through the mass media is frightening indeed. Perhaps it takes an outsider fully to appreciate this. I remember watching an apparently straight TV newscast in the United States shortly after the Bay of Pigs incident. For the first time I really felt what it must be like to live in a society where all the material for political judgement is doctored at source.

But there is one great difference which should never be forgotten. Whatever political censorship occurs in Britain or America is not written into the law of the land, and the courts are open. This is also the great difference between the racial situation in the United States and, say, the Union of South Africa. However shocking things may be in parts of America, the law is, however inadequately, on the side of freedom. The unique thing about literary censorship is that it has behind it the full panoply of the law — what the recent Report of the Working Party on the Obscenity Laws set up by the Arts Council of Great Britain called 'Big Brother wigged and gowned on the judicial bench'.

The survival of these laws (like the, mercifully obsolescent, blasphemy laws) is a hangover from the paternalistic society. In this society man, in St Paul's words, is 'under guardians'. There are those who know best, who, in the name of decency and order, decide what it is good for the rest of us to read or to see, and who are there to protect us, if necessarily against ourselves. This paternalistic society, whether benevolent or malevolent, has, until remarkably recently, been universally taken for granted, and all the classic conceptions of Utopia, from Plato's *Republic* onwards, have assumed it in their vision. It is the society, too, in which the Christian church, like every other free institution in our modern world, has grown up and lived.

It is only *very* lately that it has been widely questioned, and that in the name of the 'permissive' society. But this betrays its parentage in the very act of revolt. For who 'permits' whom? Why, the guardians, of course – who graciously, grudgingly, or even thankfully, abdicate (like the Lord Chamberlain, the father figure of English theatrical censorship, who recently made a dignified if hurried exit). But while the paternalistic society 'gives' freedom (as Britain 'gave' India her independence), the permissive society takes it – often without so much as a 'by your leave'.

It is the classic situation of adolescent rebellion, where the shrewd parent recognizes the limits of authority and relaxes the rein. Some of course let it go altogether and capitulate. Yet most try to hold what they can. But even in the so-called 'Gadarene rush' to permissiveness, the slack in our society is not very great. And certainly the guardians have not been converted. Commenting on his 'exemplary' sentence on the Rolling Stones, the judge, who rejoiced in the name of Block, said afterwards:[1]

> We did our best, I and my fellow magistrates, to cut these stones down to size, but, alas, it was not to be because the Court of Criminal Appeal let them roll free.

And of the present Home Secretary's rejection of the (Government commissioned) Wootton Report, which after a cool review of the facts tentatively advocated reduced maximum penalties for the possession and use of cannabis, *The Guardian* reported[2]:

> Few Government decisions have been greeted with such enthusiasm by MPs of all parties. Mr Callaghan was loudly cheered as he added that it would be 'sheer masochism' to make it easier for people to introduce another social evil into the country.

These quotations are taken from a recent book by Michael Keeling, *What is Right?* He shows just how unpermissive our society still is[3] and how by the respectable outlet of 'moral violence' (often associated, as above, with sexual metaphors, or with racial ones: 'a yellowed ghoul who sells the muck') people righteously take out on

---

[1] As reported in *The West Sussex Gazette*, 1 November 1967.
[2] 24 January 1969.
[3] *Cf.* Anthony Grey, the Secretary of the Homosexual Law Reform Society, speaking on 17 July 1969: 'Anyone who has the notion that in today's climate of law inforcement as it affects unorthodox minorities we are living in an over-permissive society is, I'm afraid, leading a pretty sheltered life.'

others what they cannot tolerate in themselves. He concludes:

> The question is not really, 'Is society too permissive?' but 'Is society permissive enough?'. Does society yet come anywhere near giving us enough room for moral growth and enough respect as persons? The phrase 'the permissive society' contains the answer within itself. The word 'permissive' suggests that there is a right inherent in society, or in the leading individuals in society, to exercise control over us and that they are failing in this duty, inasmuch as certain activities are 'permitted' which ought not to be 'permitted'. It suggests that the controls have slipped. So long as this suggestion can be made – and taken – seriously we have not begun to realize what the right relationship between ourselves and society is. It is not the business of society to control us. It is the business of society only to provide the basic civil liberties within which we can make our own moral decisions and discover our own possibilities for moral growth.[4]

The permissive society is a real advance on the paternalistic society. But, as that quotation indicates, it has scarcely begun to ask the right fundamental questions. Nevertheless, before moving on, we should do well to underline the gain it represents and how precarious and so far short-lived it is.

At least the permissive society, like adolescence, *demands* freedom. It does not create it and often, indeed, does not foster it. In fact it tends to smother it by massive new pressures, particularly towards teenage conformity. It is not easier for a young person genuinely to be free. But at any rate it does not prohibit it; and by its inner logic it requires it, often beyond the strength and structure of the individuals and groups unaccustomed to it. Hence the casualties, which can be tragic (especially with drugs). No sane person would argue that there is not a place for a framework of law – and good law. (The Englishman looks with incredulity at the American gun laws.) Nevertheless I believe the backlash against the permissive society and the attempt to put the clock back is worse. And when right wing forces of the church line up moralistically behind this backlash, it is necessary to quote to them the words of St Paul: 'You did not receive the spirit of slavery to fall back into

[4] *Op cit.*, p. 93.

fear, but you have received the spirit of sonship' (Rom. 8.15). And 'sonship' for the New Testament always stands not for a relationship of childish dependence, but for maturity, for 'man come of age'.

I would urge, therefore, that we press *forward* from the paternalistic and the permissive society to the mature society, recognizing at once that we have not reached it, yet seeing this as the target by which we should constantly be setting our sights. For if we do not have such an aim, then we shall merely drift like an adolescent on the loose, or more likely revert. And I should like to test out the implications of such a society by looking at what I called the next goal for liberal reform, the abolition of censorship.

This step has recently been boldly proposed in Britain by the Report I cited earlier commissioned by the Arts Council, a prestigious independent (but Government-subsidized) body, representing literature, theatre and the arts. The Working Party began by reckoning to reform the existing law on obscenity, which was itself a real advance pioneered by Mr Roy Jenkins when he was a private member of Parliament in 1959, and subsequently amended in 1964. Yet so unsatisfactory has this proved that, within a decade, they were driven to the conclusion that nothing short of outright repeal (in the first instance for an experimental period of five years, as with capital punishment) provided a workable stopping-point. I believe their logic is unanswerable, and the Report itself is a model of lucidity and good writing. Predictably the present Home Secretary made it clear that he was having none of it, and the prospect of its implementation in the foreseeable political future is dim. There is no doubt that we are not as yet a sufficiently mature society. But the Report will take its place in the honourable queue of rational statements that have apparently to be reiterated many times before the law on such subjects comes eventually to be changed. Its value, indeed, largely derives from the courage of the Working Party in firmly deciding to recommend what ought to be done, and not to recommend on the basis of conjecture what Parliament might agree to do.[5]

The heart of the difficulty which the Report exposes is that obscenity is a word quite incapable of objective legal definition. Verdicts

---

[5] For a less radical next step, if and when this is relevant, see the proposals in C. H. Rolph's *Books in the Dock*, which is useful in itself as an account of the sorry, if often amusing, history of literary censorship.

of judges and juries must therefore continue to be subjective, arbitrary and unfair – wielding censorship rather than implementing law. Nevertheless there are, I believe, within this tangled field, a number of moral distinctions to be made, and these are important for helping to discern and shape the attitudes of a mature society which is both free and responsible. I would think it relevant to distinguish rather carefully between the *erotic*, the *obscene*, and the *pornographic*.

1. *The erotic.* It cannot be said too often in our sick, sub-Christian western society that the erotic is positively good – part of that creation which God saw and pronounced to be very good. There is nothing obscene whatever in the portrayal, however explicit, of the erotic as such. The erotic is something to be enjoyed. Other civilizations, notably those of ancient Greece and India, have not found this difficult, and the phallic symbol, even in public, has not been regarded as obscene. Yet such is our fear of sex that if you adapted the advertisement 'the Guinness sensation : enjoy it' to 'the sex sensation : enjoy it' – particularly if you illustrated it – the indignation can be imagined! Yet to do it for the sheer joy of it, *to sell nothing*, would arguably be more moral than to *use* sex to export cars.

A reinstatement of the genuinely erotic as a subject of beauty and delight seems to me to be one of the priorities of our society. And it is an area where the church has reparation to make. For, as everyone knows, the church has a shameful record of being anti-erotic. What everyone does not know, and what has to be stressed again and again, is that there is practically nothing of this in the authentic Hebraic strain of the Bible itself[6] – as the Song of Songs shows and as every schoolboy searcher of the Old Testament must remember. There is nothing anti-erotic about Jesus, who was certainly not known as a puritan, and by his fearless freedom gave women an entirely new acceptance in the ancient world. Nor is there, I believe, anything anti-erotic about St Paul, who receives such a consistently hostile press at this point, largely based on phrases, like 'It is better to marry than to burn', taken out of context and misunderstood. But he is no depreciator of marriage. On the contrary,

[6] On all this see again W. G. Cole, *Sex and Love in the Bible*; also D. Sherwin Bailey, *The Man-Woman Relationship in Christian Thought*.

'It is better to marry than to be aflame with passion' (I Cor. 7.9) and persistent sexual abstinence within marriage is a bad thing (I Cor. 7.5). Certainly St Paul saw celibacy as his own vocation, and he could wish, with the world as it was (I Cor. 7.28-31), that others for their own sakes might see it too. But each man must 'do his own thing' (I Cor. 7.7). He never condemns sex as such. Indeed, he extends and glories in the Old Testament insight of carnal 'knowledge' as a sacrament of union with the divine (Eph. 5.25-33). The idea that the two loves are exclusive and contradictory was later and pagan, however pervasive. Yet such is the damage it has done that merely to 'induce erotic desires of a heterosexual kind' itself constitutes one of the tests of corruption in the latest gloss by an English judge (Lord Justice Salmon in the *Last Exit to Brooklyn* case) on the Obscene Publications Act of 1964. This makes its repeal the more urgent. But there is, of course, a far more fundamental change to be achieved in our entire attitude.

Yet this change is hindered rather than helped by the persistent exploitation of the erotic in our modern world by *eroticism*. This makes an 'ism' of it, extracting it from the total personal relationship and proper intimacy in which it is beautiful, and playing upon it for its own sake. Any 'ism' is in my judgement suspect because it fastens upon a perfectly valid part and then seeks to see the whole in terms of it, inevitably thereby distorting not only the proportion but the part. And when, like sex, it is such a powerful part, the temptation and the disbalance are the greater. It has been said that you can sell anything by nudity. In fact, in the long run, this is questionable. An article in the English journal *New Society*[7] on 'The Sex Sell' concluded:

> Sexy ads . . . fail to convince when they aren't related to products concerned with the female sexual persona. Sex is a very bad way of selling *Müllsäcken aus Kraftpapier* (strong paper refuse bags). It's quite a good way, though, of selling sex.

The purpose, commercially, of the nude female is that women should identify with it, not that it should appeal to men.

But advertising is not the only or indeed the main field for eroticism. The same article gave convincing figures for the surprisingly

[7] 15 May 1969.

limited use of sex in the really big areas of commercial advertising. The author quotes an ad man as saying, 'Of all the media, advertising has the least sex', and he adds, 'With the exception of music, I'd say he's right'.

Eroticism in fact mainly sells itself – through books, magazines, films and records. And it is important at this point to get the record straight. There is nothing intrinsically evil about eroticism, as I shall maintain later that there is about pornography, although the one may shade imperceptibly into the other. Eroticism is a distortion, by isolation, of something good.

Let me illustrate the difference between the genuinely erotic and eroticism from the current issue of *Playboy* as I write this (August 1969). It contains some marvellous cine-photographic stills of Paula Kelly dancing completely in the nude, pubic hair and all. Nothing could be more beautiful and entrancing. Further on is a highly-posed picture of Debbie Hooper sitting cross-legged, thighs apart, with a crumpled bath-towel neatly arranged in the strategic spot. A beautiful girl again, but the effect is totally artificial and merely contrived to titillate. Further on again there is a whole warren of Bunnies in equally unnatural positions, including one of Kitty Tabor balancing precariously on a railroad track 'who epitomizes the carefree spirit of the Detroit Playboy Club'. Anything less genuinely carefree I find it hard to imagine!

I say this not to condemn but to distinguish. *Playboy* has, on the whole, done a liberating job in releasing all kinds of inhibitions about sex and making the erotic acceptable in a pseudo-puritanical culture. It has overcome guilts and fears in people who could not admit them even to themselves. Moreover, by combining the erotic with high-quality articles on politics, philosophy, theology and the rest, it has helped to counteract the isolation of the erotic which lies at the root of eroticism. And never, as far as I know, has it indulged in under-cover pornography by the singularly nauseous and hypocritical ruse, beloved of the English Sunday papers, of 'exposing vice' in the unsullied name of virtue.

On the other hand, there is no doubt that it has been a powerful influence in promoting an 'ism' which I am convinced rests on an 'up-tight' view of sex, epitomized again in the look-but-no-touch Bunny. This has been said often enough before, notably in the witty but serious thesis of Harvey Cox, later included in *The Secular City*,[8] that *Playboy* is anti-sexual. One need not go as far as that to recognize that by purveying sex confessedly as 'entertainment for men' it has reinforced the abstraction of it from the total relationship of human beings in love in which alone it is whole and true. And this is the norm – of what Katharine Whitehorn has called 'sex at its best' – that we have constantly to move towards if we are going to create a genuinely mature society.

I have no compunction as a Christian in saying that we have in our generation to aim for a truly humanistic understanding of sex. (Humanism is another 'ism' which makes a valid part, man, the measure of the whole.) And this is a relatively recent possibility. We should recognize in fairness that the patristic and mediaeval fear and denial of *eros* belong to a world in which a truly human life was a very precarious achievement, constantly threatened by nature or the gods. For most of human history, sex has been viewed alternatively as the god within or the animal within, a tempestuously powerful force acting upon men and women, whether from above or below. The Rennaissance represented a bid of the human spirit to throw off this double domination, staking a claim for the autonomy of whole areas of life from supernatural or sub-human control.

The sexual area has been one of the last to win this freedom. This is largely because the mechanisms of understanding and control, physical and psychological, have not been available until the twentieth century, and are still very crude. It is an area demon-ridden with taboos and inhibitions which make cowards of us all. The liberation of sex, so that we are genuinely free in how we act and how we talk about it, is far from complete. But it is in sight – and it is being anticipated with the casualties we know.

In the first flush this liberation is a freedom *from*. Hence the assumption that 'the sexual revolution' is simply to be equated with greater permissiveness. But if this were all there was to it, there would be no genuine revolution at all. It would just be one more swing of the historical pendulum between control and licence, Apollo and Dionysus.

But I am convinced that there is more than this. For the heart of the sexual revolution in our time is that potentially now we have

[8] Pp. 199–204.

within our grasp a freedom *over* sex, as over the rest of nature, undreamed of before. One aspect of this is indeed the runaway commercialization of sex, under whose pressures and suggestions we are in so many ways less free. (It has been said that sex is bidding fair to replace religion as the opium of the people.) But with it has come also the possibility of a vastly enriched area of human responsibility and control. Whether we have children – and soon no doubt their gender – is not to be left to nature or the gods. What we do about sex becomes increasingly a matter for deliberate personal choice.

And this is where, as a humanist, I want to come back on the naturalist. To justify sex – any sex – in terms of the 'natural behavioural instincts' (in the words of an English imitator of *Playboy*) is a dismal sell-out. It is to refuse the revolution and decline its responsibilities. For the revolution demands that, whether we are Christians or not, we should re-think our attitude to sex not simply in terms of what is permitted ('how far' we go, or where we 'draw the line'), but in terms of the quality of *personal relationship*. It is the test of honesty to the relationship and real fidelity to the whole person that matters. Sex can be fully personal, as opposed to animal, only in the content of a tender, caring, responsible relationship. And it is this that eroticism undermines by detachment. Anything that works against this detachment is not only on the side of the angels, but, more importantly, on the side of integrated, mature, joyful, human living.

But it is time to move on, from the erotic, to our second category.

2. *The obscene.* The first thing to be said here is that obscenity, as such, has nothing peculiarly to do with sex. It comes from the Latin *obscenus*, which is in origin a term of augury, meaning ill-omened. When Horace used the phrase '*anus obscenae*' it had no connection, as we might guess, with anal obscenity. It means 'old hags' or 'witches' of the sort that we meet in *Macbeth*; and their obscenities were the disgusting objects with which they fed their cauldron. Indeed the basic thing about obscenity is not, as the law asserts, its potential to 'deprave and corrupt', which is extremely difficult to prove, but its undoubted capacity to disgust or offend.

But this, naturally, depends greatly on the subject and the circumstances. What some find repulsive others won't, and what is indecent, or unfitting, in some contexts could be perfectly 'proper' in others. There are many (though mostly those who had not seen it) who apparently thought the film of *Ulysses* obscene. All I can say is that I found it extraordinarily beautiful and moving. *Per contra* I remember an issue of the Roman Catholic magazine *Ramparts*[9] with a collection of photographs of children savaged by the Vietnam war which I should have no hesitation in calling obscene. This does not in the least mean that I should want to ban such photographs: I deeply desire people to be exposed to them, as there are some things on which our sensibilities ought to be shocked. And the English courts have made it clear that to 'shock and disgust' is in itself no offence, though in practice the criterion of obscenity given to juries of 'what is acceptable . . . in the age in which we live' comes close to saying it.

What, however, I believe, does need to be said is that any person has a reasonable right not to be *forced* to be shocked. In other words, society has a responsibility here as elsewhere, to respect privacy and enable people to be free. People should be protected, to some extent at least (absolutely it is of course impossible), from having things thrust at them in situations they cannot avoid which may be expected to cause them pain or nausea. What offends susceptibilities has changed and is changing constantly. But where there is reasonable likelihood of serious offensiveness it is proper that society should exercise restraint, so that people shall be free not to be damaged if they cannot take it.

Thus, I would argue that it was valid by the Street Offences Act to clear the English streets of prostitutes, even if it did mean 'sweeping them under the carpet'. For undoubtedly many people are disgusted and embarrassed by having to encounter them whether they like it or not. (This is quite different from prohibiting those who wish to seek them out.) Equally, it is valid by film classifications, television timings, and warnings before programmes to provide protection for children and others who may wish to avail themselves of it (though my experience suggests that children are pretty well able to look after themselves: it is often the adults who want to protect themselves against embarrassment). The same applies to public advertise-

[9] January 1967.

ment and shop displays, though one wishes it could apply to many of the other obscenities we are exposed to on the streets, including those of ugliness, noise and stench. But ultimately the purpose of any restrictions is to enable people to be free; and you can so protect them that they are not free.

It is not generally realized that even the latest Danish legislation abolishing all censorship retains restraint on public display, and the proposed Bill drafted by the Arts Council Working Party would protect individuals both against public indecency and against unsolicited material by post. No one should be prohibited from seeing or reading anything he wants; but equally no one should be forced to see or read anything he does not want. It would help to disarm reasonable fears of a pornographer's paradise (even if, on the Danish evidence, short-lived) to stress the requirement that no one need be compelled to share it.

And this brings us, finally, to the hard core of the subject, pornography.

3. *Pornography*, as D. H. Lawrence insisted, is 'doing dirt on sex', and this, as the name implies, includes anything that in written or descriptive form prostitutes it. Unlike the erotic, which is good, the pornographic is, by definition, evil and undesirable. The number of people it seriously corrupts is, I think, questionable. (What it undoubtedly does corrupt is sex.) We never appear to suppose that it might corrupt the juries we set up to vet it. Could a man refuse jury service on the ground that it was wrong of the community to threaten his corruption? In fact persistent pornography appeals only to those already twisted or deprived in their relationships. Others, though they may find it titillating, will soon be sated and turn away in disgust; it has no power fundamentally to change their pattern of life, which has been set by emotional factors at a much earlier age.

The only serious form of *public* effect seems the very real possibility that playing on themes of sexual *violence* may add fuel to destructive desires that would otherwise remain socially harmless. This was argued persuasively by Pamela Hansford-Johnson in her book *On Iniquity*, on the notorious Moors Trial in Britain. But even this is far from proven by any evidence that a sociologist or lawyer could accept. And it still leaves open the question of what you do about it. As the Arts Council Report points out:

> Violence has been ubiquitous in the art, literature and press of the civilized world for so long that censorship must by now be recognized as a totally inadequate weapon to combat it. Indeed laws available for the purpose including the Obscenity Acts are virtually never even invoked against it.

Nevertheless, pornography poses a real problem for a responsible society. As Lord Soper wrote in the excellent symposium edited by C. H. Rolph, *Does Pornography Matter?*,

> The work of personal redemption and the work of social redemption would be significantly advanced in an environment purged of pornography. . . . It chains those who produce it and those who indulge it to a quality of life that is both unworthy and inadequate.

I am indeed inclined to think that its most pervasive and corrosive effects are not to be found at the extremes where the law might be invoked. The real corruption of a society's attitude towards sex sets in much earlier on, with all that suggests, arouses and plays upon an attitude to love, nudity, sexual gratification and experiment, which, to quote Lawrence again, is 'trivial, cheap and nasty'. This is the charge against so much of the paperback market, the sex-magazines, the strip-shows, the suggestive advertising. It is not pornography in the legal sense, but it is the persistent exploitation of sexual stimulation for commercial gain which is the essence of prostitution. And it has the power to demoralize and to desecrate which any person, especially any young person, in our society needs a great deal of strength to withstand.

It is this that nourishes the understandable desire of most decent people to prohibit it. But most decent people have yet to learn that to disapprove and to prohibit are not the same thing. For prohibition is usually counter-productive. It feeds the problem rather than solves it – as the astonishing drop of 25 per cent in sex crime in one year after the permitting of pornography in Denmark provisionally demonstrates. It is a malaise of Anglo-Saxon society that moralists tend to be prohibitionists. If you are not a prohibitionist, you are assumed

to be lax and unconcerned for morals. Yet the question is fundamentally *how* to exercise responsibility in a *free* society. The attempt
to deal with the evils of alcohol by prohibition, is, of course, the
classic instance of the failure of prohibitionism to achieve the ends
it most desires. But the principle applies in many spheres where the
use of the law is much more limited than most people instinctively
suppose when they see something of which they disapprove.

However unhealthy we may think pornography to be, I do not
believe the function of the law is to prohibit it as such, nor to set
itself up as the arbiter of what I may read or reject. The function
of the law in the last ditch (and it is the last ditch) is to protect
freedom. And there are limits to which it can do this without having the opposite effect. It can to some extent protect persons against
the exploitation of their erotic compulsions (for an exploited person
is not free). It can to some extent protect them against forcible in-
trusion upon their susceptibilities (for a forced person is not free).
And it can to some extent protect them against things that will
result in their being *treated* as less than persons. I have so phrased
this last as to include the suppression of material likely actively to
promote racial discrimination or prostitution or violence against the
person, sexual or otherwise. But I would want to stress the publicly
verifiable effect of *action* on other persons (or in the case of drugs,
for instance, on the person himself) and not simply the presumption
by a judge or jury of a likelihood to 'deprave and corrupt'.

One of the greatest things society can do for a person is to help
him to be free. It cannot make him free. This must depend on his
own choice. But to deprive him of the choice by prohibition is itself
to deprave him, to treat him as less than a responsible person. Society's
own example in treating people as less than responsible by censorship
can have the same effect as society's own example of taking life
by capital punishment. The effect of public prosecutions (as of public executions) is, I believe, wholly bad. It was the action of the
Director of Public Prosecutions that *made Lady Chatterley's Lover*
pornographic for many. There is much that I would not wish to
defend or encourage but which equally I think it wholly regrettable
to proceed against by law. And I would take exactly the same
attitude in regard to blasphemy.

I am sure that the Arts' Council's Working Party was right in concluding that 'the proper sanction for breaches of taste ... should be social reprobation and not penal legislation'. It would help to allay the fears raised by the rational arguments that it mobilized so beautifully if such an influential body could also go on to suggest positive ways in which this reprobation might be channelled through the disciplines it claims to represent. There is place for more voluntarily adopted professional codes to counter the so-called 'conspiracy to corrupt'. But standards must be exercised in the interests of personal freedom, not of anti-sexual repression. For the way a mature society functions is not, except in the very last resort, by suppression (that way lies a much worse death), but by encouraging values and relationships which will make people *not want* to do dirt on sex or anything else.

The responsibility of helping to shape such a society lies particularly on all those involved in publishing and the press, advertising and the arts, as well as on the more direct influencers of individuals like parents and teachers, priests and psychologists. But for the creative exercise of any of these roles freedom (short of the freedom to destroy freedom) is ultimately the most precious as well as the most dangerous commodity. We need the law to protect it rather than to prohibit it.

5

Mystique and Politique[1]

'Everything begins in mysticism and ends in politics' (Peguy). There must be many of my generation of politically committed Christians who have grown up with this saying from George MacLeod. Prayer and picketing are poles of the same response: the one must issue in the other.

It was in trying to trace the source of this quotation that I discovered, alas, that it had no such meaning. It comes from a *Cahier* written by Peguy in 1910, called *Notre Jeunesse*, and I reproduce it in the translation of Marjorie Villiers' fascinating biography, *Charles Peguy: A Study in Integrity*.

> Men have died for freedom, as men have died for faith. You say that elections are a ridiculous formality, and you have good reason for saying this, . . . but men have suffered, men have died, a whole people have lived so that today the greatest idiot should have the right to accomplish this 'rigged' formality. . . . There was a heroic age when the sick and the dying insisted on being carried in chairs to place their vote in the ballot box. Everything starts with a *mystique*, with its own *mystique* . . . and everything ends in *politique*. What is important, what is essential is that in each order, in each system, the *mystique* should not be devoured by the *politique*.

Mrs Villiers defines the two categories as follows: 'By *mystique* he meant an unqualified and disinterested adherence to spiritual values. . . . By *politique* he meant the sacrifice of these absolutes to

[1] *New Christian*, 21 September 1967. I have not attempted to bring the political illustrations up to date.

les raisons d'état.' So far from being complementary for Peguy, they were contradictory. Indeed, there are passages which could be taken to suggest that he was a – political or even anti-political. To join a party, he said, was the quickest road to becoming a criminal.

Yet this would be to ignore the fact that Peguy was a dedicated socialist and revolutionary. More balanced was his recognition that there was a *mystique* at the true heart of every party, be it Republican or Royalist. Whether the flame of its *mystique* was alive was ultimately far more important than whether it gained the majority of votes. The final prostitution was to use *mystique* for the benefit of *politique*: 'To be a politician engaged in politics is one thing, to engage in politics and describe it as a *mystique* is unpardonable.'

All Peguy's thinking is conditioned by the fact that, for him, the classic encounter of *mystique* and *politique* was the Dreyfus case. Though this was eventually won, the manner of its winning threatened constantly to turn it into a defeat:

> The initial stand of the anti-Dreyfusards had been: 'One man must suffer injustice for the maintenance of the *status quo*': the final stand of many of the Dreyfusards had been 'the man must be reinstated to ensure the fall of the government and of the influence of the army upon the political life of France'.

For Peguy *everything*, including the character of Dreyfus himself, was irrelevant except the fact that he was innocent.

But, though the Dreyfus case clarified the issues magnificently, it also oversimplified them dangerously. For the cause was a simple moral issue of justice done or not done to an individual, even though it had to be translated into an expensive political decision. But the interrelation of *mystique* and *politique* really becomes intriguing when the moral or spiritual issue is itself a political one, in the sense that it involves the *polis* and readjustment in the structures of social and economic power.

The classic instance of this is the revolution, where the *mystique* is swallowed up by *politique* with depressing inevitability. But there is also a whole range of social and political issues where the moral question is fundamentally simple and the political question incredibly complex, in which the differing responses of parties and individuals reveal the subtle interplay of *mystique* and *politique*. Such issues have included recently Suez, the abolition of capital punishment, *apartheid* in South Africa, integration in the United States, the status of South-West Africa, and Rhodesia. These are the kind of issues that set a man against his brother and disclose, often quite unpredictably, with whom *mystique*, and with whom *politique*, prevails.

Rhodesia has provided the focus of a fascinating confrontation. On the one side have stood those who from the beginning saw this as a question of principle on which there could be no compromise. And the linking of independence to majority rule was for them entirely unaffected by the far from encouraging record of African self-government. As Peguy said of Dreyfus, 'There was no reason why he should also be possessed of all the virtues.' Indeed, 'it is a good rule that the victim should not be a believer in the *mystique* of his own case'.

On the other side have been ranged the advocates of a 'sensible' *politique*. Most shades of this reaction have been represented in the Conservative Party, which, with a few rare exceptions, has by comparison shown up the pragmatism of Harold Wilson as almost pure devotion to principle. It has ranged from the scarcely veiled racism of the 'kith and kin' blood-group (which is perhaps best understood as a near-fascist *mystique* disguised as *politique*), through cynical accommodation to a *fait accompli*, to a disingenuous willing of the ends but not the means. It will probably appear as discreditable as anything in the Tory record – especially as it is always easier, as the Liberals have demonstrated, to be principled in Opposition.

Nevertheless Rhodesia has been, and continues to be, a political problem to which there must sooner or later be a political solution – which inevitably means compromise and the language of priorities. The purist of *mystique* alone merely reveals that he does not understand politics and condemns himself to futile protest.

But with the extension of the Rhodesian question to the United Nations another encounter of *mystique* and *politique* emerged in which both government and opposition found themselves united, even at the height of mutual recrimination, in a common dishonesty. This was the attempt to dissociate the Rhodesian issue entirely from the South African and to pretend, in George Brown's words, that 'we have no quarrel with South Africa'.

But, of course, the two are morally as well as politically deeply intertwined. The Union of South Africa represents the only previous instance of the granting by Britain of independence before majority rule and stands as the most awful warning. The dismantling of the entrenched clauses for which Britain was responsible represents as cynical an act of *politique* as Hitler's re-militarization of the Rhineland. And for a British Labour government to say that it has no quarrel with a régime which is the purest example of *Herrenvolk* dictatorship in the world today beggars belief. And all this is quite apart from the fact that the South African government is blatantly flouting mandatory sanctions. If South Africa were economically negligible, and above all if the suppressed race were white, everyone knows perfectly well that there would be an almighty quarrel – and that it would have been settled, by force, long ago.

And yet here, too, there is a genuine power-political situation to be reckoned with. The arguments from Britain's economic weakness – and political unpreparedness – cannot be ignored, any more than it was a political possibility to provoke Hitler to a show-down in 1938 with a handful of anti-aircraft guns to defend London and a nation morally divided and debilitated. What was unpardonable was to buy him off at others' expense and then to cloak it all with the *mystique* of peace where there was no peace.

The lesson is surely that a *politique* that refuses to grasp the moral nettle will in the end fail even as politics. Rather than go through the sickening pretence that Vorster can be an ally in restraining Smith (as Mussolini, the established gangster, was in the early stages used by the democracies in an attempt to restrain Hitler), the only possible line of integrity for Britain today is to accept the real confrontation, which is not with 200,000 White Rhodesians but with an evil philosophy that is poisoning the whole of Southern Africa. Integrity demands that we accept the economic cost, go all out to off-set it by international agreements, educate the U.N., the U.S., and above all British public opinion to the real issues (as the statesmen of the 'thirties so signally failed to do), and recognize that Britain's *distinctive* contribution to world peace is now not east of Suez but south of the Sahara.

And what in this entanglement of *mystique* and *politique* is the role of the individual radical – if by that is meant the man who insists on going to the real root and refuses to be shifted from it? Obviously he will be especially sensitive to any 'sell out' – and

tiresomely and persistently so. For he will refuse to allow the issue
to be shelved as closed (this was Peguy's quarrel with the later Drey-
fusards). He will exasperate those who want to turn from it in relief
to more 'relevant' problems. He must be ready for the charge of
being a moral bore, particularly from those who hate all *mystique*
because of its *grandeur*, because it belongs to a different dimension
from theirs. Indeed, he must recognize in himself the constant temptation to be 'righteous overmuch'.

Such a man will never be a good party member. He will put integrity before orthodoxy, fidelity before loyalty. He may find himself
often in the position of having to be against the party – or the church
– in order to be for it. He will be a radical who is *also* a Socialist,
or a Liberal, or a Conservative. His unity, as Peguy put it, will be
with 'a few Catholics who do not cheat; a few Protestants who do
not cheat; a few Jews who do not cheat; a few Free Thinkers who
do not cheat'.

Where is such integrity to be found and what is its root? As a
Christian, I should like to be able to say that this was the character-
istically religious contribution to politics. Alas, it cuts right across
this line also – though it is still, I think, fair to point out that the
number of Christians behind, say, the Freedom Movement in America
or the Liberal party in South Africa has been quite disproportion-
ately high.

But this moral and spiritual response to the unconditional –
'Here stand I, I can no other' – is very close to the quick of what in
a previous age would have defined itself as belief in God. The fact
that for humanists and for increasing numbers of Christians today
the traditional God-talk simply fails to articulate – or to add to –
this response reflects the fact that this language scarcely any longer
relates to the real, let alone to the *ens realissimum*.

Equally, the old morality has lost the power to channel the cate-
gorical imperative. On the face of it, the so-called new morality
looks lax and relativistic. The old morality at any rate appears to
stand for absolutes, for rules that never can be broken. But, as
Moral Re-armament demonstrates, it hardly comes out as radical
or even as conspicuously honest – merely as reactionary, politically
and morally. The radical is in fact in a different camp from the rigorist.

I am convinced that the renewal of our theology and of our morality – the *definitions*, that is to say, of our commitment – will, in fact, spring not from working over the creeds and codes that form the shells of previous responses, but from whatever now is most real – to Christians, to believers in other faiths, and to humanists alike. There will be fundamental differences – as there will be between Socialists, Liberals and Conservatives. But it is the *mystique*, not the *politique*, which quickens and unites – and, then, as constantly, re-divides.

Postscript (1969)

IS GOD RIGHT-MINDED?

From time to time articles appear in journals like *The Readers' Digest* under such improbable titles as 'Is the universe left-handed?'. I am not sure that I know what such a question means. But evidently it is worth someone's while debating whether there is or is not some fundamental bias written into the constitution of things.

In the same way, I lie awake sometimes pondering playfully on the phenomenon of left- and right-mindedness – on the mystery that 'every little boy and gal that's born into this world alive, is either a little liberal or else a little conservative'. Is this, as Gilbert's policeman thought, a matter of heredity – or environment – or what? For there does seem to be something here which corresponds to left- and right-handedness. Much of the time you may not notice the difference – but throw a person a ball and which hand does he catch it with? Similarly the left- and the right-minded may be indistinguishable on most questions, but throw in a Suez, or a Rhodesia, or indeed most questions connected with 'gut' issues like race, sex or war, and which way does he jump or come off the fence?

Men equally concerned and sincere can apparently look at the same situation so differently. Some instinctively respond one way, some another. Or rather, as though by selective radar, some seem to pick up some factors, some values, others, just as sensitive, other factors and other values. Do you (in education, for instance) go primarily for equality or primarily for quality? Do you give priority to justice or to order? Do you instinctively say 'yes' to change or 'no'? Do you, for example in the classic situation of Antigone, take your stand on a sticking-point however 'unreasonable' or do you conform 'sensibly'? Are you temperamentally a radical or a fundamentalist, a 'protestant' or a 'catholic', a 'love' man or a 'law' man, a 'kingdom' man or a 'church' man? Or, in the terms of the distinction Kenneth Harris mentions at the end of his hilarious book *Winged Words* as the basic difference between the Americans and the English, 'Are you descended from those who came away or from those who stayed behind?'

Of course, in this testing for reactions, you may respond in different ways on different things, just as I am left-handed for some things and right-handed for others. In fact, in taking up a new game, I am not sure in advance which hand I shall use for different actions. (In tennis I serve left and play right: in squash I serve right and play left!)

Also, of course, you can change. Against everything one is told, I was made to switch to writing right-handed (though there was a transition period when I still *drew* left, which requires more of a straight steady hand than finger movement). Similarly, of course, people move from left-mindedness to right-mindedness. In fact this is the usual progression as you get older and more 'mellow'. But it is not automatic, in the way that the eyes invariably focus more distantly with age. Roger Fulford once wrote of Queen Victoria's uncle, the Duke of Cambridge, that 'like all those who do not understand politics, he drifted imperceptibly to the right'. But clearly it is not simply a matter of 'understanding' either.

Moreover, some, as traditionally with parsons' sons, react to environment by opposites, others by going along. I was a parson's son, but happily went along. On the other hand, politically I responded by reaction. I was brought up an unthinking Tory and I can date my conversion exactly. What finally pushed me over the edge (though, as with Saul's conversion, there was doubtless a hidden build-up) was Winston Churchill's electioneering speech in 1945, in which he said that if Labour got in we should have a Gestapo. This was really going too far, and I canvassed for the radical left-wing Common Wealth party. Ironically, though I have grown more not less radical with age, I have found myself going from Common Wealth, to Labour, to Liberal – which only shows that the party complexes do not necessarily correspond with left- or right-minded-ness, and that the radical is in any case a bad party man.

But these crossings of the lines by the individual and blurrings of the edges do not invalidate the fact that there are these basic camps, and their constitution and membership has something of the mystery and inscrutability of divine election.

Which brings me to my facetious title 'Is God right-minded?'. There is no doubt of the Establishment bias. Just as all the good words are right-handed, like dexterity, and the bad ones left-handed, like sinister, so 'all right-minded men' leaves no doubt as to whose side God is thought to be on. And certainly he appears to have created many *more* right-minded (like right-handed) creatures. They, as it were, provide most of the stuff of creation, and the slowly drifting land-masses of historical movements are made up preponderantly of men and women of conservative leanings. Revolutions soon revert to becoming right-wing, and, on the basis of not inconsiderable experience, it is the Tories who think of themselves as having the God-given right to rule. (It was William Temple, a man of the left, who acknowledged that the norm of British government was a Conservative administration, interrupted from time to time by a corrective from the Liberals or Labour.)

If, then, God is on the side of the big battalions, there is no doubt that the universe is right-minded. But there is also the disconcerting fact that the new directions, the creative leaps in the process, come from the left. And if the Prophets, those troublers of the Establishment, are distinctively 'men of God' and above all if the prophet of Nazareth, the archetypal radical, is the Son of God, in whom all the fullness of the Godhead dwells, what does that have to say? Does the Christian revelation not give the last word to the left?

Yet a watch needs both a mainspring and an escapement. One appears to work against the movement of the other. But the watch-maker sees that each is necessary. Exasperating.

6

The Credibility Gap in Politics[1]

My assignment is the credibility gap, in the sphere where the phrase originated – in politics.

At all sorts of points in the world today we see the same simmering phenomenon – a growing and dangerous disaffection of the young, and particularly the most sensitive and articulate young, with the political establishment. Poland, France, Germany, Czechoslovakia, Ulster, and here in England – wherever you look, there is the same syndrome of disillusionment and disengagement, leading to anarchy or apathy. But the country where the phrase 'the credibility gap' was born – the United States – is where the whole thing is writ large and where it is easier for us, from the outside, to see and to share the feeling it induces. One has only to imagine oneself faced with the choice between Nixon, Humphrey and Wallace to realize how utterly disenchanted vast numbers of people – and not only young people – must at this moment be feeling.

To be clear that we know what we are talking about, let me quote some comments from an interview, that appeared in last week's *Guardian*, with a student group at Yale – and Yale is among the most liberal and gracious of all American universities, where there are few of the frustrations and tensions that contort the campuses of Berkeley or Columbia. Here are a few excerpts:

> The war is so scary; there is no prospect of a good President: no miracle will happen. If you really start looking, you know there is nothing you can do. Even if you burn yourself in front of the Pentagon, well, big deal, it's been done before; and so what?
> We are beyond liberalism. You can't be talking about negotiations in Vietnam when the only issue is how to get out. You can't be

[1] Sermon preached at Great St Mary's, Cambridge, 20 October 1968.

talking about civil rights when the problem is black power. We are told to support Humphrey as the least of all evils. People are tired of finding out just how bad the lesser evils are.

'We are tired' is a recurring phrase.

When you are outside the system, it doesn't really matter who you vote for.

Mass movements are stupid; what we have to do is to live as close as possible to our private conception of life. To be conscious of how America subverts you, that in itself is important.

In our society the only way to be noticed is to be a freak. That's why we wear long hair, why we have hippies. Drug-taking too is part of the attempt to break away from the mass media and from mass conditions. It is a way of creating individual reactions.

In the words of the heading to the article: 'Leave us alone: heal yourselves.'

What are we to make of this? In one sense, it is all very old. People have been disabused of politics and politicians often enough before. In fact, it is the typical pre-fascist situation. And there are sufficient parallels to the temper of mind that let in Hitler to be really worrying. There is the neo-Nazi revival in Germany, the neo-Stalinism of the Warsaw powers, the panic reversion to de Gaulle in France, the ominous American backlash with its rush for guns and 'law and order' (not to mention the ugly respectability of George Wallace), and, last but not least, the ground-swell of Powellism in this country. There can be no doubt that much the most likely threat to democracy today comes from the right. And if it materializes it will be difficult to absolve the apathetic, anarchic 'include-me-outism' of the left. To that extent I regard this as a real menace, and it won't be the first or last example of the *trahison des clercs*, the betrayal by abstention of the educated classes.

And yet I am convinced that this is not the whole story. Traditionally the source of the fascist revolution is the lower middle classes (as traditionally the source of the socialist revolution is the urban proletariat). And today indeed it is the Alf Garnetts, the 'poor whites' and their equivalents, who are likely to swing the political lead. But the educated élite – focused in the students – is obviously doing far more than abstain! I believe that Herbert Marcuse is right in saying that we have a new situation, in which the catalyst and instrument of the revolution can no longer credibly be the working proletariat or the lower middle classes. If society is to be changed it must be through those with the education and intelligence to see how the masses – all of us – are being subverted and pulped by the mass media. The majority now signifies nothing. Consensus politics is the bogus consensus induced by those who control the instruments of communication. The real situation is not going to be changed by the ballot box – as the American election shows. The only hope is a revolutionary élite, prepared to stand out, or sit in, until something gives – as the Sorbonne showed.

I am sure there is a vitally important truth here, and it will be a tragedy if what throws up the Rudi Dutschkes and Cohn-Bendits or what is focused upon figures like Marcuse and McCarthy is simply silenced or soured. The Che Guevara myth shows that it will not easily be.

And yet the dangers – of violence and even more of counter-violence – are there for all to watch. The so-called principle of 'selective tolerance' – that is, of being intolerant of those *you* think intolerant or intolerable, is obviously wide open to abuse. And the view that there are 'no enemies to the left' but *only* on the right seems singularly naïve. Yet as an analysis of what is happening in our society – or rather to our society – the ideology of 'the new left' must, I am certain, be taken seriously. No amount of personal integrity or charismatic leadership can in itself bridge the credibility gap. As Reinhold Niebuhr said from the 'old' American left, 'No degree of goodwill alone can cure a deficiency in glandular secretions; and no moral idealism can overcome a basic mechanical defect in the social structure.' There is no substitute – not even the Christian gospel – for hard analysis. And the neo-Marxist one is as hard as any on the market.

But having insisted on this, what word is there to be spoken from a pulpit? Is there anything to be said which is distinctively Christian?

At this point let us go back to the passage I chose for the reading (I Kings 19.1-18). Elijah had already won the reputation with authority as 'the troubler of Israel'. A career of moral protest had reached its climax in a head-on clash with the prophets of Baal who lived off the corrupt queen's court. In a mass teach-in fraught with suppressed violence he took on 450 of them in public, and his henchmen ended by massacring the lot. In a situation of high political tension he was given twenty-four hours to live, and he fled across the frontier. His career as a freedom-fighter seemed finished. All he wanted was to drop out. Like the students at Yale, he was 'tired' – utterly. Like them he had reached the point of saying: 'No miracle will happen . . . there is nothing you can do. Even if you burn yourself . . . well, big deal, it's been done before.' 'It is enough: Lord, take away my life; for I am no better than my fathers.' In acute depression he refuses food, and on the odd scrap maintains a precarious existence in the mountains for a month.

Then comes the moment of truth – a revelation into the meaning of power. He had been living at first hand with all the tearing violence of nature – a raging mountain storm, an earthquake, a forest fire. Yet in none of these manifestations did he find what spoke to his deepest need. The experience of the students is again strikingly similar. 'Mass movements are stupid. What we have to do is to live as close as possible to our private conception of life.' The still small voice within – this alone, he came to see, provides a fulcrum from which to move the world.

Yet observe the corollary in Elijah's case. It was not to drop out. 'What are you doing here, Elijah?' was the question he heard. It was indeed a burning passion for his people's rights that had driven him to this point – and now it seemed a dead end. Yet there could be no release: 'Go back by way of the wilderness to Damascus, enter the city and anoint Hazael to be king of Syria; anoint Jehu to be king of Israel, and Elisha to be prophet in your place.' In other words, 'Get back into the political fray; set up rebel régimes; secure the movement's succession – and be ready for a great deal more violence.' In fact there was a long struggle ahead, and Elijah himself only lived to achieve his third objective. There were two more kings after Ahab before Jehu, an army officer, seized power by a bloody *coup d'état*; and Hazael, described in an inscription as 'the son of a nobody', only got to the throne by smothering the king with a wet blanket. It was a colonels' revolution of the crudest kind. Don't let us be under any illusion about these biblical characters. Theirs was not a pretty life. No one can say that they didn't live in the real world.

Yet through all this sordid familiar mess – which lacked only the television cameras to bring it up to date – something majestic shines through, which lifts the story of Elijah above the level of the patriot's diary. There is a dimension here of radical integrity, of responsiveness and responsibility in face of the unconditional, which singularly fails to come through in the students' interview. There's no contemptuous 'leave us alone: heal yourselves', no nervous need to 'create individual reactions' by freakishness or drugs. For what really takes a man out of himself is a love and a justice which grasps him with a claim that will not let him go. It does not allow him the luxury of apathy or absenteeism. And above all it gives him a sticking-point beyond which he will refuse to sell out.

And this I believe is the rarest commodity in the whole political scene today. Where is the credibility gap most patent? Why – in simple credibility. No one really believes that Mr Wilson or Mr Heath will not sell out. Take the issue on which I personally resigned from the Labour Party – the Kenya Immigration Bill. This was a clear case of deliberate breach of promise – in a different class from the other immigration problems. Yet from either front bench only Mr McLeod[2] showed that he had a sticking-point. The Government panicked, and in the process created as great a rush of immigrants in a fortnight as might have come in years. And if Mr Heath had had the courage from the start to disown the alarmist remarks of Duncan Sandys and Enoch Powell from his own back-benches there would probably have been no crisis. (Incidentally, I joined the Liberal party at the time, partly because on this issue at any rate their MPs were prepared as a man to stand up and be counted, but largely because, as I said earlier, the greatest menace today is, I believe, the attitude which merely says 'a plague on all your houses' and pulls out.)

Or take the dismal D'Oliveira affair and the MCC.[3] Whatever the strange reasonings of the selectors, known only to themselves,

[2] The Conservative colonial secretary at the time when the pledge was given.

[3] Against all expectations, Basil D'Oliveira, a coloured South African cricketer, was not selected by the Marylebone Cricket Club, the governing body of English cricket, to tour South Africa with the English team in the winter of 1968–9.

the crucial mistake of the MCC was not to have insisted (on the advice of their president, Sir Alec Douglas-Home, otherwise one of the most respected of today's politicians) on a clear understanding of principle in advance that there would be no question of a colour-bar. In the event, this cowardice was compounded by the utterly disingenuous re-election of D'Oliveira, under pressure, in place of a bowler, when originally it had been said that he was not chosen because, overseas, he was useful only as a batsman. Hateful as are Dr Vorster's principles, one at least respected him for having some in putting a stop to the tour.

The sub-title given for this sermon was 'Christian democracy – or what?' I cannot complain, because I accepted it. But I think it's a bad title. For I don't think there is such a thing as Christian democracy – any more than Christian economics or Christian sociology. There is democracy, of different varieties, to which Christians seek to contribute their insights and sticking-points. And, despite its failings, I believe in it. There are far too many valuable things in our democratic tradition to throw away to the anti-liberal forces of the right or the left. Yet there is a real either-or confronting us today. As Elijah said to the people on Mount Carmel, 'How long will you go limping with two different opinions?' – or, as the draft of the New English Bible has it, 'How long will you dance to two tunes at once?' And we read: 'The people did not answer him a word.' The Bible has no illusion that the majority is always right or that the *vox populi* is the *vox dei*. In fact Elijah feels himself in a minority of one: 'I only am left.'

Yet by his sheer integrity he had the power to close the credibility gap.

So also did Jesus, who was seen by many as the new Elijah. He too was taken by the authorities for another freedom-fighter and nailed up between two of them. Yet he closed the credibility gap. But he did not do it by political astuteness – still less by political apathy. He rendered to Caesar the things that were Caesar's – and to God the things that were God's. Once again, he did it simply by being transparently credible – and utterly involved. He did it because there was a dimension to his life which was not at the mercy of men – while at the same time he was totally open to men. He had no price – but he spared no cost.

It is this quality, I believe, that is most desperately needed in our world – and above all in our political world – today. I would not presume to say that only Christians can give it – let alone pretend that most Christians do give it. Yet I am haunted by some words describing the peculiar function of Christians in the world – and that a far from democratic world – which were penned by an unknown writer probably within fifty years of the New Testament itself. Let me close with them, as a pen-portrait of what a modern Christian layman, writing out of the New Left, has called 'the secular saint'.[4] They are frequently quoted, yet they describe that combination of attachment and detachment, of immanence and transcendence, which I believe to be the most precious phenomenon in the political scene today. Would that it were, as the writer suggests, the distinctive contribution of those who call themselves Christians!

Christians are not distinguished from the rest of mankind either in locality or in speech or in customs. For they dwell not somewhere in cities of their own, neither do they use some different language, nor practise an extraordinary kind of life. . . . But while they dwell in cities of Greeks and barbarians as the lot of each is cast, and follow the native customs in dress and food and the other arrangements of life, yet the constitution of their own citizenship, which they set forth, is marvellous, and confessedly contradicts expectation. They dwell in their own countries, but only as sojourners; they bear their share in all things as citizens, and they endure all hardships as strangers. Every foreign country is a fatherland to them and every fatherland is foreign. . . . They obey the established laws, and they surpass the laws in their own lives. . . . In a word, what the soul is in a body, thus the Christians are in the world. . . . The soul is enclosed in the body, and yet itself holds the body together; so Christians are kept in the world as in a prison-house, and yet they themselves hold the world together. . . . So great is the office for which God has appointed them, and which it is not lawful for them to decline.[5]

[4] Michael Novak, 'The Secular Saint', *The Center Magazine* (published by the Center for the Study of Democratic Institutions, Santa Barbara, California), June 1968.

[5] *The Epistle to Diognetus*, 5 and 6 (translated by J. B. Lightfoot).

7

Liberation and Reconciliation[1]

'For freedom Christ has set us free' (Gal. 5.1)

This service recalls a memorable day in your island history. And when you consider that at this moment the Czechs are also recalling on that very same day, 9 May 1945, the 'liberation' of Prague by the Russians, you have double reason to be thankful. To some no doubt the relief of liberation still seems as vivid as though it were yesterday. To others of you, a quarter of a century later, it must belong to a different age – as far away as the end of the first world war at that time was to those of us who never knew it.

My task this morning, however, is not to reminisce but to be what the Bible calls 'the Lord's remembrancer', to put you in mind of the great themes of God which remain true from ages past to endless years the same. And the two themes on which I have been specially asked to dwell are those of liberation and reconciliation. These are two great words which are conjoined in Christ – and in particular in the cross of Christ. But they are brought together in him. Though we may think of them as twins, they start very far apart.

Liberation is a theme that runs right through the biblical story. Never for long were the Jews a free people. Most of their history was spent under some occupation or threat of occupation. And when liberation came it was like honey in the mouth. 'Our soul is escaped even as a bird out of the snare of the fowler: the snare is broken, and we are delivered.' And then again, two psalms later: 'When the Lord turned again the captivity of Sion, then

---

[1] Sermon preached at the annual Liberation Day service, St Peter Port, Guernsey, Channel Islands, 9 May 1969.

were we like unto them that dream. Then was our mouth filled
with laughter, and our tongue with joy.' You can sense the relief
and the release still.

Yet this sentiment had little to do with reconciliation. Indeed,
the two were almost completely opposed. The typical paeon of
liberation was what the biblical scholar calls the 'taunt song' – like
the song of Miriam for the release from Egypt: 'Sing to the Lord,
for he has triumphed gloriously, the horse and his rider has he
thrown into the sea.' Not much nonsense about reconciliation with
Pharaoh! And even more is this true of the superb but blood-
thirsty song of Deborah to celebrate Jael's dastardly murder of
Sisera, the commander of the occupying army (what a delightful
lot these biblical dames were – with Esther and Judith to come
later!). As poetry it is as magnificent, and incidentally as old, as
anything in the Bible, and as such, despite its theology, I cannot
resist quoting it:

> Most blessed of women be Jael the wife of Heber the Kenite, of
> tent-dwelling women most blessed. He asked water and she gave
> him milk, she brought his butter in a lordly dish. She put her
> hand to the tent-peg and her right hand to the workmen's mallet;
> she struck Sisera a blow, she crushed his head, she shattered
> and pierced his temple. He sank, he fell, he lay still at her feet;
> at her feet he sank, he fell; and where he sank, there he fell
> dead. . . . So perish all thy enemies, O Lord! But thy friends
> be like the sun as he rises in his might.

Again, not much reconciliation there. Yet, as Israel was to discover, true liberation and reconciliation are complementary not
contradictory. Indeed, in the long run there is no real freedom
without reconciliation. And this is why there could not have been
a better way of celebrating liberation – which like forgiveness takes
time – than the invitation here as your intercessor for the first
time this morning of one who served as a chaplain to the occupying
forces.

For liberation which does not lead to the reconciliation of the
foe from whom one is freed remains precarious and incomplete.
That is what the Jews have still to learn today. After one of the
swiftest and most complete liberations of any war in history they

are finding no true freedom, because there has been no reconciliation. As a Jewish acquaintance of mine (Aubrey Hodes) has argued in a recent book *Dialogue with Ishmael*, unless Israel seeks reconciliation with the Arab neighbours she will remain surrounded by a desert of hostility, unable to achieve fulfilment as a nation or a significant role in world affairs.

The classic illustration of this is recorded near the start of Israel's history. Jacob is liberated from servitude to Laban and returns to his homeland laden with oxen, asses, flocks, manservants and maidservants – with everything apparently that he wants; yet he is not freed from fear of his wronged brother Esau whom he will meet on his homecoming. He spends a night in agony with God, wrestling in conscience till he is a broken man. Then with the morning he sees Esau coming out with four hundred men to meet him. Prostrate with fear, he throws himself on his mercy. 'But,' we read in words that remind us of the parable of the Prodigal Son, 'Esau ran to meet him, and embraced him, and fell on his neck and kissed him, and they wept.' Then follows one of the most graceful reconciliation scenes in history with Jacob urging the reluctant Esau to accept his present, for 'truly to see your face', he says, 'is like seeing the face of God'.

This alone is true liberation. And the same Isaiah who wrote that marvellous chapter we read earlier with its, 'Comfort, comfort my people, says your God; speak tenderly to Jerusalem, and cry to her that her warfare is ended', was also to see the implications for Israel of being the suffering servant among the nations, the instrument of healing by her chastisement.

But, as I said, it is only in Christ that the two fully coincide. Jesus also lived in an occupied country. He was perhaps more closely connected with the liberation movements of his day than our evangelists suggest and he died to all appearances as a freedom fighter. Yet he knew that liberation by means which did not make for reconciliation truly freed no one. The way of the Zealots and the way of Jesus both led to crucifixion, but the conversation with the bandits on either side of him reveals the difference.

Jesus comes through the pages of the Gospels as the genuinely free man, moving among his fearful and defensive contemporaries as the one who was not only free *from* – the law, fear, self – but above all free *for* – free for others, indeed free for all whatever their nationality, sex or respectability. (Our use of the term 'free for all' shows how trivially we think of freedom.) And when his disciples came to tell his story they told it as the story 'not only of a supremely free man but of the free man who had set them free' (Paul van Buren). So when St Paul was led to meditate on the meaning of that life and death, the language of liberation, deriving ultimately from the liberation of Israel from Egypt, mingled imperceptibly with the language of reconciliation. For there is no at-one-ment by one without the other.

He then went on to draw the consequence. As God through Christ has reconciled us to himself, so he has given us the ministry of reconciliation. '*For freedom* has Christ set us free.' Truly to show what freedom is, as opposed to licence, in a permissive society is one of the most vital ways in which the Church is called to spell out the Gospel today. Really to be free one must know what it is to be unfree; and, like the Jews in Jesus's time, men cannot accept that they are not free: 'We have never been in bondage to anyone. How is it that you say, "You will be made free"?'

'We have never been in bondage to anyone': how *could* they say that with their history? It was indeed because they had so often been in bondage, physically and spiritually, that the Hebrews had more to teach mankind about the meaning of freedom than any of the ancients. The ordinary Englishman is also inclined to say 'We have never been in bondage to anyone' (or at any rate not since the Romans and the Saxons and the Danes and the Normans!). But here in the Channel Islands you cannot. And that perhaps is the lesson which you should have to teach to the rest of us, your fellow Britons – the real meaning of freedom, discovered through the ecstatic experience of liberation crowned and made complete by the still deeper joy of reconciliation. It is a lesson, God knows, which not only in England but throughout our taut and unfree world we desperately need to learn.

8

The Mastery of Time[1]

'He that believeth shall not make haste' (Isaiah 28.16)

'He that believeth shall not make haste.' That is to say, he won't get rattled or hustled; he won't let time get on top of him or dictate to him. Doesn't that speak to all of us of something which deep down we wish were true of ourselves? Time, the enemy. . . . How often do you hear people saying, how often do you find yourself saying, 'Oh, I haven't got time!' I haven't got time. No, we haven't, for time has got us, or most of us. In this western world we have planned to master time. We think we have got it where we want it – around our wrists or on the wall, there at our disposal by turning a radio knob or dialling on the telephone. We have invented machines to measure it with incredible accuracy (a clock was recently imported for the American missile programme – I'm happy to say, from Britain – claimed to be accurate to one three hundred thousand millionth of a second), yes, and every kind of gadget to save it – so that we can get ever more and more into the twenty-four hours. If someone were to patent an invention for condensed sleep, so as to get the effect of eight hours in two, he would probably be hailed as the greatest benefactor of mankind. Time would have received its knock-out blow.

And yet I wonder. For the net effect of all this is that we have only become more and more the slaves of time. The quiet, unhurried serenity has gone. We cannot do anything without glancing at our watch or consulting our diary; and it frightens me to think of the extent to which my whole waking routine is controlled by

[1] A sermon from an earlier period preached at a number of different centres in England and America.

what is surely the most ugly of all noises that grates upon the ear each morning. And if there is a symbol of our age, perhaps it is something that every factory worker does each day of his working life – clocking in. Very soon probably he won't even have to do that; the clock will itself observe him by radar. In the ancient world when a man entered a temple, he made a votive offering to a god or a goddess at the door. As twentieth-century man files into his shrine, he obediently pays his due to the god that regulates his life – the clock. It is the clock that measures man, that silent witness that keeps his going in and his coming out and relentlessly records his every movement. That is where all our organization and machinery to free us from time, to save us time, has brought us. Never before have we had such control over things, and never before have we been so enslaved by them. And of nothing is this more true than of time.

And so we take a holiday, a vacation, to gain release from this bondage for a space, to stand back from the rush of things and breathe again. But a holiday is a respite, not a cure. The more we need holidays, the more certain it is that the disease has conquered us and not we it. More and more holidays just to get away from it all is a sure sign of a decaying civilization : it was one of the most obvious marks of the break-down of the Roman empire. It is a symptom that we haven't learned how to live so as to re-create ourselves in our work instead of being sapped by it. A car should always be charging its battery as it runs. If it simply uses up without putting back, it has to go into dock to be recharged. It is not a sign that we are running particularly well if we are constantly needing to go into dock.

Jesus is never recorded as taking a holiday. He retired for the purposes of his mission, not from it. He was never destroyed by his work; he was always on top of it. He moved among men as the master of every situation. He was busier than anyone, the multitudes were always at him – yet he had time, for everything and everyone. He was never hurried, or harassed, or too busy. He had a complete supremacy over time, he never let it dictate to him. He talked of 'my time', 'my hour'. He knew exactly when the moment had come for doing something and when it had not.

And so it has been in lesser degree with those who have caught his spirit: they have time. What is this secret of unhurried souls? It is quite simply that, like Jesus, they have learned what it means to live with him who is the Lord of time, with the One who himself is never hurried or hustled or perturbed. How does it happen, why is it that a person whose life is thus rooted in God and eternity acquires this mastery over time? For two reasons:

1. Because then life takes on a new simplicity. We get harassed when life gets too complicated. We become distracted and distraught as one thing after another comes crowding in upon us. We never have time for anything, because we have lost the power to do one thing. You get the impression of Jesus that he knew at any moment what was the single thing that mattered. For you've always time for what you really think important. Have you got time for this? The answer is: How important is it to you? Next time you catch yourself saying, 'Oh, I haven't got time for that,' remember you are giving away your priorities. It may be quite right that you haven't – but then you shouldn't be harassed about it. What has happened when we say we have time for nothing is that there is no one thing that has an absolute priority in our lives. We do lots and lots of things, we are constantly rushing around frantically busy with this, that and the other, taking on more and more – very often precisely so that we shan't have to stop and face the choice: What are the few really important things in life?

That's the first reason why a life lived in God is a life that masters time. One can see the distractions for what they are and centre down on the things that really matter. But of course this doesn't mean that Christians do less than other people. Look at Jesus again, and think of those people – many of the busiest – you have known who have had something of this quality. And that leads me to the second reason for the mastery of time.

2. Those who live in God have not only got their priorities straight; they have learned that to live with God is to live always in the present, with him who is the eternal Now. We all know people who live in the past – and we usually laugh at them – for they are pretty harmless. But it is much easier, and much more dangerous, to live in the future. Remember how Jesus coupled mistrust of God with *anxiety* – always worrying about the morrow. And that applies

not only to the morrow but to the next job. The reason why we get harassed, again, is that we are always thinking of what we have still to do rather than of what we are doing. The secret of the busiest people who are also the calmest is that they are able to concentrate everything on the thing of the moment, without a constant side-glance at the clock or a worry whether they shouldn't rather be doing this, that or the other instead. Not only are they able to centre down upon the things that really matter, they are able to do each in turn. They acquire the power to do one thing, and also the power to do one thing at a time. They keep their eyes fixed on the present and don't dissipate their energies on worry or regrets.

Living in the present means squarely accepting and responding to it as God's moment for you now, while it is called Today, rather than wishing it were yesterday or tomorrow. There is a verse in Deuteronomy: 'In the morning thou shalt say, "Would God it were evening!" and at even thou shalt say, "Would God it were morning!"' Haven't we all caught ourselves wishing the present away like that? And if you do this, it will be because, as the Deuteronomist says, 'Thou shalt have none assurance of thy life' – a lack of trust, trust of the Father in whose hands the times and seasons are. A wise man[2] once said: 'Only a Christian can live wholly in the present; for to him the past is pardoned and the future is safe in God.' The past is pardoned: the Christian life must be a life without regrets, without remorse. If you have made a decision, and you still feel, taking all in all, it was the right one, then don't look over your shoulder on what might have been; if it was wrong, ask for forgiveness and accept the present consequences, happily and without remorse. Nothing is more sapping than remorse, nothing more corrosive of the powers you should be using to meet the present.

God is eternally living and working in the now. He doesn't say, 'Oh, if only men hadn't got my purposes into such a frightful mess, I might be able to do something for them.' Patiently he uses every situation, however tangled it may have got by human sin, and, like the potter with the plastic clay in his hands, creates out of it a wholly new moment, a fresh situation of opportunity, in which his will

[2] Søren Kierkegaard.

can be answered and his design furthered. The Christian is the person who sees every time and every situation, however dreary and repetitive, as God sees it – a fresh creation from his hand, demanding its own response in perhaps a wholly new and creative way. Under God he is free over it. He has won through to a purchase over events; he has risen with Christ.

Don't we envy the people who never get flurried, who always, however busy, seem to have time for us and for what they want to do, who are always on top of the clock? I know I do, for they seem to me to possess one of the greatest liberties of our age. Well, that is not an accident in any person, nor is it merely a matter of temperament. It is a quality of saints. It comes from a singleness of purpose; it is given to those who have sunk roots deep into eternity, to those who have made up their minds about God and his purpose for them, who see life whole and therefore see it steadily. It is these who can rise above time and its slavery. It is he that believeth that shall not make haste.

9

The World that God Loves[1]

'God loved the world so much that he gave his only Son'
(John 3.16, NEB)

'The world that God loves' – that is the theme which you of the Church Missionary Society have taken for your work this year. And that theme is, of course, founded on this text.

I say 'of course'; but it will probably come as a surprise to you, as it did to me, to realize that there is no other text in the Bible on which it could be founded. Never elsewhere are *'the world'* and 'the love of God' brought into conjunction. God in the Old Testament is 'loving unto *Israel*' and he is described as having set his love upon his *people* (Deut. 7.7); and in the New Testament the nearest parallel to our text is St Paul's words: 'Christ loved the *church* and gave himself up for it' (Eph. 5.25).

Of course it is implied that God's love in Christ knows no bounds, but only in this passage of St John is it actually said that he loves *the world*. This is the more remarkable when we recall that the whole tenor of St John's theology is the other way. Much more typical is his statement that Christ 'loved his own who were in the world' (John 13.1). And indeed in this gospel he is not recorded as loving anyone else: Jesus the friend of publicans and sinners belongs entirely to the Synoptic portrait.[2]

It has often been noted that love in the Johannine writings, however deep, is limited in scope to the Christian brotherhood.

[1] Sermon preached before the Church Missionary Society at St Martin-in-the-Fields, London, 28 January 1963.
[2] The incident of the woman taken in adultery in John 7.53–8.11 is, of course, not originally part of the Johannine text.

Characteristic is the apparent smugness of the words, 'We know that we are of God's family, while the whole godless world lies in the power of the evil one' (I John 5.15). Christians are told not to pray for the world (John 17.9): indeed, they are actually told not to love the world (I John 2.15). Yet in the midst of all this we have the most quoted Johannine text – and we suppose the most typical: 'God loved the world so much that he gave his only Son.'

How does it all hang together? Of course, St John is using the word 'world' with subtly different nuances, and an adequate Bible study would require us to wrestle with these. But the short answer is given by St John himself when he represents Jesus as saying to the Father about 'his own': 'I pray thee not to take them out of the world. . . . As thou hast sent me into the world, I have sent them into the world . . . that the world may believe' (John 17.15–21).

In other words, the love of God in Christ for the church is always *for the sake of the world*. The church is loved, and the church exists, only for the world which is *not yet* the church. Or we may put the matter in another way by saying that the church exists only for the sake of *the Kingdom* – in which ultimately there is neither world nor church, for both will have become one.

Nothing is more important for a truly biblical outlook or for a truly Christian 'style of life' than that we should have our doctrine of the church properly related to that of the Kingdom – for otherwise the church becomes an end in itself and everything else is subtly distorted. The church is the instrument of the Kingdom, and stands always between the Kingdom accomplished and the Kingdom acknowledged.[3] Its entire existence is orientated towards that area of life where the universal kingship of God in Christ is *not yet* accepted.

This means that it is by its very nature the *missionary* community, which is only another way of saying that it is the *eschatological* community (for it lives under the judgement of the day when church and Kingdom will be identical and the temple will be no more) or that it is the *secular* community, existing for the sake of life in this age (or *saeculum*) in which Christ is King but not yet crowned.

[3] See O. Cullmann, 'The Kingship of Christ and the Church in the New Testament', in *The Early Church*, chapter 5.

This has profound practical implications for the life and mission of the church. For I am more and more convinced that unless we constantly remember that God first loves the world, *and the church for the sake of the world,* all the fruits of revival which we see in our time may indeed taste sweet to our mouth but will turn sour in our stomach (Rev. 10.10). God has renewed the face of the church in our generation in many glorious ways. There has been a notable revival, not merely *in* the church (as has often happened before in separate sections of it, frequently at the expense of breaking the Body), but *of* the church. *And yet there is much less talk of the kingdom of God than there was 30 years ago –* and a great deal more talk of the people of God.

Much of this indeed is more biblically based. But if we stick there – if we remain church-centred rather than Kingdom-centred – then I fear that we shall hear the whisper in our soul: 'The fruit that you longed for is gone from you' (Rev. 18.14). The forces making for renewal will have become curved in upon themselves, and all will be lost. Let me speak of that fear in relation to the four great movements of renewal in our day.

1. *The Liturgical Movement.* I need not dilate upon all that the Spirit has been saying to the churches. There has been a marvellous revival in our understanding of the relation of communion to community, of liturgy to society. For the first time since the early centuries of the church we are seeing the significance of St Paul's seminal insight that it is *because* of the one loaf that we who are many are one body (I Cor. 10.17 – a verse whose meaning has been seriously obscured from English eyes by the rendering of the Authorized Version – 'for we being many *are* one bread, one body'). We have come to see that we can share in the body of Christ in the sacrament only as we share in his body the church – and *vice versa.* The eucharist is through and through the act of the whole people of God.

All this is pure gain, and we rightly rejoice in it. And yet in the rejoicing we seldom remember that the primary context of the eucharist in the institution of Jesus was not the church but the Kingdom. In the New Testament it points forward always to 'the time when it finds its fulfilment in the kingdom of God' (Luke

22.16, 18; Mark 14.25): it exists to 'proclaim the death of the Lord until he comes' (I Cor. 11.26). It is the eschatological meal, bounded always by the Kingdom and orientated towards the world which is not yet the church.

Liturgy and evangelism are simply the inside and the outside of the one act of 'proclaiming the Lord's death'. And not only, as we are finding in our parishes, is liturgy central to evangelism but, as Douglas Webster has insisted in his splendid contribution to *The Parish Communion Today*,[4] evangelism is central to liturgy – or it will die on us, while the meat is yet in our mouths (Psalm 78.31). It will become church-bound, it will lose its roots in the soil of the secular. And the Holy Communion is nothing if it is not the making holy of the common.

But how terribly easily liturgy can simply create 'another world' of its own, where everything is done according to the latest (or the oldest) models, but which merely goes on side by side with real life. As Eric James has said in his pamphlet *The Roots of the Liturgy*[5]: 'The great danger is that liturgy creates a world of things over against the secular, instead of a vision of the sacredness of the secular.' It can so easily become theatre, with an independent life of its own 'neither natural nor necessarily supernatural'.

Only if liturgy makes us more sensitive to the holy in the common, to the Christ in the hungry, the naked, the homeless and the prisoner, do we not eat judgement to ourselves. Otherwise it merely increases the damnation of the 'church-bound', of those who claim to have 'known' and to have said 'Lord, Lord'. The renewal of the *church* through the liturgical movement is going to depend in the long run, I am convinced, on a sense of the priority of the *Kingdom*. And this I do not readily detect.

2. *The Ecumenical Movement.* Again, what riches and glory! Blessed indeed are the eyes which see the things which we see! After a week of prayer for unity borne along by larger hopes than any before it, we cannot be wrong in believing that we have begun at last to see Satan falling. And yet experience shows that the quest for unity will go sour on us if it remains church-centred. We can

4 Ed. D. M. Paton.
5 *Prism* Pamphlet No. 1.

share in our Lord's prayer for unity only if it is subordinated to the petition 'that *the world* may believe' (John 17.21). Otherwise all we shall get could be a bigger and better ecclesiastical combine.

The ecumenical venture will retain its vision and keep its course only if it has a higher doctrine of the church than it does of the ministry and a higher doctrine of the Kingdom than it does of the church. Reverse these priorities, as so much church-bound debate does, and how sterile it becomes! If, as Anglicans, we are a 'bridge-church' in the sense of being a bridge merely from church to church, and not from the world to the Kingdom, we shall find, as we are already in danger of finding, that no one will want to walk on us.

The ecumenical movement sprang from the missionary drive to 'speed the coming of the day of God' (II Pet. 3.12), and in its early 'Life and Work' conferences it 'looked forward to new heavens and a new earth, the home of justice' (II Pet. 3.13). Now the International Missionary Council is merged in the World Council of Churches (rightly – but is the church to be missionary or the mission churchy?), and we hear ominously more of 'Faith and Order' than of 'Life and Work'.

The renewal of her unity: there is no more urgent point of obedience for the church. But always, always, we must ask: 'Unity for what?'

3. *The Biblical Revival.* Again, what a gift to the church! But how easily once more it can become an enterprise pursued for its own sake, in a closed world walled round by volumes of Kittel's *Theological Wordbook of the Bible*! I have been committed to this revival as keenly as to the other three and I will not go back on it, but already I detect signs of 'biblical theology' becoming a dirty word. And that will be a tragedy for the church. For it represents a permanent advance not to be cast aside, any more than that of biblical criticism. It is not yet an advance in depth, and our thinking could all too rapidly lose again its biblical perspective. And yet there are real dangers.

Ted Wickham, the Bishop of Middleton, has observed how little of the theology which pours from our presses has any 'bite' on the modern world. We desperately need more 'applied' rather than 'pure' theology. It must indeed be biblical through and through. But let it start from the questions and perplexities of *the world that God loves*. Let it be what Paul Tillich, its towering exponent, calls an 'answering theology'.

The revival of biblical theology has been a tremendous force of renewal. It will be a fearful irony if the biblical theologians themselves ignore the implications of their own controlling category, which they have done so much to deepen for us – 'the kingdom of God'. Karl Barth changed the title of his *magnum opus* from *Christian Dogmatics* to *Church Dogmatics*. When will he or anyone else give us a 'Kingdom Dogmatics'?

4. *The Recovery of the Laity.* We are witnessing in our day, again for the first time since the primitive church, the *Laos* really coming to its own. Once more, let us rejoice and be exceeding glad. It is still a stripling, and in most places, let us face it, a weakling child. But already, I believe, we can see the dangers of deformation. The enterprise can so easily be viewed simply as waking the sleeping partners of the clergy and creating better members of the organization church. The great danger of the thrilling movement for lay training beginning to stir in our churches is that it should become congregation-centred rather than world-centred.

There are, as Mark Gibbs pointed out in an article in *Frontier*,[6] two kinds of laymen – the minority whose primary interest is in the life of the church and the majority whose primary interest is in the life of the world. And all lay training schemes, whatever their good intentions, are likely to be swamped by the first – for these are the parson's captive audience, and a starved audience at that. Of course we must feed them, but without leaving to the rest merely the crumbs that fall. For we can so easily define 'laicity' (to use Congar's word) in terms of churchmanship (or even of non-clericy), whereas, as both he[7] and Bonhoeffer[8] insist, it must be defined in terms of worldliness – holy worldliness.

The true layman is the man for whom the things of the world

[6] 'Two Kinds of Laity', *Frontier*, Spring 1962, Vol. 5, No. 1.
[7] Y. Congar, *Lay People in the Church*, pp. 17–21.
[8] D. Bonhoeffer, *Letters and Papers from Prison* (1967 ed.), pp. 198-202.

exist for their own sake. They don't first have to become religious in order to be interesting. They have their authenticity simply because they are part of the world God loves. And it is for this world that the church exists, as it was for this world that God gave his Son.

That was how God showed himself to be God and that is how the church must show itself to be the church. The rallying cry 'Let the church be the church' is safe only if we really know what 'being the church' means – the world's priest, but also the world's deacon. Ronald Gregor Smith has said: 'The church cannot stand over the world with a whip; nor can it get behind it with a load of dynamite. The whip and the dynamite, where available, would be better used on itself. The world is not, I think, "hungry for God" in the sense of popular conservatizing evangelists, who really mean by that a hunger to hear their own words in the old accepted terminology of their fathers – or rather their grandfathers (for their fathers knew better). The world is very suspicious, and rightly so, of those who cry "The temple of the Lord are these", for it has had long experience of the unbridled ambitions of the church over against the world. What the world would really see gladly is an honest and complete recognition, without any ulterior motives, by those who claim to carry forward the message of Christianity, of the existence of the world with all its principles of movement, hopes and possibilities.'[9]

That, I believe, is what *loving* the world means as God loved it – for its own sake. It is the first prerequisite of any Christian mission. And that 'sacred secularity', as he called it in one of his recent *News-Letters*,[10] is, I believe, the greatest insight (of all the many) of which Max Warren has brought to the Church Missionary Society and through it to the world church. What a transformation he has wrought – and yet how I fear it is only skin-deep in us all. As he passes on his tremendous burden after twenty-one gruelling years as General Secretary he bequeaths to us a heritage on which we cannot and dare not go back. For *sic deus dilexit mundum* – that was the way in which God loved the world.

[9] *The New Man: Christianity and Man's Coming of Age*, pp. 68f.
[10] *CMS News-Letter*, September 1962.

10

The Ecumenical Consequences of *Humanae Vitae*[1]

The morning following the publication of the papal encyclical *Humanae Vitae* on contraception an English newspaper commented (and it was the universal first reaction): 'Ecumenically, of course, the encyclical is a total disaster.' I disagree.

Of course, it is tragic beyond words. No one could have wished it this way. Yet in fact what has been shaken is what had to be shaken if ecumenical progress is to be made. The *way* it has been shaken is going to demand all the prayerful patience and loving understanding of the total Christian Church, Catholic and Protestant, if renewal and wholeness is to come out of it rather than backlash and disintegration. And this will be the task not of a day nor even of a generation. Yet certain things have been undermined – more suddenly than any could have dared to expect – that in the end must give. I would cite six.

1. The first is a concept of authority which is as alien to the New Testament as it is an anachronism to the second half of the twentieth century. The imposed, heteronomous authority of *Roma locuta est, causa finita est* (Rome has spoken, the issue is settled) was in any case fast on the way out. *Whatever* the Pope had said on birth control would have been accepted or rejected by the majority of educated Roman Catholics to the degree that it authenticated *itself* and *not* because Rome had spoken. To that extent the traditional Roman Catholic concept of authority had already been subtly but decisively changed. What is new is that a totally unsubtle attempt

[1] Written originally for the American Roman Catholic magazine *The Critic* (October 1968), and reprinted in *New Christian*, 31 October 1968.

to exercise it has damaged it beyond visible hope of repair.

The tragedy is that the papal writ will run for the most part only in places where its damage will prove greatest – among the poverty-stricken and uneducated and among authoritarian governments (whose *use* of contraceptive techniques to depress personal freedom was ironically one of the dangers the encyclical aimed to avert). Elsewhere it will have little effect, except to debase the currency of intellectual honesty. The deeper tragedy is that an unrivalled opportunity has been missed (since on this subject *everyone* would listen) for a creative act of statesmanship in transforming from within an understanding of authority that was in any case becoming powerless from without. The dilemma in which the Pope was placed was indeed acute; but with imaginative leadership there can be little doubt that the theological resources were there in the church for a genuine transcendence of the old that would *not* have to be covered by the face-saving formula 'as the Catholic church has always taught'. But that opportunity has been missed, never to recur in this form again. Indeed the clock has actually been set back. For as Charles Davis has pointed out, 'What is involved is not just the rejection of contraception, but the rejection of the notable advance in Catholic moral thinking that led to its acceptance'. But if that is the only way in which a false concept of authority can be overcome, so be it.

2. The second idol to be shown to have feet of clay is the closely associated image of the papacy as an individual infallible oracle. However much, technically speaking, this has never been Roman doctrine, which has therefore not been affected by the present case, there is no doubt whatever that the whole incident has been a slap in the face for collegiality and for the *consensus fidelium* and a reversion to the pitting of one man's judgement against the considered wisdom of the church. Even though the encyclical is not technically an infallible pronouncement, the very concept of infallibility has received a knock from which it will not recover. Few will now bother to ask whether the Pope is infallible. The credibility gap is too great. They are much more concerned with whether the pill is infallible.

The demise of the notion of infallibility (belonging to the same world as the indelibility of orders and the divine right of kings) has been going on quietly for a long time. Some weeks before the Pope's latest pronouncement I was giving a series of lectures to the Roman Catholic Catechetical Institute in London. It was a highly intelligent and receptive audience, drawn from many parts of the world. Pinned to the College notice-board was the press-cutting: 'Pope reaffirms infallibility.' And one knows why students – even in this case very mature students – pin cuttings on notice-boards.

There have of recent years been Anglican, and other, voices suggesting that there is nothing ultimately inimical in the papacy as a focus of Christian unity. But it would have to be a papacy stripped of any pretensions to plenary inspiration or oracular infallibility. The very fact that these claims have been so crudely reasserted and so visibly shaken is a portent of ecumenical significance and hope. If in the ensuing agony the *magisterium* can genuinely be redefined in terms of the *ministerium*, the lord and master in terms of the servant of the servants of God, then much good may yet emerge for Christian unity. Alas, further recognition of the primacy of Rome cannot now come in this pontificate. But that was probably too much to expect anyhow. Yet the process of acceptability begun by Pope John could actually be speeded rather than stopped by his successor's attempt to stem the tide. But this brings me to my third, closely related, point.

3. The papacy will have to be dissociated not only from anachronistic concepts of authority and infallibility but from the dynastic monarchy of the Roman court. And that dissociation, too, must have been hastened. The automatic succession of Italian popes is surely now finished. Cardinal Montini was the very best from that stock – indeed he was strongly backed by reformers in preference to Pope John. Yet for all his cosmopolitan concern he has proved in the event mentally too unadaptable, too muscle-bound, to transcend the limitations of his origin. The same newspaper I quoted earlier[2] ended its editorial with the words: 'The birth control question called for the vision and understanding of a Holy Father. It has evoked the reflex responses of a Bishop of Rome.' The reflex responses of an unconstitutional monarch, however benevolent, cannot, alas, be trusted with the pill any more than politically

[2] *The Guardian.*

they can be trusted with the button. It is painful to see a humane man crushed in the hinge of such a fate. One is tempted to echo Tacitus' obituary of the Emperor Galba: *'omnium consensu capax imperii nisi imperasset'* (by universal consent capable of empire, had he not been emperor). But that would be unfair. Paul VI will surely be remembered as a good pope. As in the classical Greek tragedy, it is the one flaw of his inflexible integrity which has proved his undoing.

The sadness is that nothing *else* he says on the international scene – particularly in his chosen field of peace and poverty (so inescapably bound up with population) – will now be heard. The rest of his reign has inevitably been neutralized. For the very reason that he has now shown himself beyond doubt to be a conservative reformer rather than a radical (and hitherto the contrary could, just, be argued), he may still be able to put through significant reforms of the Vatican machine. But as a creative world-force – even within the Roman Catholic church – his power must wane. His greatest remaining contribution could be to set a tradition by being the first pope to retire (the first Archbishop of Canterbury only did so forty years ago) – at the seventy-five years he has designated for others – and to use the next four years to facilitate a genuinely international election. In this way he could earn the gratitude of the entire ecumenical church. For a truly supra-national focus of loyalty and leadership is the corollary of that indigenous local catholicism, in liturgy and life, which must increasingly be the pattern of Christian presence.

4. The fourth casualty of recent events is the traditional concept of natural law – the basis on which the papal decision was commended. This, like the other foundations whose weakness has been exposed, has also been under attrition for some time. What should theoretically command the rational assent not only of all Christians but of all right-thinking men has increasingly held suasion only for Roman Catholics, and of these a diminishing number. Something has clearly gone wrong. When St Paul appealed to the law of nature written in men's hearts, he made the point – the essential point – that 'their own conscience bears witness' to it (Rom. 2.15). It must be able to commend itself with the argument being used in the Ministry of Transport's current road-safety campaign: 'You *know*

it makes sense.' And that is the kind of self-authenticating conviction that the prohibition of contraceptives singularly fails to carry.

So far from shining in its own light, the ban is bolstered by argumentation that is not even logical. In the following key passage of the encyclical the first sentence appeals precisely to the assent that I have mentioned. But the 'hence' joining it to the second is clearly a non-sequitur (the Latin in fact only has *pariter*):

> It is justly observed that a conjugal act imposed upon one's partner without regard for his or her condition and lawful desires is not a true act of love, and therefore denies an exigency of right moral order in the relationship between husband and wife. Hence, one who reflects well must also recognize that a reciprocal act of love, which jeopardizes the responsibility to transmit life which God the Creator, according to particular laws, inserted therein, is in contradiction with the design constitutive of marriage.

The Pope continues:

> Upright men can even better convince themselves of the solid grounds on which the teaching of the church in this field is based (by reflecting on) the consequences of methods of artificial birth control.

For such methods, he asserts, open a wide and easy road to exploitation of women by men and of individuals by the state. He does not apparently recognize that the (hoped-for) pill perfecting the 'natural' rhythm would render a woman equally safe as an 'instrument of selfish enjoyment', nor that the real, revolutionary new freedom which contraceptives offer is in fact not to men but to women. But the essential point on which one has to insist is the elementary moral principle that *abusus non tollit usum* – abuse does not deny the proper use. In the original wording of a resolution put to the 1968 Lambeth Conference,

> the consequences of a rational and disciplined use of artificial methods of birth control do not of themselves lead to moral degradation, but far more often to personal maturity and to the achievement of the highest aims of Christian marriage.

Indeed, to suggest otherwise is an insult to the intelligence and sensibilities of those of us who *know* from personal experience. This, of course, is the burden of those Roman Catholic couples who wrote so poignantly in *The Experience of Marriage*, edited by Michael Novak, and whose position was endorsed by the great majority of the Pope's advisory commission.

The trouble is that the traditional concept of natural law has yet to catch up with the understanding of personality in the modern world. What is 'natural' is defined in sub-personal, biological categories rather than in terms of what makes for deep, free, mature, responsible personal relationships. So far from exceeding the morality of the secular humanists, the Catholic theology of natural law falls far short of it. A valid natural theology is more than ever necessary in morals as elsewhere. But it will have to be spelt out in terms of what love – the highest respect for persons as persons in their particular context – really requires. The case for such a contextual ethic has not been better put than by Fr John J. Noonan in his article, 'Authority, Usury and Contraception', in *Cross Currents* (Winter 1966):

> What acts are just and charitable depends on the concrete circumstances of a society. . . . What has been thought to have been essential may be seen as essential only in a given context. Such re-examination occurred with respect to the usury rule.

He urges the same reconsideration in regard to contraception.

> The church is always free to look again, to see if, in a new environment, the rule is still the best specification of the commandment of love.

The tragedy of *Humanae Vitae* is that one man has temporarily tried to block that freedom. The hope is that the old static concept of natural law has finally been exposed as subnatural. Roman and non-Roman Christians can now work *together* on putting something better in its place. This is a real advance on a situation in which Christian ethics has been from the point of view of Catholic-Protestant relations one of the most segregated subjects in the syllabus.

5. The fifth barrier to ecumenical understanding to fall is surely going to be the place of the confessional as a pastoral condition of

receiving Communion. One of the tragedies again of the new situation is that it must inevitably derogate from the true value and integrity of sacramental confession. Both priests and penitents will be faced with severe dilemmas of silence and dishonesty. Unease at the confessional will impound the guilt it is meant to cure.

The advice 'Whatever you do, don't cut yourself off from the sacraments' means in effect that the individual is left to decide whether he is in a state of grace to receive. If it had been openly said that contraception was an issue of personal conscience, then of course the liberation would have been positive and constructive. As it is, the uneasy toleration is negative and psychologically erosive. But for good or for ill I believe that a break-through has been made. The place of the confessor as an arbiter of conscience will never be the same again. Since non-Roman Catholics have never subscribed to that place, they cannot but mutely rejoice, while sharing the agony of conscience now imposed on so many of their brothers and sisters in Christ.

6. The sixth consequence I see much less clearly than the others. It could mean a real hastening of the break-up of the church *as a religious organization*. The religious club is becoming more and more peripheral in a secular world and its preservation by no means obviously stands in a 1 : 1 relation to turning the world upside down in the power of the kingdom of love. For this latter task structure, strategy, organization and institution are still indispensable. But the particular 'body' in which the church has lived in the pre-secular 'religious' centuries with which its existence has so far coincided is becoming historically more irrelevant. The casing by which it is incapsulated is increasingly insulating the life within it from the society it is meant to be leavening and transforming. I said in a recent article[3] that the church must die to this body either by a hardening of the skin or by a bursting of the skin, and I reckoned that if things were simply allowed to take their course the former was more likely.

On the face of it the Pope's action represents a depressing hardening of the skin. But the effect of a sudden hardening – or of a dramatic disclosure that the skin is beyond the point of organic change –

[3] 'The Exploding Church', *The Observer*, 14 April 1968, reproduced in substance in the second half of chapter 12 below.

can be a cracking. Whatever now happens or does not happen, Charles Davis has been proved right to the extent that those who want renewal of the Roman Catholic Church will have directly to confront papal authority or relinquish their efforts. The skin of the most hardened religious institution in Christendom is cracking all over. This does not mean that the body will break up – such an outcome is highly unlikely – nor that it will not form a new skin which can become just as encrusted. But for those deeply concerned for ecumenism it is of real and hopeful significance. For as traditionally understood the ecumenical movement is in danger of running out of steam. Among the younger generation, as Fr Eugene Bianchi, S.J., puts it in his essay in *American Catholic Exodus,* edited by John O'Connor, 'Institutional ecumenism . . . is not much more attractive than are the institutional churches themselves.' And Robert McAfee Brown adds: 'Ecumenism is going to move in a new direction in our day, the day of increasing involvement in the secular order. Unless it does this, it will become increasingly precious and ingrown.' Perhaps Pope Paul by making institutional ecumenism more uninviting has struck a decisive blow for secular ecumenism. And in that 'ecumenical movement of those who hope to diminish the number of stunted lives' (Michael Novak), Christians and non-Christians, religious and non-religious, can equally be involved.

Writing in that same symposium Professor Wilhelmsen of Dallas contributes a superbly uninhibited counterblast from the radical right. 'If the heretics in our midst,' he says of the post-Conciliar reformers, succeed in their efforts, 'the Roman Catholic Church as we have known it will disappear.' It could be said that by one letter Paul VI has ensured that result more effectively than they all. Of course, one must not exaggerate. But *as we have known it* the old Roman Catholicism, in the six respects I have mentioned, has, I believe, received a mortal blow. Naturally a body of that size takes a long time to notice the effects. Indeed in this sheer size I actually see grounds of hope. A smaller religious organization – as one sees from the English Free Churches – uses up almost all its recuperative powers in attending to its wounds. It becomes preoccupied, defensive and insecure. The Roman Catholic Church can afford to be much less worried. One would hope, if it is not presumptuous to say so, that it might even learn something from the more organic and flexible way of absorbing change that has always characterized the Anglican tradition.

But in any case we must all in future learn of each other. For, as someone has said, 'We're all RCs now' – whether that stands for Roman Catholics, Reformed Churchmen or Radical Christians. An Anglican has long since got used, vis-à-vis the Protestant churches, to an ecumenical scene in which the important lines of agreement and disagreement run across rather than along the denominational frontiers. He has still to pinch himself a little to believe that this is true also in the case of Rome. Yet that is increasingly borne out in my experience. My best press these days seems to come from Roman Catholics and the great majority of my ecumenical invitations. Though I am under no illusions that I should have had the freedom to begin to speak or write as I have done as a bishop of the Roman obedience, I frequently find myself in the embarrassing position of apparently being asked to say things to Roman Catholics which they know they cannot hear from their own hierarchy. And with the mouths of the hierarchy full now of the Pope's latest and hottest potato one must, I suppose, expect this to increase. But at my consecration, as a reminder that one was being called to be a bishop not merely in the Church of England but in the Church of God, I set at the centre of my pectoral cross the symbol of the World Council of Churches. Little did I expect, within a generation, an ecumenical situation in which that symbol would be manifestly too small.

11

Theological Freedom and Social Responsibility

A concern that has marked much of my work has been the combination of theological freedom and social responsibility. Indeed, this could be regarded as one of the characteristic contributions of the Anglican tradition in which I stand. One could instance the notable (even if at times notorious) succession in the bishopric of Birmingham of Charles Gore, E. W. Barnes and Leonard Wilson. Each in his different way stood for a distinctive and courageous fusion of the two.

It was therefore with pleasure and honour that I accepted the invitation of the Protestant Episcopal Church of the United States to submit evidence to its advisory committee on 'Theological Debate within the Church'. This had been set up under the chairmanship of Bishop Stephen Bayne to try to bring some wisdom out of the unhappy attempt to arraign for heresy the then Bishop of California, James A. Pike, himself a notable, if also at times notorious, combiner of the two strains. Its Report, *Theological Freedom and Social Responsibility*, was a model of Christian maturity and good sense. It was published, with a selection of the supporting evidence, by the Seabury Press in 1967. Since it is not widely available, I have included my contribution here. The questions are those to which answers were requested by the committee.

1. *What obligations does the church have for encouraging theological inquiry and social criticism? What procedures should it provide to fulfil those obligations?*

The short answer to the first question must surely be 'many in every way'. I doubt in fact whether the church ever has an obligation to *discourage* either theological inquiry or social criticism. For both belong to its very life as the *avant-garde* of the kingdom of God. They represent essential functions of its *prophetic* ministry to the world. By the same token they are manifestations of the Spirit, and cannot be subject to the call and command of the church. The task of the church is to encourage the movement of prophetic inquiry and criticism, to listen to it, and then to test, acknowledge, and act upon whatever in it is of God. And the primary way in which the church gives encouragement is by allowing the maximum possible freedom – both in the conditions and security which it affords to its thinkers and agents and in its refusal to suppress voices, however uncomfortable or embarrassing. These may indeed be genuinely embarrassing (as, of course, may be the voices of those who are theologically or socially reactionary). And there must be equally full opportunity for those who think them inadequate or wrong to state the contrary opinion.

All exploration, whether in the theological or the social field, involves the risk, indeed the certainty, of mistakes. But it is at least arguable, from the study of church history, that more damage has without exception been done in the long run by the suppression of opinion than by any error given rein by freedom. At any rate the church must always act on the assumption, till proved otherwise, that freedom will in any instance be less harmful than the attempt to curb it. And this is even more true in an age in which any kind of authoritarianism is, rightly, suspect. The church's record in this matter is such that there is the heaviest possible presupposition that it has more to gain, both in respect and in honesty, from erring in the direction of liberality. But its basis for this is not merely prudential. It is grounded in the genuine trust of truth, represented in the attitude of Gamaliel – that any new movement will flourish if it be of God and wither if it be not. And it is an attitude which has historically been one of the glories of the Anglican church at its wisest and best.

Moreover, in encouraging theological inquiry and social criticism, the church has the task of doing all it can positively to foster the conditions in which schools of prophets may arise and flourish. Unless it is prepared to support enterprises both in thought and action which will be risky, divisive, and undertaken increasingly in conjunction with non-Christian agencies, the church cannot rightly expect to have the wisdom to meet new challenges. There will indeed be particular occasions when the official church may take the initiative in commissioning pieces of research or criticism. (To an outsider, it seemed an admirable example of this when the Anglican Church of Canada invited Mr Pierre Berton to write, in complete freedom, his critique of the church contained in *The Comfortable Pew*). For the most part, however, it has to recognize that most creative theological inquiry and social criticism will start from the bottom rather than the top. The ministry of the Establishment is to make it possible for this to be heard (however awkward, one-sided or wrongheaded it may appear) and to preserve the ring-fence of free and responsible debate.

The question is made more complicated – though it is not fundamentally altered – when the individual initiative in theological inquiry or social criticism comes from within the ranks of the Establishment itself, and in particular when it is voiced by a bishop of the church. Again, I believe the church must start by insisting equally strongly on the right, and indeed the duty, of a bishop, like any other member of the church, to exercise his ministry of prophecy. The need even to say this reflects the truth in the cynical observation that the way the church kills its prophets nowadays is not by stoning but by consecration.

The validity of the bishop's right to exercise his individual gift of prophecy has been more readily recognized in the field of social criticism than in that of theological inquiry. William Temple was able to make it abundantly clear that he continued to speak as an individual even after he became archbishop. Indeed, so emphatic was he on the difference between that which he advocated as an individual and that to which he would wish to commit the church, that he said that if anyone got up in Convocation to propose in the name of the Church of England the programme of reform set out in his *Christianity and Social Order* he would rise to oppose him. And there is a long and honourable record of bishops on the picket-lines or in prison for acts of social witness on which they would never presume to suggest that every loyal member of their church must agree with them.

When it comes to theological inquiry the matter is further complicated by the tradition that bishops, by virtue of their order, are, in some unique way, the repositories and guardians of doctrine. This tradition has much historically to explain it and no doubt at the time to justify it. But I doubt if it can seriously be defended in a church which takes seriously the consensus of the whole people of God. Of course, bishops have extra responsibility in this as in all respects not to lead astray the flock (and of this I shall speak further in answer to the second question). But it would seem to me vital in the present situation to make it more than ever clear that a bishop when speaking on doctrine is *not ipso facto* speaking as the *vox populi dei*. He can, and should (according to his capacity) be exploring, probing, and raising questions he cannot answer, as much as anyone else. And the church should have the wisdom and the wit to recognize this as normal, not exceptional (let alone eccentric), within the total life of the Body. This carries with it additional risks, but where these risks are declined the dangers of dissolution and death are the greater.

2. What obligations should be assumed by those who participate in theological inquiry and social criticism?

In general, there would not seem to me much to be said here that is not obvious. Clearly the freedom of which I have spoken carries corresponding responsibilities. There is the self-evident obligation to encourage and respect the freedom and judgement of others. There is the requirement laid upon all participants to show that maturity of converse and of controversy which should characterize any Christian pursuit of and care for the truth in love. Both in social criticism and theological inquiry there is the need for rigorous discipline to respect facts and sound learning and not to rush in on the basis of press reports or journalistic summaries. This is so obvious as hardly to deserve mention, were it not an aspect of Christian ethics for which the clergy are not always notable. (It was a church newspaper in England that found it necessary to say that it would not publish letters on *Honest to God* by those who had not read the book. Its rival evinced no such scruple!)

Perhaps I may confine my comments to the additional responsibility which it seems to me that a bishop should reasonably be expected to show in this matter. He will be the more aware that his lightest word is liable to be taken up – and distorted – by the public media. The inordinate attention paid to what he says – which is largely a secular phenomenon – derives almost entirely from his office, and his utterances and actions will therefore appear, particularly outside the church, but also to embarrassed faithful within, to commit many others than himself. This means that he must exercise special prudence and imagination (though ultimately how things will be taken up is beyond his control and often beyond anyone's imagination!). And he will have the theological responsibility, not only of being as well-read and well-informed as his time and capacity allow, but of being careful to insist when he is speaking with the authority of his office and when he is not. But in the last analysis the responsibility of the bishop in doctrine is different only in degree not kind from that of any other baptized Christian, just as the responsibility of the priest in politics differs from that of the laity only in degree, not kind.

3. *What is heresy? How should the church define, detect and deal with it?*

I find myself having very little to say on this that has not been said far better by John Macquarrie in his article 'Some Thoughts on Heresy' in *Christianity and Crisis* of 26 December 1966. Indeed, I would urge that this be reproduced in any published report of the Advisory Committee.[1] My comments are simply footnotes to it.

While heresy remains a living theological category, genuine and serious heresy is, as Macquarrie insists, extremely rare. Far more damage would seem to be done by throwing the term around in popular ecclesiastical debate than by letting it lapse into desuetude. For it carries with it, especially in such combinations as 'heresy-hunt' and 'heresy-trial', overtones and associations which are today

---

[1] It was. Macquarrie defined the purpose of his article as being 'to show that the concept of heresy has become a very elusive one, that heresy trials are definitely an anachronism in the twentieth century, and that the church must find a more adult way of dealing with threats to the integrity of its faith'.

almost wholly unfortunate. Moreover, it suggests, well nigh un-
avoidably, a criterion of truth (namely, conformity to proposition
or formula – and past propositions and formulae at that) which is
per se false to the nature of Christian faith, and it is associated with
methods of persuading men to the truth (anathemas, imprimaturs,
indices, excommunications, inquisitions, and the rest) which belong
to a world that is not even humanist, let alone Christian. Even
'rebukes' in the name of ecclesiastical authority are, as Macquarrie
points out, of very doubtful value. The only answer to bad theology
is better theology. If, for the sake of example, Bishop Barnes' book,
The Rise of Christianity, was genuinely heretical, which is surely
very doubtful, its errors were contained far more by its failure to win
any serious body of support from scholars (and by such reasoned
replies as that of C. H. Dodd) than by archepiscopal rebuke. This,
as Macquarrie points out, does not mean that church leaders should
not seek to give responsible guidance to their numbers, if only to
make clear, both in doctrine and in politics, the limits to which a
man is committing the church as a whole.

The church must also give positive witness to the fact that integrity is a more fundamental theological virtue than orthodoxy (at
any rate as that word has come to be defined in the Western church).
A man of unimpeachable orthodoxy but uncertain integrity is a far
greater threat to Christian truth than the man of questionable
orthodoxy but undeniable integrity. Moreover, the man who, however mistakenly or inadequately, genuinely intends what the church
means (and this is implied in the desire of the heretic, as opposed
to the apostate, to say what he says from the inside) is unlikely in
the long run to damage it seriously.

One could, indeed, plausibly argue the opposite case and say that
the most serious damage to the cause of Christian truth today is done
by those who refuse to question the deposit of tradition, socially or
theologically. The point has been made in the World Council of
Churches' discussion on 'The Missionary Structure of the Congregation' that heretical *structures* are today far more destructive of
the mission and ministry of the church than any conceptual
heresy and that these are in fact upheld and perpetuated by the most
conservative rather than the most radical. And there is a parallel
in the doctrinal field to the heretical effect of structural fundamental-

ism in the ecclesiastical. It is arguable, for instance, that the belief that Jesus was in every respect *like* a man but not *really* one of us is today a much more insidious menace to the Faith than the parallel heresy that he was not really God but like God. For, unless Jesus was genuinely man, the Gospel simply cannot begin to speak to the human condition, never mind where it ends. This, of course, has always been insisted upon with the utmost emphasis by Christian orthodoxy. But it is hardly open to question that it is the most traditionally orthodox statements of the sinless perfection of Christ's manhood that give modern man gravest cause to doubt whether Jesus's was a genuinely human existence, let alone a uniquely human existence. It is those who are *not* taking the risks of exploration and restatement in this field who paradoxically may find themselves in the greater danger of encouraging heresy.

Finally, there is implicit in the category of heresy, at any rate as popularly understood, the assumption that the final bar of Christian truth is the church and its juridical authority. But if theological inquiry and social criticism is properly part of the church's prophetic ministry this can never be the complete truth. For the prophet is answerable not simply to the church but to the kingdom of God. Congruence with the church's formulations is only one aspect by which prophetic activity must be judged. Indeed, there are many instances, especially in the area of social criticism, where witness to the Kingdom has meant witness *against* the church in the name of the world. The prophet has historically often been most free when he has been protected from the church and has enjoyed relative independence of ecclesiastical authority. And many are feeling this to be more rather than less true today, as the church wrestles with a genuinely engaged theology of the secular. Both social critics and theological inquirers are sensing that they can speak with an authentic voice only if they have at least one foot, economically and academically, within the structures of the world. To be completely answerable to the religious institution is to be living, it often appears today, in something less than the genuine solidarity with men out of which alone the prophet can be heard.

For this reason, therefore, as well as others, 'heresy' is of limited relevance as an adequate or final criterion of Christian truth. For where, within the secular order, is the bar of heresy to be found?

12

The Next Frontiers for Theology and the Church[1]

How do we remain theologians after 'the death of God'? How do we remain Christians after 'the death of the church'? These, I believe, are the two questions that will underlie most of the discussion in the days and years immediately ahead of us. It does not, I suggest, matter precisely in what sense we think God or the church to have died. I do not myself subscribe to the more literal or final views of their demise. And yet I believe that something has happened to each that cannot simply be reversed and to which the biblical metaphor can be applied: the corn has fallen into the earth, and the casing has begun to disintegrate. From one point of view this is death, from another point of view it is release and life. I do not want to argue about terminology. I want to explore what, if this is the situation, we do next.

1

One of the significant things about the 'death-of-God theologians' is that they go on calling themselves theologians. 'God' may be dead, but one must still theologize. Now I should like to set that conviction alongside some sentences from the latest (1967) revision of Sir Julian Huxley's *Religion without Revelation*. In a fresh opening chapter, entitled 'The New Divinity', he writes this:

> Though gods and God in any meaningful sense seem destined to disappear, the stuff of divinity out of which they have grown

[1] Lecture to the Edward Gallahue Conference, Princeton Theological Seminary, 17 April 1968. Reprinted from *Theology Today*, July 1968.

and developed remains. This religious raw material consists of those aspects of nature and those experiences which are usually described as divine. Let me remind my readers that the term *divine* did not originally imply the existence of gods: on the contrary, gods were constructed to interpret man's experiences of this quality.[2]

A humanist evolution-centred religion too needs divinity, but divinity without God. It must strip the divine of the theistic qualities which man has anthropomorphically projected into it, search for its habitations in every aspect of existence, elicit it, and establish fruitful contact with its manifestations. Divinity is the chief raw material out of which gods have been fashioned. Today we must melt down the gods and refashion the material into new and effective organs of religion, enabling man to exist freely and fully on the spiritual level as well as on the material.[3]

In other words, that dimension of reality which caused men to create gods remains valid. But the theistic mould has been shattered. The shaping of the stuff of that experience into gods existing as beings, or into a God existing as a Being, in another realm above or beyond this one, is no longer credible. Nevertheless, the matter of divinity is not thereby destroyed: human life is constantly summoned to self-transcendence. And Huxley ends his book with the credo: 'I believe in transhumanism'.[4]

Another British humanist, James Hemming, has expressed a similar view in this way:

Both scientific and religious viewpoints are, today, humanisms. But neither is only a humanism because each accepts that existence itself is shrouded in mystery. Each may wish to put something different into that mystery. One group may put a personal God there; the other a question mark; but each will agree that the ground of man's being is humanism within a mystery. This is the new starting-point. It provides a vast unifying common ground in terms of human involvement and purpose.[5]

[2] *Op. cit.*, p. 4.
[3] *Op. cit.*, p. 5.
[4] *Op. cit.*, p. 195.
[5] 'Moral Education in Chaos', *New Society*, 5 September 1963.

Finally, let me cite the French Marxist, Roger Garaudy:

What makes us atheists is not our sufficiency, out satisfaction with ourselves and with the earth, with some sort of limitation on our project. The reason is that we, from our experience, similar to the Christian's, of the inadequacy of all relative and partial being, do not conclude to a presence, that of the 'one necessary', which answers to our anguish and impatience.

If we reject the very name of God, it is because the name implies a presence, a reality, whereas it is only an exigency which we live, a never-satisfied exigency of totality and absoluteness, of omnipotence as to nature and of perfect loving reciprocity of consciousness.

We can live this exigency, and we can act it out, but we cannot conceive it, name it or expect it. Even less can we hypostasize it under the name of transcendence. Regarding this totality, this absolute, I can say everything except: It is. For what it is is always deferred, and always growing, like man himself.

If we want to give it a name, the name will not be that of God, for it is impossible to conceive of a God who is always in process of making himself, in process of being born. The most beautiful and most exalted name which can be given to this exigency is the name of man. To refuse it to him is to strip him of one of his dimensions, and his essential, specific dimension, for man is precisely he who is not. This exigency in man is, I think, the flesh of your God.[6]

I believe that these statements point to a new and encouraging situation. What they indicate is *not* that those who used to be distinguished as theists and atheists are now saying the same thing. That, as Garaudy insists, is seriously to over-simplify, and would be repudiated from both sides. What they indicate is that the theistic container has been shattered which clearly marked off one position from the other. The casing has been breached and the situation is thoroughly fluid. The frontier is open, and the difference between the positions is to be determined more by their centres than by their edges. The centres are indeed different. Feuerbach and Teilhard de Chardin, for instance, occupy quite distinct positions, the one re-

[6] From *Anathema to Dialogue*, pp. 82f.

quiring for its essential expression what has traditionally been 'man' language, the other what has traditionally been 'God' language. Yet each author is freely and gratefully drawn upon by proponents of the other side. Similarly, Roger Garaudy and Leslie Dewart speak from different centres; yet they have more in common than either has with the 'old theology' of his own camp.

Before going further I should like to try to indicate – though certainly not to define – what I believe the two 'centres' are. Each side is concerned to do justice to what it recognizes as a real dimension of transcendence, of openness, of 'exigency', of 'mystery', which makes a closed or static humanism equally uninviting to both. But each attempts to catch the mystery of this reality from a different aspect.

Here, for instance, to balance the earlier quotations from the humanists, is an attempt to describe the transcendental qualities of experience from within a way of speaking and thinking that works with 'God' language. It comes from a book written during the second world war by S. L. Frank, a Russian Orthodox contemporary of Nicolas Berdyaev, *God with Us*. I confess that I had ignored it completely until it was drawn to my attention in a review as anticipating rather remarkably some of the things I had said in my own recent book, *Exploration into God*. The similarities are indeed fascinating. In his chapter 'Faith in a Personal God', Frank argues for the same utterly personal 'panentheism' (including the term iself) with which I sought to replace classical theism. But here is his description of what he calls 'experience of the transcendental', which he takes to be valid of *all* experience but pre-eminently of what we call religious experience:

> The gist of the matter is that religious experience – like every other – has the dimension of *depth* or of *distance*. In ordinary visual perception we see not only that which is quite close to us, but also discern more or less clearly what lies in the far distance and is scarcely visible. In tactile perception we not only apprehend the open surface of things but can also vaguely feel that which lies underneath; tapping, touching, etc., plays an important part in the medical examination of bodily organs concealed from the eye. In a somewhat similar fashion in religious experience we

vaguely – as it were in darkness and in the distance – discern or 'feel' at any rate the fundamental and essential aspects of the reality it contains. But of course this analogy too is inadequate. In religious experience we have a peculiar and clear combination of intimate nearness with remoteness, or, in philosophical language, of the greatest immanence (which in this case is actual possession, a mergence of the object of experience and ourself) with transcendence. It is the very nature of religious experience that in it our soul inwardly senses, is in immediate contact with, and penetrated by, something which is recognized as coming from an unfathomable depth and infinite distance. As St Augustine puts it with characteristic force and brevity: 'Thou criedst to me from afar . . . and I heard as the heart heareth.'[7]

It is characteristic of this approach that it sees experience as *response* to a 'Thou', to a cry, to a call. The other approach pushes out from the infinitely open possibilities of man himself. Thus Roger Garaudy goes on:

> We are undoubtedly living, Christians and Marxists alike, the exigency of the same infinite, but yours is presence while ours is absence.
> Is it to impoverish man, to tell him that he lives as the incomplete being, that everything depends upon him, that the whole of our history and its significance is played out within man's intelligence, heart and will, and nowhere else, that we bear full responsibility for this; that we must assume the risk, every step of the way, since, for us atheists, nothing is promised and no one is waiting?[8]

The difference is clear. Yet I believe profoundly that the two approaches are complementary rather than exclusive. 'The exigency in man,' says Garaudy, 'is . . . the flesh of your God.' *Hoc est corpus meum*: 'this (of yours) is my body'. The '*est*' is not the identity of metaphysical substance: it is an affirmation of faith – the *Christological* faith that the two sets of languages, the man-talk and the God-talk, do coincide. Indeed, I suspect that we shall have to restate

[7] *Op. cit.*, pp. 59f.
[8] *Op. cit.*, p. 83.

the problem of Christology not in terms of two natures in one person but of two sets of language about one nature. And the Christological act of trust is that it does not in the last resort matter from which end one starts, since ultimately there is a convergence. It also means trusting that the truth is to be found by pushing out from each centre *to the limit*, not by trying to qualify one set of language by the other. For the Christian faith is that the mystery at the heart of reality can be described *wholly* in terms of the Son of man and *wholly* in terms of the Son of God. In fact it stands for the conviction that it must be described in terms *both* of Son of man *and* of Son of God. But it is insistent that one does not arrive at this conviction by setting up one over against the other, or by limiting one by the other, as if one account could ever be valid at the expense of the other. As John Oman insisted in his classic book, *Grace and Personality*, *all* is of God (and can so be described) and *all* is of man (and can so be described).

The future of Christian theology is bound up therefore, in my judgement, with taking seriously the heart of its Christological faith (and I predict that Christology will be the next focus of debate). This involves the acceptance on both sides that we are *free* to talk man-language or to talk God-language *completely*, respecting the fact that any one person or set of people may not be able to use the other and at the same time respecting the right and freedom of others to do so even if we cannot. Furthermore, I am persuaded that we shall make progress in theology to the extent that we avoid the ancient pitfalls, and do not seek (1) to preclude one set of terms by a monophysite insistence that only one (this time man-language) can be valid; or (2) by 'confusion of natures' to transform one into the other (saying that all God-language is really man-language); or (3) to retain the God-language by finding a place for it in the gaps or inadequacies of the man-language. We must maintain both the validity and the adequacy of each.

But, having said this, I do not believe that we can go on talking of God *and* the world in the way that we have tended to do in our theistic past, as though these were two separate entities. When we could think of God as *a* Being, who had a world, then we could speak as if the distinctive subject-matter of theology was 'God' (in contrast with knowledge of the world) and then sub-divide this into doctrines of the three Persons of the Trinity. But I do not believe we can any longer simply say that theology is 'about' God, or Christology 'about' Christ, or Pneumatology 'about' the Holy Spirit. For the answer to Bonhoeffer's question: 'How do we speak of God in a worldly fashion?' is not to be confined to the realm of language or to the viability of the word 'God' in a secular age. It means posing the question of God afresh as a question about the world. It means understanding the world theologically – that is, as absolutely 'open' to the Beyond in the midst. It is what I take it Hans Ruedi Weber of the World Council of Churches intends when he insists (in what I assume to be a good Barthian statement) that the Bible is fundamentally anthropology from the point of view of God, not theology from the point of view of man. It is what C. A. van Peursen, the Dutch philosopher, seeks to draw out in his fascinating set of lectures called 'Him Again' reproduced in a recent number of *Risk*,[9] the magazine of the Youth Department of the World Council of Churches, that the word 'God' acquires identity only as a constantly re-encountered dimension of the ordinary events of nature and history. It is what, if I understand him aright, Leslie Dewart is attempting in redefining omnipotence, for instance, as an attribute not of a heavenly Being but of 'a world totally open to *future creation by man*'.[10] 'In God,' he puts it, 'nature can do anything';[11] '*with* God . . . all things, all history, is possible to man.'[12] The frontier here between Dewart and Garaudy is very thin.

In the same way, we must insist that the subject-matter of Christology is not just 'the Person of Christ' – whether primarily conceived as the historical Jesus or as a meta-historical divine Being. For Christology is not simply about *a* being, it is about being, all things, recapitulated in the Word made flesh. It is about the universe as fulfilled, or destined to be fulfilled, in Christ. Henceforth one must talk Christologically about all things. Of everything one may ultimately say that whether one uses man-language or God-language it comes to the same thing in the end. In the last analysis, the two coincide; for all things have been 'reconciled' in Christ – even though historically there may yet only be one place to which

[9] 3. 4 (1967).
[10] *The Future of Belief*, p. 193. Italics his.
[11] *Ibid.*   [12] *Op. cit.*, p. 197.

one can point for their convergence. This means that we must be able to translate the traditional language of the cosmic Christ, existing supernaturally as a metaphysical Being, into the worldly language of a Christic cosmos. It is because Teilhard de Chardin has pursued this translation most thoroughly in our generation that he is able to speak not only to those who use the language of 'God' but also to those, like Huxley and Garaudy, who can only use the language of human potentialities.

It is also only by this translation, I suspect, that we shall be able to restate for men and women today the proclamation of the living Christ, and therefore of the Resurrection. To say 'Jesus lives' is for most people today literally unimaginable. (How far our church language is from ordinary parlance is illustrated by the story of the man who was asked what he thought of the death of Christ: 'Oh, I'm sorry to hear of that, I didn't even know he'd been ill.') To say that Jesus is alive suggests either that he must have been physically resuscitated or that he is somewhere around the universe as an invisible metaphysical Being – both of which are to most people merely fantastic. The only way now, I suggest, of beginning to make intelligible this central Christian affirmation is to see the Resurrection, as indeed the New Testament does, cosmically – that is, primarily as a statement about the world. It is not just a truth about *a* man or *a* being, but about the renewal and transformation of the entire body of history. The gospel of the Resurrection is the gospel of a new world, a new order of creation, a new possibility of human existence, at the level of spirit – the spirit disclosed and released in and through Jesus Christ. Just as from the beginning of the evolutionary process St John's Gospel sees everything as 'alive with his life', so the Epistle to the Ephesians sees all things as 'filled' with Christ. 'The second Adam,' says St Paul, 'is a life-giving spirit' – 'man remaining man, but transcending himself, by realizing new possibilities of and for his human nature.' The words are Julian Huxley's definition of 'transhumanism'.[13] The Christian sees these new powers, what the Author to the Hebrews styles 'the powers of the age to come', as released not simply in science, which at the profoundest level can 'change' nothing, but in the transformation of man and his relationships through the spirit of Christ 'from one

[13] *Op. cit.*, p. 195.

degree of glory to another'.

This leads into how we can do our theology today of the third Person of the Trinity. As long as we go on speaking of the Spirit as a separate metaphysical entity or 'Person' I doubt whether we shall ever begin to communicate. Indeed, I wonder whether in English, as opposed to Greek, the very article 'the' is not misleading and distorting. It is just as characteristic of biblical usage to speak of 'spirit' in an anarthrous way, without an article. Thus it says, 'God is spirit' (*not*, as in the Authorized Version, 'a spirit'), or it talks of 'fellowship, or participation, in holy spirit'. One of the contributions, I believe, to modern theology is the way in which Berdyaev speaks about 'spirit', especially in his books *Spirit and Reality* and *Freedom and the Spirit*. Marghanita Laski, at the end of her important study *Ecstasy*, deplores the lack of vocabulary in which to speak of that open frontier with which we are here concerned:

> It is, I think, significant that we have no neutral adjective to distinguish the range of emotions, values, moral compulsions, felt truths that arise from ecstatic experience. *Spiritual* implies acceptance of presuppositions rejected by rationalists, and those who reject such pre-suppositions have sought rather to deny importance to ecstatic experiences than to examine them on the basis of their own pre-suppositions and to supply a vocabulary in which such examinations could be made.[14]

Yet, for all her doubts, I suspect that 'spirit' and 'spiritual' (in contrast to 'religious' which is sometimes used in this way – e.g., 'the religious dimension in art') is the vocabulary we have to redeem. 'The spirit of man is the candle of the Lord' was a text beloved by Benjamin Whichcote, the Cambridge Platonist, and by other Christian humanists. It stands for the truth reiterated in the New Testament (and especially in St Paul's great passage in Rom. 8.14-28[15]) that spirit is on both sides of the relationship, that it is at home as much in the world of man-language as of God-language. It is where the depths of God and the depths of man meet.[16] *Sophia* and *logos* have also in the history of Jewish and

[14] *Op. cit.*, p. 373.
[15] Particularly as brought out by the New English Bible.
[16] 1 Cor. 2. 10f.

Christian theology performed a similar function, and it is significant that Marghanita Laski, for whom the ecstatic is to be described wholly in human terms, should be 'content and happy to believe', in her closing words, 'that the god [men] sometimes believed they had perceived in these experiences was indeed the *logos*'.[17] But, whatever our words – or probable lack of them on this boundary, where Bonhoeffer urged upon us the wisdom of silence – we must learn to speak of spirit in a worldly way. Indeed, after being the Cinderella of theology for so long, it may well be the way into it today, when 'God' and 'Christ' (for all Jesus's own preference for 'the Son of man') have lost their cash-value in the coinage system of 'man'-language.

Perhaps I could sum up the first half of this lecture and lead into the second half on the future for the church by relating what I have said to the category which in the Bible forms the link between God and the church, but which has been strangely neglected as the keystone of Christian theology, namely, the Kingdom. Here, alas, is a word that is probably unusable in secular circles today – if only because kingdoms are even more 'dead' than gods or churches. But what it stands for is, I believe, decisive for our task of rethinking. For if the subject-matter of theology is not God who *has* a world but the world-in-God, then the biblical term for the world-in-God is the Kingdom.

Let me return at this point to S. L. Frank. The purpose of his book *God With Us*, as the title indicates, is to emphasize the fact that the subject-matter of theology is not the existence of God in himself but what in *Exploration into God* I called 'the divine field', or Teilhard spoke of as the *milieu divin*. It is the area of God's *shekinah* or presence, 'the kingdom of his love', so that one can say that to 'dwell in love is to dwell in God; for God is love'. And this is Frank's comment:

All these expressions symbolically reveal one fundamental fact: God is not a self-contained entity; He is like the sun, the very being of which consists in radiating light and warmth, and therefore from the very first must be thought of as the centre of a bright and life-giving realm of being distinct from but directly

[17] *Op. .cit.*, p. 374.

related to Him. In theological thought, i.e. on the plane of the logical categories of ground and consequence, that realm of 'heavenly being' is derivative from the being of God, and faith in it depends upon faith in God. But we must have the spiritual courage to recognize that in living religious experience, in the actual spiritual act of faith, it is, in a sense, the contrary relation that holds. A simile of it may be found in our apprehension of the difference between night and day. In our ordinary experience, that difference consists not in the fact that at night we do not see the sun and in the daytime we do (for matter of that we never see the sun clearly, at any rate, not in its full brilliance) but simply in the alternation between light and darkness, between being in an environment in which the outlines of objects are clearly seen, and being plunged into a kind of dark abyss in which we helplessly grope about like the blind. In a somewhat similar fashion the basic, decisive difference between a believer and an unbeliever consists not in the fact that one 'recognizes' God's existence and the other does not. The real criterion is whether a man's spirit is in touch with the treasure of God's kingdom, with the gifts of the Holy Spirit, whether the rays of divine love give it warmth and light. To dwell in the life-giving rays of the sun and to feel its light and warmth is in practice far more important and essential than to see the sun itself.[18]

I believe that this is an important emphasis, when the casing of the divine container, the theistic concept of God as a supreme Being, is in the process of dissolution. Frank puts it in God-language – and I personally am content to follow him. For others, for whom the sun is hidden, the environment in which man's life is lived may seem better described without reference to such loaded terms as 'the treasure of God's kingdom', 'the gifts of the Holy Spirit', 'the rays of divine love'. But, as Frank says, 'the real criterion is whether man's spirit is in touch', whether the stuff of 'divinity', to use Huxley's phrase, is indeed a reality in which we 'live and move and have our being', or whether there is no openness to the unconditional, no 'absolute future' (as Karl Rahner calls it), no 'omega point' (in Teilhard's phrase).

[18] *Op. cit.*, pp. 73f.

2

The category of the Kingdom leads naturally, as I said, into the second question, that of how we remain Christians after 'the death of the church'. As with 'the death of God', I do not believe that this means that the church is finished. But its falling into the earth means a real death to the body in which it has so far existed. And there is, I think, a close parallel here with 'the death of God'. Corresponding to what I called the theistic container, which has shaped divinity into *a* God existing over against the world, is the religious organization, which has shaped the church into *a* community existing over against the secular order. And, like gods, the religious organization is in the process of being melted down, eroded, or cracked open, according to which way one looks at it. This means nothing less than the disintegration of the mould by which throughout its history so far the Christian church has been given form and substance.

One has only to say this to be taken for a prophet of gloom, siding with the enemies of the church. But this is not my intention. I believe in fact that what is dissolving is the *casing* of the church, and that this process could be one of release and liberation. Just as, in the God-debate, 'the end of theism' meant the end not of God but of one way of expressing the divine reality, so I believe that the decay of the religious organization is the decay of one body in which the church has hitherto lived and whose demise may be necessary for its resurrection.

I do not suggest that this will be a sudden or discontinuous process. The new body is much more likely to be built up within the shell of the old – as well as outside it. Nor is there anything *wrong* with the religious organization as such – any more than with the theistic projection if it communicates the reality of God. Where the religious organization serves as the carrier of real, outgoing life I have no wish to see it die. But I suspect that it is reaching the term of its historical usefulness.

An illustration will point the distinction I am trying to make. There is a poster at the moment on the hoardings in Britain for the Salvation Army. It depicts a scene of human dereliction and carries the caption: 'For God's sake care. Give us a pound'. Imagine that poster put out by the Church of England or indeed by any other religious body, except perhaps the Quakers. 'For God's sake care. Give *us* a pound.' The credibility gap is too great. For the ordinary man suspects that of every pound given to the church 95 per cent will go towards keeping *itself* going. And he is not far wrong. Of the total annual income of the Church of England – according to the most recent available figure, £42¾ million – £40½ million is spent on servicing itself at home or abroad, while half of the remainder goes to maintain its own schools and colleges. Similarly, an overwhelming proportion of its ministers' time is absorbed not in washing the world's feet but in servicing a religious organization centred on its own buildings.

Of course, the purpose of the organization thus serviced is to be a force for good in the community at large, and such is the devoted, caring, unselfish work carried out by the average parson that his calling is still rated for good in the public opinion polls above even that of a doctor. (It is also true that other studies[19] have revealed churchgoers as more conformist, more prejudiced, more intolerant and more 'deterrent-minded' than the average non-churchgoer.) But the point is that, however beneficent the by-product, the amount 'given off' by the religious organization is quite disproportionate to what goes in. Indeed, so self-absorbing is the life of many a local congregation that it would be difficult to say whether they support the church or it supports them. The minister finds himself, whether he likes it or not, the manager of a religious club which it is his prime burden to keep open and flourishing.

This club is what is left of what used to be a much more embracing institution, supplying welfare, education, culture and recreation that could not easily be had elsewhere. Now it has one line, which nobody much wants. 'I'll do anything for you, vicar, except come to church.' He has heard that in England, especially from the working-classes, for long enough. The difference is now that he may hear it from the curate.

For there is a revolt afoot, especially among the younger clergy and the more radical laity. The church may expect a rapidly increasing brain-drain. For many of the most lively minded are losing faith in the relevance of the religious casing. The image of the

[19] E.g. those quoted in P. Berton, *The Comfortable Pew*, pp. 32–9.

church which has identified it with organized religion is becoming a positive liability. That image will have to go. But many are puzzled or threatened because there seems nothing to put in its place.

By inheritance the church is well equipped for standing over against the secular world as a separate religious organization. It is singularly ill equipped for permeating that world from within as the salt and leaven it is supposed to be. Yet people today are looking for points of meeting and commitment that will not take them out of the world – and will bring them together face to face, rather than face to back as in the traditional pew. They respect agencies that directly do the job – like Oxfam or Shelter, Christian Aid or Christian Action (to use the obvious British illustrations) – with the minimum of overheads and openly appointed executives. They do not want static hierarchies and imposing edifices and pulpits six feet above contradiction. They want embodiments of Christian presence where the real, shifting needs of human beings in community can be interpreted and met. Worship, prayer, structure, must be allowed to grow out of these, as form follows function.

The church's greatest assets and its greatest liabilities are its buildings and its manpower. No other voluntary organization, political or social, has anything like its wealth of strategically-placed sites – at the heart of every village and urban neighbourhood. Yet in the burden of plant it carries it can only be compared with the cinema circuits or the railways. Moreover, it is the masonry that largely determines the deployment of its personnel. For (in Church of England terms, though it applies everywhere) men are tied to stipends and stipends to benefices and benefices to buildings.

In theory again, the church is stupendously well off for manpower. No other voluntary organization has such a network of full-time residential agents, and in many an inner-city area or new housing estate the church is the only professional or caring body with a paid representative actually living amongst the people it serves. Yet the minister's presence is negatived by his lack of organic relation to the secular structures. He is minding a pool of his own rather than helping to direct the main-stream of life. It has been said recently: 'No commercial firm has so many employees all doing the same thing to so little effect at so great cost',[20] and, it could be

---

[2] J. Pellow, *The Concrete Village*, p. 167.

added, with practically no freedom to sack or redeploy them.

Both in plant and personnel the resources of the church must be realigned to serve the kingdom of God rather than the religious organization. It would be crazy to throw away the advantages of central sites, many of which (to cite the British scene again) provide the only opportunity, through housing associations, of breaking the council-list monopoly for the benefit of professional people prepared to live among those for whom they care. There is place still – as Coventry cathedral has shown – for big buildings adapted and staffed to modern needs. And in each natural grouping of 30-50,000 people one can envisage ecumenical centres focusing the Christian presence and response on a large scale. In between there remain widely varying opportunities for points of meeting and service geared to more local or functional needs. Then, of course, there can be numerous house-church groups that require no overheads. Especially in the suburbs, there will doubtless still be room for the self-supporting religious organization which is a going concern and can hire its own minister. But such cannot be the main call on the resources of the servant church.

Similarly, the ministry of the church – clerical and lay (if the distinction seriously survives) – must be shaped by the constantly changing priorities of human need and will surely be exercised for the most part through secular employment. There are areas where, except in a co-ordinating or 'episcopal' capacity, full-time ministers paid by the church are a selfish luxury. There are other spheres where the church should be providing sacrificially what society fails to supply – men and women *free and available* to love and serve and care wherever the need or the action is.

Within the total ministry of all Christian people, ordination is admission to an order. It is not a concealed cheque for so much a year for life. No one should in future be ordained without a secular qualification. Retraining for the many now equipped to be nothing except ministers of religion is an urgent priority. Of course some ministers will continue to be required, at different stages of their careers, for full-time ecclesiastical employment, but there is no reason why bishops and other leaders should have to be chosen from these. It might make more sense to recruit them, by advertisement, from pastorally and prophetically minded men already used to executive responsibility in the secular world.

I have illustrated these possibilities not to predict a programme but simply to show that the disintegration of the religious organization is far from necessarily negative or depressing. Fr Thom Janssen, a Dominican from Holland (where the process I have described is viewed most uninhibitedly), has spoken of 'the exploding church'.[21] If the casing gives, there is a lot of radio-active material waiting to get out. In the New Testament analogy again, 'unless a grain of wheat fall into the earth and dies, it remains alone; but if it dies, it bears much fruit'. An eggshell cracked open by pecks from within has after all long been the symbol of the church's Easter message.

A suggestive description of the shape of things to come is the account in *The Concrete Village* by John Pellow of the response of his tiny Congregational church to the 'new' Stepney in the east end of London :

> What the shape of that new community was going to be we did not then know. The only thing we could attempt was to put ourselves in such a position in that new community that we became subject to those forces as should determine the shape of the community. This is not just so that we might become one of the determining factors, but so that there might be a basic understanding between us and the world, which it is our duty to serve. . . . We determined to do nothing apart from the new community which could not be done with it.[22]

In that quotation lies the spirit of tomorrow's church. Its 'religious face' in a religionless age will not be very prominent. Least of all will it exist to gather the religious out of the world. Yet everything will continue to centre in the making holy of the common, which is worship. And worship, the shaping of God's worth, will no less than before have to be forged, through sacrifice, out of the bread and wine of ordinary human relationships transformed by Christ.

The next five or ten years, I suspect, will tell which way the church must die. Either we shall see a bursting of the skin or a hardening of the skin (and the latter could easily be intensified by

[21] See the interview in *Frontier*, Summer 1967, pp. 122–4.
[22] *Op. cit.*, pp. 108, 124.

ecumenical grafts). All the institutional pressures, legal and finan-
cial, unless redirected, will be on the side of the second. Those of
us who believe that the pains of disintegration are salutary (and
they are none the less painful for that) will be accused of abetting
gloom and despondency. Indeed, I am certain that things have got
to get worse before we can expect a real break: the system must
be seen to be unworkable, as it already is in many inner areas.
Meanwhile I am convinced that all will depend on there being
sufficient people tapping away constructively, both from the inside
and from the outside, open and flexible enough to seize the opportunities when they offer.

Within every religious denomination today two churches are struggling for supremacy. One wants to contain things, to preserve the
religious club, to stem the process of dissolution. The other (and it
consists of many clergy and laity and of many who have voted with
their feet) longs to release what life there is from a casing that
threatens to stifle it. Most of the time there is not a clear either-or,
and much of the job of maintenance consists, as I well know, of
loosening bolts.

Yet it would be an error to see this simply as the dismantling of
'organized religion', as if there were something *wrong* either with
organization or with religion as such. Organization, and efficient
organization, is essential if the Christian presence is to be related
effectively to the principalities and powers of this highly collectiv-
ized world – as the examples I have given from the field of Christian
action demonstrate. What needs to be questioned is organization
that strengthens the container marking off the church as *a* community from the rest of mankind in Christ; and this is something that
affects much more than its religious face. The whole existence of
the church as an *ecclesia,* or gathered fellowship, is being queried
as radically as the 'death of God' theologians have questioned the
word 'God'. Fr Janssen, whom I quoted earlier, has gone on
record as saying: 'Perhaps we shall not talk about the "Church" at
all in the future. The word "Church" is not very helpful!'[23] Maybe
the church, too, is something that has to be 'melted down' – like salt
in solution – without its power being lost. And, like the demise of

[23] *Op. cit.,* p. 123.

gods, this question-mark against the gathered community reflects a fundamental change in the culture in which we live. To bring this out, let me cite from one of the 'secular meditations' in Malcolm Boyd's *Free to Live, Free to Die*:

> It used to be easier to speak of community. In fact, in-groups were even accepted as a part of life which wasn't questioned. Community was understood in terms of *this* group or *that* one; people doffed their hats in respect and went their own way, away.
>
> But now community has many more complex meanings. Most people have come to realize that community isn't a *place* but a state of being, fluid and ongoing, marked less by a post-office address than an attitude shared by persons.
>
> Maybe the real secret of community now is that no one can arbitrarily be excluded. A so-called believer (in good cooking, social justice, God or *The New York Times*) doesn't want to be shut off from so-called unbelievers. There's a mystical sense of being involved together, and, just as much to the point, wanting to be. Whether one is speaking of fulfilment, salvation, or joy, no one wants it on a private preserve, shut off from others. Persons are claiming each other. Walls are coming *down*. A person is a signpost to another.
>
> We are beginning to see that no one makes a community; he accepts community, where and as it *is*.[24]

Is the job of Christians to make a community or to accept community where and as it *is*? This seems to me a fundamental question which we are only just beginning to ask seriously. It lies behind the whole notion of 'non-church'. This, as I understand it, is not inspired by the old-fashioned individualism that wants Christianity without the church – though this undoubtedly is how it *looks* to most of its critics. It is concerned with responding to community, accepting the responsibility of community, where it is, in the world, rather than with organizing *a* community over against the world. I believe that this concern may be much closer to the New Testament than our inherited presuppositions have allowed us to see.

If we ask, 'Is the church a community? Is it meant to be a com-

[24] *Op. cit.*, pp. 8of.

munity?', the answer to the first question will probably be 'No'. The answer to the second question will almost certainly be 'Yes'. But is this what it is meant to be? Is *a* community a Christian category?

It is noteworthy that the church is never described in the New Testament as 'a community'. *Koinonia* is not a group of persons but a quality of relationship, a sharing, a participation. It is well known among students of the New Testament that the primary reference of *koinonia* is participation in a divine reality – in God, in Christ, and above all in Holy Spirit. The phrase 'the fellowship in or of Holy Spirit' refers to participation in this divine reality, not in the first instance to fellowship between Christians (though that, of course, must follow), let alone to *the* fellowship of Christians. The church is meant to be the embodiment, the carrier, the incarnation of this *koinonia* of Holy Spirit, as it is of the grace of our Lord Jesus Christ and of the love of God. But it is not a fellowship as such (any more than it is a love or a grace).

This may appear a somewhat academic distinction; and indeed there has been no great need to distinguish until the meaningfulness of a closed community, a structured fellowship, whether religious or secular, is questioned, as it is questioned by Malcolm Boyd. But the issue has been raised: Does the witness to holy community (that is, to community with a difference and a depth which the world can neither give nor take away) necessarily mean being involved in creating, keeping going, *a* community in the sense of a separate religious organization with institutional structures, definitions and boundaries – which a person is either 'in' or 'out' of? Hitherto our answer has been 'Yes'. But is this correlation essential? May not 'the fellowship' often be a witness against rather than for 'community where and as it is'?

To accept community where and as it *is* is, in Christian terms, to respond to the presence of the Kingdom, wherever it meets one, in the midst of life, wherever two or three are gathered. *Koinonia* is, theologically, the equivalent of the Kingdom, not of the church. The church is meant to be its instrument, its embodiment, its servant. But the church is constantly judged by the Kingdom, by holy community, and can never be equated with it, in the sense that you can say in advance, 'Here is where you will find it, but not there'. In fact, said Jesus, when men say to you of the Kingdom (or of any sign or aspect of it), 'Lo, here, lo there', go *not out* – that is, do not be drawn out of the world, out of the secular structures, in order to find or create it; for it is in your midst.

We assume too easily that the ideas of 'church' and of 'fellowship' coincide in the New Testament. Ideally and ultimately they do – because the church as *a* group dies to itself in the fellowship of Holy Spirit, is negated and universalized in the Kingdom. But short of that there is in fact a tension, rather than a coincidence, between the two. Church, or *ekklesia*, is in origin an Old Testament idea, and it means those 'called out'. It designates those who respond to the summons 'Come out from among them' to be separated people, representative of the sacred as opposed to the secular, the holy as opposed to the common. But the great fact of the New Age, the *koinonia hagiōn* (holy community, holy communion), represents the making common of the holy – and therefore the end of the church as a peculiar people.

This is an eschatological idea, but like all eschatology in the New Testament it is meant to be realized in the here and now and not simply in the future. The New Testament itself continues to regard the church as a 'brotherhood' of those within as opposed to those without (this is particularly noticeable in the Johannine and the Pastoral Epistles). This may be necessary and inevitable in the penultimate stage. But 'the non-church' movement may be a reminder of something essential in the Gospel, which has been overlaid, namely, that the Christian's freedom is to *respond* to community where and as it is rather than having to *create* it in an 'ecclesial' group. To that extent the non-church may be a perennial minority witness, like, say, that of the absolute pacifist, to an aspect of the Gospel which is always judging the institutional church. On the other hand, just as the change that Malcolm Boyd is drawing attention to is a genuinely new factor on the secular scene, so the non-church *could* represent a breakthrough in the 'coming-of-age' of the church, part of the 'new formation' which Charles Davis has spoken of as struggling to be born.

To ask 'With what body will it come?' is to invite St Paul's retort, 'You silly man!'. Our job is not to worry too much about the body of the church – whether the present one or the future one.[25] God may be destroying the church in one body, only to raise up quite another form of his presence in the world. Our only trust as Christians is that there will always be a form, a body, through which the response to God, the Spirit, the Kingdom, can be made. We take the church seriously as we do not take it too seriously; it is simply the instrument of the Kingdom – disposable in the hand of God. Our commitment should be marked by a certain divine carelessness. So far from becoming depressed or oppressed by the many signs of the death of the church in our day, we should have that lightness of tread, that resilience of spirit, that marks St Paul's classic passage in II Cor. 4.7-5.6. And I would like to close by citing from it, asking you to have in mind not simply the individual Christian, but the church:

> We are no better than pots of earthenware to contain this treasure, and this proves that such transcendent power does not come from us, but is God's alone. Hard-pressed on every side, we are never hemmed in; bewildered, we are never at our wits' end; hunted, we are never abandoned to our fate; struck down, we are not left to die. Wherever we go we carry death with us in our body, the death that Jesus died, that in this body also life may reveal itself, the life that Jesus lives. . . . No wonder we do not lose heart! Though our outward humanity is in decay, yet day by day we are inwardly renewed. . . . For we know that if the earthly frame that houses us today should be demolished, we possess a

[25] Here in a suggestive paragraph which I have since come across from the article 'Catholicisme Seculier?' by Anna Morawska, my Polish publisher and translator, in the French summary *Le Signe* 19 (January-June 1967), p. 6., of the Polish magazine *Znak*:

> The church, it is said, must give itself to the service of the world, to the promotion of the justice, unity, and well-being of the human family. But it is evident that the present structures of the church are quite unadapted to this, and that not only in a superficial sense but in a sense which at points touches essentials of the doctrine of the church itself. In what way, then, must it change? To be a 'sacrament of the unity of the world' should it be a pressure group, powerful and centralized (like other such groups which are really effective), or a constellation of purely spiritual 'centres of light', or again a 'religion of the United Nations', or perhaps nothing but a federation of small fellowships (*shalom*) or guerilla groups, which would operate where and as they found best? And how far can one go in these changes? With this question, clearly, one is back at the heart of the doctrine of the church.

building which God has provided – a house not made by human hands, eternal, and in heaven. In this body we do indeed groan; . . . we are oppressed because we do not want to have the old body stripped off. Rather our desire is to have the new body put on over it, so that our mortal part may be absorbed into life immortal. But God himself has shaped us for this very end; and as a pledge of it he has given us the Spirit. Therefore we never cease to be confident.

13

Meeting, Membership and Ministry[1]

I start from three points of confusion, not to say crisis, in the pastoral discipline of the present-day church. These are not confined to the Church of England, but they find their focus in the current uncertainty within my own communion (of which alone I can speak with any direct authority) about Baptism, Confirmation and Ordination. On each some fundamental self-questioning is taking place.

1. With regard to Baptism, the situation has recently been highlighted in the report of an ecumenical conference, sponsored by 'Parish and People', entitled *Crisis for Baptism*.[2] The whole question of infant Baptism is once again wide open, as it has not been since the seventeenth century. It is not merely that indiscriminate Baptism in a post-Christian society troubles pastoral consciences. Many are doubting the propriety today of infant Baptism at all. The conference revealed itself as deeply split on this issue. Some clergy are refusing Baptism even to their own children. And the question is frequently raised whether there should not be some alternative service of dedication or blessing.

2. On Confirmation, the uncertainties have not yet seriously broken surface, though the Convocation of York has asked for a joint committee on the whole subject.[3] But under the surface there is much questioning. There is the perennial confusion stemming from the fact that the theology of Confirmation (and its relation to Baptism) has never really been settled in the western church. Hence the irresolution in all our traditions about the meaning of, and age

[1] *Prism* Pamphlet No. 31, 1966 (revised).
[2] Ed. Basil Moss, 1965.
[3] This was subsequently supported strongly by the Convocation of Canterbury, and after much delay an Archbishop's Commission is being set up. See also *Confirmation Tomorrow*, the report of a working party of the Diocese of Southwark, and *Crisis for Confirmation* (ed. M. Perry, 1967).

for, Confirmation or its equivalent. But there are also new occasions in this generation which have caused many to think again. I instance here simply two:

(i) There has been the revolution associated with the parish or family communion. My own experience as a boy contrasted with that of my children illustrates sufficiently the change that has come over the scene. When I was confirmed I was taken by my mother the Sunday before to 'the early service', to see what it was like. Our own children were present at the parish communion virtually every Sunday of their lives from the carry-cot onwards. As they continued to come up to the altar-rail with their mother, the question became more insistent: why should they not partake, with the rest of the family of God? They were not nearly ready for Confirmation, but they were ready for communion. 'Mummy, it would help if I could have the bread and the wine too.' But by now the child who said this has, for the time being at any rate, lost the desire both for communion and for Confirmation. A theology of non-communicating attendance, condemned for adults, is being imposed on our children with most unhappy results.

(ii) There has been a revolution at the other end also – after Confirmation – in regard to lay training and lay ministry. The equipping of all God's people for the work of the ministry (Eph. 4.2) has come to be recognized as an integral and continuous part of the life of the body of Christ. It is reshaping our theology of the laity and our teaching methods. Inevitably, it is leading to questions about our traditional practice, whereby Confirmation marks the point where most laymen *stop* training. And its person-centred rather than content-centred approach to teaching raises queries about the time-honoured methods of catechetical instruction. Lay training at present largely consists of redeeming the casualties of previous mistakes. Is this rescue operation after the lapse of a number of years and the majority of candidates really the best that we can do?

3. This last question of the lay ministry is closely related also to that of Ordination. There is deep heart-searching on the ordained ministry and its distinctive function. It is the underlying question, in my experience, at almost all clerical gatherings. It is partly sociological. What is the role of the priest or minister in modern secular, welfare society? Where is he really wanted, and what should be his

particular expertise? But it is also theological. At last the church is beginning to take seriously the fact that not only clergy are 'in the ministry'. But this constantly raises the question of the differentia of the ordained ministry. And psychologically the extension of the lay ministry is seen as a threat to what was previously the prerogative of the clergy: as the one increases, the other, so it seems, must decrease.

Moreover, the theological falterings at these three points have been accompanied in England (though certainly not in England alone) by what could be a dramatic 'fault' in the hitherto gentle curve of statistical decline. It will be interesting to see if church historians observe in retrospect a sudden shift in the early 1960s. Not unexpectedly, it is particularly marked in the urban areas.

If the figures are to make their impact it is necessary to set them out, even summarily, in a little detail. I have brought them up to date as far as possible from official Church of England sources.[4]

First, and least significantly, there are the numbers for infant Baptism. From 1892 to 1956 these were never below 600 per 1,000 live births and never much above 700. Then:

1956	1958	1960	1962	1964	1966
602	579	554	531	526	511

– a drop of 15·1% in ten years. But in the Metropolitan area the figures not only begin lower but decline more rapidly – in fact at double the rate. For the diocese of Southwark they were:

1956	1958	1960	1962	1964	1966
538	536	483	432	407	376

– a drop of 30·1%. And for the diocese of London:

1956	1958	1960	1962	1964	1966
464	444	413	360	346	312

– a drop of 32·8%.

Nothing quite like this has occurred before. Partly no doubt it is

[4] The Statistical Unit of the Church Assembly, which is often sniped at, deserves the greatest praise for providing the data from which accurate self-knowledge can be arrived at.

a victory for pastoral policies of baptismal responsibility. If it were happening for the right reasons, there would be little ground for concern. But in any case it points to a very different Church of England a generation hence.

It may be said that the figures for infant Baptism merely reflect the fat which any established church has to carry, and that its melting away is not serious. But clearly the same cannot be said for Confirmation and Ordination – the muscle and the bone of the religious organization. And for these the figures are still more ominous.

Up to and including 1960 the average Confirmation rate in the Church of England was surprisingly stable – virtually unchanged since the end of the first world war. In each of the six years 1955-60 it had run at 34 per 1,000 of the population aged 12-20. Then:

1960	1961	1962	1963	1964	1965	1966
34·2	32·9	30·4	27·0	25·9	24·1	23·2

– a drop of 32·2% in six years, which is over three times the national rate of decline for Baptisms.

But in Southwark the dip has been steeper still:

1961	1962	1963	1964	1965	1966	1967	1968
7,038	6,481	5,914	4,765	4,931	4,350	4,060	3,581

– a drop of 48·9% in seven years.[5]

It is the same pattern with Ordinations (though it comes out later because of the time-lag of about three years for the period of training). Until 1963 they were gradually rising from the wartime trough. Then:

1963	1964	1965	1966	1967	1968
636	605	592	576	496	478

– a drop of 24·8% in five years.

But the significant figure for the future is of those recommended for training.[6] Here the numbers were:

---

[5] It is exaggerated a little by the fact that 1961 corresponded, 12-14 years later, with the end of the post-war bulge in births.

[6] The figures are for those definitely recommended. It is only fair to add that the proportion of those conditionally recommended has increased – a welcome sign that the selectors are being more stringent.

1963	1964	1965	1966	1967	1968
586	508	351	324	303	239

– a staggering drop of 58·9% in the same five years (or nearly eight times the rate of decline for Baptisms).

All these figures reflect too short a period from which to draw long-term conclusions. They could represent a temporary dip, and they would need qualifying and balancing by closer research. But the trend is unmistakable, and it is not confined to the Church of England. A similar drop in ordinands has taken place, not only among the other English churches,[7] but in almost every other country in the world. And the same sharp dip in the curve is convincingly confirmed by the figures of converts to Roman Catholicism in England and Wales. In the six years up to 1959 these had climbed steadily from 11,920. Then:

1959	1960	1961	1962	1963	1964	1965	1966	1967
15,794	14,483	14,174	13,280	12,728	12,348	10,308	9,121	8,293

– a drop of 47·6% in eight years.

There is obviously a connection between the statistics and the theological uncertainties of recent years. But it is easy to jump to hasty conclusions and blame the damage on those who have been articulating and bringing to consciousness what has been going on underneath. In any case, the statistics suggest that the decline had set in earlier – round about 1960 rather than 1963, the point when the theological crisis broke. The theologians have simply been more sensitive to the obstinate questionings and know that nothing is to be gained by battening down the hatches or behaving like Canute.[8]

[7] Cf. the following figures for ordinands:

	1961	1962	1963	1964	1965
Roman Catholic	944	909	899	899	743
Methodist	85	88	90	89	54

(The Roman Catholic figures are for all men in training, the Methodist figures for new candidates.)

[8] The function of the theologian may perhaps be likened to that of the white rabbits in the striking passage from Gheoghiu's novel *La Vingt-Cinquième Heure* (quoted by M. Jarrett-Kerr, *The Secular Promise*, pp. 148–9). The hero, himself a novelist, describes how:

I once went on a cruise in a submarine. I stayed under water for about forty-five days. In submarines there is a special apparatus for indicating

Moreover, these signs of malaise are symptoms not causes. The critical point has been reached because at these three sensitive places the inherited pattern of church life is palpably not relating to the world as it now is. The statistical shocks and the theological headaches, like pain, reflect malfunction. Though unpleasant, they are merciful, because they can alert us, if we do not try to cover them up, to the causes and thus, hopefully, to the cures.

At this point I want to switch from the contemporary scene to the church of the New Testament. For this may help us to recognize that the pattern of Baptism, Confirmation and Ordination which is under such threat is itself part of a structure that presupposes a particular, far from permanent, relation between the church and the world. If we merely accept this pattern as normative without asking further questions, we shall get very depressed about the church. For by this norm the church is failing with galloping progression. And our response will simply be reactionary – to try to stem the flood, reverse the figures, and silence the theology.

But this norm assumes a connection between the church and the world which is as remote from the first century as it is from the twentieth. It is little wonder that pastoral ordinances based upon it are fast being exposed as irrelevant. Indeed, it is astonishing that they have served so far. For they were all designed for an established Christendom in a settled society that has long since passed away.

The figures for Baptism, which by any qualitative test of membership are far too high, look as catastrophic as they do only on the assumption, from which they started, that every member of the nation was ideally by birth a member of the body of Christ. Whether the religious establishment has been official or unofficial, this is the assumption by which in western Christendom, Catholic and

---

the exact moment when the air has to be renewed. But a long time ago there was no such apparatus, and the sailors took white rabbits on board instead. The moment the atmosphere became poisonous the rabbits died, and the sailors knew then that they had only five or six hours more to live. . . . In the submarine I went in there were no white rabbits, but there were detectors. The captain noticed that I could sense every diminution of the quantity of oxygen. At first he pooh-poohed my sensitiveness, but in the end he did not use the detectors: he only had to look at me. . . . It is a gift which we have – the white rabbits and I – to feel six hours before the rest of human beings the moment when the atmosphere becomes unbreathable.

Protestant, thinking on both the other sacraments has in consequence been shaped.

For in this situation where, as Kierkegaard complained, all men are Christians, it has been necessary to have an inner circle of 'full' membership, involving commitment, Confirmation and Communion. Ideally, again, this should include all who have been baptized – and still in Sweden today more than 90 per cent of the nation have not only been christened but confirmed, despite the fact that less than 10 per cent go to church. Confirmation has been viewed as a 'passage rite' for those attaining the years of discretion. Indeed, in the Book of Common Prayer the onus is not on the individual to decide for Christ but on the godparents to 'take care' that the child 'be brought' to the bishop to be confirmed as soon as he is basically literate in the faith.

But, thirdly, within this second circle there has been an inner élite of those who have 'entered the Ministry'. And this is where the line has really been drawn. 'There are two kinds of Christians,' wrote Gratian in the twelfth century. And by this he meant not good Christians and bad, but clergy and laity. The 'clergy line', which has run also along the 'professional line' (reserving the priesthood with few exceptions to those deriving their living from it) and the 'sex line' (excluding women from any 'holy order'), has in effect confined real ministry with the body of Christ to a professional, male and (still in the largest church in Christendom) celibate caste.[9]

All these ordinances stem from a situation in which the world is inside the church instead of *meeting* it from without, where *membership* of the two theoretically coincides, and where *ministry* is the prerogative of an élite in church as in state. The wonder is

If our thinking about what should replace it is to be radical and surely that the cracks in the system have not opened up well before this.

not merely reformist, we must go to the roots as these are to be found in New Testament Christianity. And here too we may detect a threefold division in the relation of the individual to the life of the church. But it is not the same division that subsequently

[9] I have written at greater length about this in, 'Taking the Lid Off the Church's Ministry', in *New Ways with the Ministry* (ed. John Morris), pp. 9–21, and in *The New Reformation?*, pp. 56–60.

became stylized in Baptism, Confirmation and Ordination. It may be described under the three heads just mentioned, of Meeting, Membership and Ministry. And since, linguistically, these relationships correspond closely in Greek and Latin to different case-endings and prepositions, one could speak here of a grammar, not so much of assent, as of association.

1. *Meeting.* This relationship is that which is represented grammatically in Greek and Latin by the prepositions *pros* and *ad* with the accusative. It describes a person in the position of facing towards the life of the church or the Kingdom rather than turning his back on it. It is the attitude expressed in the word *prosechein* – an attitude of response or attention, such as the Samaritans gave to Philip (Acts 8.6, 10f.) or Lydia to Paul (Acts 16.14). Lydia is also described as a 'God-fearer' (*sebomene ton theon*); and God-fearers were a group who stood precisely in this relation to Judaism. Proselytes, in contrast, as the derivation of the word from the perfect tense of *proserchomai* implies, are those who *have* come over (though the combination of *sebomenoi proselytoi* of Acts 13.43 could possibly represent a more tentative attachment). But the *degree* of association is secondary and indeed very wide, covering any, in Quaker terminology, from 'seekers' to 'attenders'. They comprise what Chinese Christians, I am told, call 'listening friends', as opposed to 'learning friends' (the catecumenate), 'church friends' (the baptized) and 'feasting friends' (communicants). They are also, more widely, what Tillich designates as 'the latent church' or 'the spiritual community in its latency'.[10] They include the many in our day who make no profession and accept no membership, but whose 'desire' is towards rather than away from what the church stands for.

The restoration and deepening of this relationship of Meeting would seem to be one of the priorities of the contemporary church, discovering itself once more, as Karl Rahner has insisted,[11] in a *diaspora* situation. During the period of Christendom it was a relationship which was almost totally neglected. Consequently, the church today has no inherited structures to give it embodiment.

[10] For definitions and references see my *New Reformation?*, pp. 47–9.

[11] 'A Theological Interpretation of the Position of Christians in the Modern World', *Mission and Grace* I, pp. 3–55.

It does not know what to do with infants except baptize them. It has never worked out marriage or burial rites for the many who desire its ministrations but not its membership. And when it sets up liturgical commissions it never occurs to it to instruct them to start here. In fact they could well begin, as a pastoral priority, with an alternative service to offer in place of infant Baptism. This should include, I suggest, the notes of thanksgiving, naming, blessing and dedication (the last not of the infant but of the parents to bring their child up 'to the best of their faith'). And, unlike infant Baptism, it could properly be based in Jesus' reception of young children in Mark 10.13–16.

But this relationship is, of course, far more than a matter of services. Indeed, it is precisely this aspect of the church as a religious organization that men today are likely to turn from rather than to. The relationship of Meeting includes all that is implied in the words (already unfortunately in danger of deflation as jargon) 'openness', 'dialogue', 'presence'. It seeks the removal of stumbling-blocks rather than the pressing of definitions and credal commitment. Moreover, it is a relationship which should be recognized as normative for the church's entire being in the world, affecting the presuppositions of its thinking about Membership and Ministry, just as the assumptions behind universal Baptism determined the pattern of previous thinking about Confirmation and Ordination. When this norm really shapes its structures of thought and organization and is translated into buildings and budgets and forms of service (rather than services), then the church will seriously begin to live in the twentieth century.

2. *Membership.* This is the rich complex of relationship denoted by the genitive in Greek and by the genitive and ablative in Latin. It is represented by the Greek prepositions *en* and *syn* and by the Latin *in* (as also, to describe the process of entry, by *eis* and *in* with the accusative). It is the relationship of belonging, of incorporation into the Body of Christ, of participation in the fellowship of Holy Spirit. The person in this relation is described in the New Testament as called 'to share in life of . . . Jesus Christ' (*eis koinonian . . . Iesou Christou*: I Cor. 1.9). And this controlling category of *koinonia* includes both Baptism and Communion. Par-

taking in the body and blood is implied in dying and rising with Christ. There is no 'church friend' who is not a 'feasting friend'. As was recognized in the report to the Convocations of Canterbury and York, *Confirmation Today*,[12] there is no basis in the New Testament for a difference between 'membership' and 'full membership'. It is a distinction which comes from regarding the Church as an organization rather than an organism.

There is, incidentally, even less justification for the usage of the Free Churches in describing the instruction of baptized adolescents as classes for 'church membership'. And the confusion is made even greater when the Confirmation rite is used as an admission service for non-conformists to the Church of England. If the Anglican church wishes to confirm those who are already communicant members of non-episcopal denominations, let it do so. But let it differentiate this quite clearly, as does the Church of Rome, from the act of reception, for which again the Liturgical Commission could be asked, as a matter of urgency, to produce a simple service.

How the western church is to resolve the dilemma it has got itself into by the division of Baptism and Confirmation is a question of choice. It could simply adopt the eastern Orthodox use of denying any division and administering everything (including Communion) in a single act. There is a very great deal to be said for this. But there is undoubtedly a factor in New Testament Baptism that cannot be contained exhaustively in any infant rite – that of personal repentance and confession of faith. But the element of adult commitment is hardly safeguarded in the Anglican rubric, or in the Roman practice of confirming about the age of eight. At the moment the western church seems to be getting the worst of both worlds. And this is especially true, perhaps, of the Roman Catholics, who have destroyed the primitive liturgical sequence Baptism – Confirmation – Communion and yet place Confirmation so soon after Communion as apparently to gain little advantage from doing so.[13]

What is the way out? In the light of the New Testament perspective I suggest the following theses:

[12] 1944, p. 15.
[13] For the present situation in the Roman Catholic Church see Charles Davis, 'Baptism, Confirmation and the Eucharist', in *Crisis for Baptism*, pp. 97–102.

(i) The theological (and liturgical) norm of Christian initiation is adult Baptism, Confirmation and communion administered together. This, as the Liturgical Commission of the Church of England has recognized, should govern our thinking about any other arrangement.

(ii) Initiation, as its name implies, belongs to the beginning of the Membership relation. Nothing should be delayed for non-adults except what it is possible for an adult *alone* to give or to receive.

(iii) There is nothing that it is not possible, at any rate sacramentally, for a non-adult to *receive*. What he cannot *give* is a fully responsible profession or commitment.

(iv) But this latter is, properly, not so much an aspect of the Membership relation (the genitive of belonging and dependence) as of the relationship of Ministry (the dative of giving and outgoing) still to be considered. It should, therefore, be accorded separate sacramental expression and not regarded as part of the initiation rite.

(v) Everything that belongs to Membership should be given to the Christian as he is incorporated into the Body of Christ. He must be able to hear the gospel: 'All things are yours because you are Christ's.' There is no case for a distinction between membership and full membership, let alone for parcelling out the Spirit by measure (such as is implied in much popular rationale of the Baptism-Confirmation divide). Communicant status and a share in the Spirit-filled community are implied by the very relationship of membership in Christ.

(vi) That part of Confirmation as presently understood which is the completion or closing act of Baptism should be restored where it belongs. This is the element of 'sealing' or 'anointing' (i.e. chrismation = 'Christing' or Christening), which like 'washing' stands in the New Testament as a name for Baptism as a whole (I Cor. 6.11; II Cor. 1.21f.; Eph. 1.13; 4.30; I John 2.20, 27; Rev. 7.3f.; 9.4; etc.).

(vii) The other aspect of Confirmation – all that has come to be seen in it as 'the ordination of the laity' – should be placed where it too belongs, namely, with whatever action or rite is appropriate to give expression to the relationship not of Membership but of Ministry.

The practicalities of this are derivative rather than fundamental. But, briefly, if I were asked how I would see it working out in the Church of England, I would answer:

(i) Instruct the Liturgical Commission to provide in their revised draft of the Baptism and Confirmation service for a signing with oil as an integral part of the total rite. Since this is unfamiliar in the Anglican tradition, at any rate in the Church of England, it would be wise to make it permissive at the experimental stage, and so allow it to win its way. Its minister would be the parish priest, though as in the eastern Orthodox Church and in the Church of Rome (which also recognizes presbyteral Confirmation in special cases) it would be appropriate, and symbolic of the unity of the church, if the oil used were specially consecrated for this purpose by the bishop. But the bishop is peculiarly the minister not of Initiation but of Ordination, for which indeed (in the broad sense to be discussed later) the symbol of the laying on of hands would better be reserved.

(ii) Meanwhile, admit to Communion on the basis of Baptism, as does the Church of Rome. It might be considered desirable to make a special ceremony of first Communion (as the Romans do), particularly in the initial period of transition. But as children grow up into the new situation there seems no reason why they should not begin perfectly naturally to communicate with their parents when and as they are old enough to manage it physically. Certainly in my own experience of a family *Agape* it would have been wholly artificial to have stipulated a certain age or moment. The children shared the bread and wine as it came round simply because they were there and were members of the family. To have passed them by would have been an intolerable breach of fellowship. The fact that the unconfirmed would at present have to be excluded is a major reason why we have not felt able to celebrate the Eucharist rather than an *Agape*.

(iii) In the same way, I doubt if there is any sense in attempting to recommend a particular age for Baptism-cum-Confirmation. There are some for whom it will remain entirely fitting that they should be made members of Christ in the context of a Christian home from birth. But with an alternative to the Baptism service available for other than committed Christian families, infant Baptism may be expected, no doubt gradually, to become less and less frequent, though in the light of our pastoral history (and the church's own confusion) any rigorist fencing of the font is surely to be deprecated. For the rest, I assume that Baptism (with whatever preparation is suitable for the years) will take place at any age at which a person wishes to make the step from Meeting to Membership and so begin to share in the communicant life of the church.

3. *Ministry.* This, as has already been indicated, is the relationship described by the dative, and also by the prepositions 'to', 'for' and 'from'. It brings together both mission and service, and is the other side of the coin of belonging and dependence. It is active profession and going out, on behalf of the Body, for the world. It covers such great New Testament words as *diakonia, martyria* and *apostole.*

It goes without saying that for the New Testament those words apply as universally to every Christian as do the complementary categories of Membership. There is no question of an élite which alone is 'in' the Ministry. Since this relationship is clearly more costing in terms of commitment, there will always be those who do not take seriously the corollary of their belonging. But the presupposition is that *all* are called to the relationship of Ministry as of Membership.

This is a presupposition that has been heavily obscured by clericalization, and I do not believe that it can effectively become operative again until we see the abolition (no doubt by painful degrees) of the clergy line. By this line I do not mean the entirely proper distinctions within the life of the Body between the liturgies and functions of different orders and members – Bishops, Presbyters, Deacons, Readers, Catechists, etc. By it I mean the line, alien to the church, but entrenched by the Constantinian settlement (when it became necessary to determine who should inherit the prerogatives and privileges of the heathen priesthood), between 'clergy' on the one hand and 'laity' on the other. Until this line disappears, any real ministry or sense of responsibility for ministry will effectively be confined to one side of it.

The strength of this line can undoubtedly be weakened by the breaching also of the others which have helped to reinforce it – the professional line and the sex line. A substantial increase of worker-priests (by which I mean not primarily clergymen taking secular jobs but laymen ordained in their regular employment) and a break-through in the ordination of women, of which there are at last signs, not only in the Congregational, but in the Methodist and Presbyterian communions (and who knows now where it will stop, even in Rome?), will certainly do something to blur the edge of clericalization. But I suspect that the greatest single blow could be struck by the 'laicization' of the Diaconate and its assimilation to Confirmation.

There may, to be sure, still be need for special officers in the local or national church with the kind of assignment given to the Seven in Acts 6. By all means let us call them deacons if we wish (as the author of Acts does not) – though we should recognize that they have little in common with the traditional diaconate or with the 'deacons' mentioned in the Epistles (to base the diaconate on Acts 6 is as precarious as to base Confirmation on Acts 8). There are, indeed important functions in this field. But it is possible that they may better be served by offices of limited appointment (e.g. of churchwardens or stewardship directors) than by a regular order. For the main part, however, it is surely necessary to recover the insistence that *diakonia* is the basic ministry (as our very use of it for the general concept implies) common to all God's people. Purely liturgically, the traditional ministry of the deacon can certainly be shared out among the laity as a whole. This has indeed long since happened in the case of the server (merely another word for deacon) and is increasingly happening with the administration of Communion. But it is outside the sanctuary that the ministry of the servant church – to be like its Master the world's deacon (Mark 10.45) – really comes to its own. And it is this that needs strengthening and drawing out.

I believe that the needs of our age would be served by a general, and not merely – as in the Ordinal – a particular, sacrament of Ministry as of Membership. The previously mentioned report *Confirmation Today* made much of Confirmation as 'the means of conferring upon those who receive it due authority to exercise the office and work for a layman in the Church of God'.[14] It was

[14] *Op. cit.*, p. 13.

subsequently criticized for this, and indeed there is nothing in the existing service, nor much in the tradition, to suggest that this is what Confirmation is doing. But that something of this sort is needed there is little doubt. Whether, indeed, it should be called Confirmation is questionable. The word 'to confirm' occurs, though in a non-technical sense, in II Cor. 1.21f. in conjunction with those of anointing and sealing, and it seems better to keep it, as it was originally employed, for the completion of Baptism. The right word, I suspect, for what is wanted is Commissioning, with its associations with authorization, commitment and mission. Its proper minister is the Bishop, and its appropriate sign the laying on of hands. By this it can be seen to be part of the total ministry of the church, of which indeed it is the foundation, and *within* which the setting apart of men to particular ministries of word and sacrament then takes its natural place.

In training for Ministry, too, there is need for much greater integration. At present those to be ordained are selected and insulated for their preparation from on-going contact with the laity and the world they are to serve. Lay training is dangerously isolated from training for Holy Orders (in the Church of England the former is not even under the Council for the Church's Ministry, but part of the Board of Education). But the Ministry is one, as Membership is one. Instead of training an élite and neglecting the rest, as the church has done following the bad example (till recently) of the state, I believe that we must work towards a more 'comprehensive' pattern. The basic training for *diakonia* – what I would designate as 'applied lay theology' – should be shared by everyone who is willing to take his Christian commitment seriously. It should be done in the locality (widely enough conceived to draw upon the best facilities both of the church and the secular community – for much of the equipping of God's people to serve the world is best supplied by the world). It should be demanding and sustained, with, say, eighteen as the *minimum* age for the Bishop's commission. This commission should include, if possible, the equivalent of a 'title' without which traditionally a man cannot be ordained – i.e. an assignment to a sphere of service – and the equivalent also of post-ordination training and supervision.

From this basic training as a layman in the church of God a

man or woman can then go on to further training for specialist ministries, pastoral, liturgical, theological, administrative or charismatic – all prepared for as supplementary to (rather than as a substitute for) a secular trade or profession, however they may subsequently be exercised. Some of these ministries may be purely functional and temporary, others appropriately marked by ordination, i.e. enrolment in an order. But any hard distinction between the two is divisive. If we are to recover the wholeness and cross-fertilization of ministry within the body of Christ known to the New Testament, we must restore the glorious 'indifference' of St Paul's '*some* apostles, *some* prophets . . . *some* teachers', etc. (Eph. 4.11; cf. I Cor. 12.28). With the clergy line will have to go the mediaeval notion of indelibility, which at the moment introduces a difference in kind and not merely in degree between, say, a deacon and a reader, even though their functions largely overlap. Once a man is commissioned a layman, or a reader, or a presbyter, he is indeed always such. There is no case for re-admission, any more than there is for repeating the sacrament of Membership. But in every instance the particular exercise of Ministry could and should be renewed and reviewed. One of the difficulties, for instance, about having a really local episcopate – e.g. making rural deans bishops – is that at present it would freeze mobility. The body of Christ must retain flexibility in terms of what *every* joint supplies.

The implications of this threefold relation of Meeting, Membership and Ministry could be expanded at many points. But I have said enough, I hope, to indicate that, dismaying as the present trends may be (and calamitous if they are allowed to continue unattended), there is a real possibility that the decay of the old could make way for the emergence of a new pattern, or rather for one which in principle is much older. The early church could be very relevant for the coming great church, not indeed, as the Reformers thought, for supplying a blueprint of faith and order, but for shaking us out of presuppositions which could easily paralyse us into despair.

14

The Church of England and Intercommunion

One of my continuing concerns has been to press for responsible freedom in the matter of intercommunion between Christians on the road to organic unity. Two articles in my earlier book *On Being the Church in the World* were devoted to this topic: 'Intercommunion and Concelebration' (chapter 6) and 'Episcopacy and Intercommunion' (chapter 7). I subsequently wrote a third, 'The Church of England and Intercommunion', published in *Prism* in March 1962 and subsequently as a *Prism* Pamphlet (no. 2). I finished drafting it on the day that an Open Letter to the Archbishops of Canterbury and York was published on the subject from Thirty-two Theologians. This was to give considerable fresh momentum to the debate, and was a decisive factor in leading to the appointment of the Archbishops' Commission on Intercommunion, of which I was a member. Its Report *Intercommunion Today* (1968), incorporates in its majority recommendations all that I was asking for. But its recommendations have yet to be turned into regulations and I believe the theological arguments bear repetition. I have therefore included this essay here, and its introductory paragraphs, starting from the Open Letter of 1961 to which I referred, may serve to place it in historical context. As I indicate in the next chapter, which represents my present thinking, I detect recently a rapid change of climate. This was already reflected in the very positive debate and resolutions of the Lambeth Conference of 1968, where the principle of reciprocity in intercommunion was fully accepted. What follows is what I wrote back in 1962.

For some time now there have been signs that the situation with regard to intercommunion in the Church of England cannot simply be left where it is. For the Resolutions adopted in 1933 by the Upper Houses of Convocation 'for the guidance of the Bishops . . . in the discharge of their duties' (Archbishop Lang) are clearly becoming strained after nearly thirty years of ecumenical activity.

Up to the appearance of the Open Letter the most public sign had been what the General Secretary of the British Council of Churches called the 'great debate' in that Council in October 1960, occasioned by the ferment at the Ecumenical Youth Assembly in Lausanne the previous July. In the editorial of its Bulletin[1] he posed the question: 'How much can you expose young men and women to intense ecumenical experience and still leave the question of intercommunion where it was?'

This same ferment led to the convening of a high-level consultation in March 1961 at the Ecumenical Institute at Bossey under the chairmanship of Bishop Stephen Bayne.[2] This was primarily concerned with Communion services at ecumenical conferences, but it was recognized that the issue was very far from being confined to these. Some searching questions were also addressed to the member churches of the World Council of Churches about their own domestic disciplines. One of these ran: 'How can existing rules of Communion discipline rightly be maintained without thorough re-examination if they were framed before the ecumenical situation arose? . . . The urgency of this is shown by the fact that the rules are being strained and broken; the churches know this, but some of them persevere in silence. Why?' One can hardly be wrong in seeing this question addressed among others to the Church of England.

It was the urgency of this same pressure that led to the explosion of the Open Letter. The fact that so many of its signatories were Cambridge men is not due to the peculiar theological spots in which that University has come out, nor to a doctrinal difference from Oxford, but to the fact that those of us who worked in college chapels there knew this pressure ever about us. Indeed, if it were not for the fact that the 1933 Resolutions specially provided a

[1] *The Church in the World*, January 1961, p. 3.
[2] Its valuable findings were published in *The Ecumenical Review* for April 1961, 13. 3, pp. 353–64.

safety-valve for this situation (permitting an open invitation to Communion to all baptized and communicant members of the college society), the tension would have been intolerable and destructive. And this tension is increasingly being felt, as I well know, in the parishes. But it is still felt in a pathetically small number of places, and what came out in so many of the letters that followed was not that their authors (quite legitimately) held a different doctrine of the Ministry or came to a different practical conclusion but that they had obviously never really felt the wind of change which had driven the Theologians to their considered outburst.

The second point is that the Theologians deliberately chose to take their stand on 'certain beliefs about the Ministry'. And inevitably it is these beliefs rather than the conditions of intercommunion itself that have proved the storm-centre. I should be the last to suggest that the doctrine of the Ministry is not a vital issue in the whole question of intercommunion, and I welcome the invigorating debate on it which their Letter has produced. But I believe we may get further by asking whether changes in the situation itself do not require modification of our working rules, *whatever* our doctrine of the Ministry. If we had to wait until the point of view advocated by the Thirty-two could command a majority in Convocation we should have to wait a long time. And this we cannot do. What follows does not depend on one particular doctrine of the Ministry; and I am not seeking to challenge previously agreed statements, but rather to build on them and draw fresh conclusions from them.

First, then, I would note at least four developments within the regular life of the church which have changed the picture considerably over the past thirty years.

1. There has been far more Communion. The weekly parish Communion has become a widespread feature of the Church of England, and in all our separated traditions the Eucharist has come to occupy a much more central place. The situation, therefore, described by Bishop Lesslie Newbigin in the new preface to his *Reunion of the Church*,[3] in which within the ecumenical movement 'Christians can do together most of the things which churches ought to do except the administration of the sacraments', becomes steadily more unsatisfactory and frustrating. 'What,' he asks, 'will be the

[3] Second ed. (1960), p. xii.

long-term effects of a situation in which everything is there except the centre, in which the most significant relationships we have are those with "Christians not in communion with us"?' The more convinced we are of the centrality of the Eucharist to our own church life, the more insistent is the question of intercommunion when we work and meet together. The limits to non-sacramental co-operation are reached very much sooner in a generation brought up on the liturgical movement.

2. There has been far more co-operation. The Bishops in 1933 limited themselves to considering 'special occasions, if and when they arise, when groups of members of the Church of England and of other Christian denominations are joined together in efforts definitely intended to promote the visible unity of the Church of Christ'. What was evidently envisaged was occasional forays of small groups from camps that were for the most part living denominationally to themselves. That this is still the situation in the majority of places is, alas, only too true. But gradually the principle urged upon the churches at the Lund Conference on Faith and Order is beginning to take effect, that we should do together everything except what we are required by conscience to do separately. This has had a double consequence: (a) There are now many local parishes in whose regular life and work there is at least as much basis for intercommunion as in occasional gatherings of persons not otherwise in contact with each other; (b) Many of the activities by which Christians of different traditions are welded into the closest community (e.g. an ecumenical work-camp or a joint parish mission) may not have the *direct* object of 'promoting the visible unity of the Church of Christ' to which the Upper House of Canterbury (but not York) confined its permission. Yet, spiritually speaking, the conditions for breaking one bread together may be as compelling here as anywhere.

3. Since 1933 the separated churches themselves have been on the move. There is, most notably, the fact of the Church of South India, which is only prevented from exposing the anomalies of our divided state by the requirement on which Convocation insisted that ministers of the C.S.I. should celebrate in Anglican churches only if they waived their right to do so in the Free Churches. But there is also the situation envisaged in the Reports of both the Presbyterian

and Methodist conversations, that there comes a stage, between churches pledged to seek union, at which intercommunion wears a different aspect. Intercommunion between churches, as between Christians, who have no serious intention of becoming one is very different from intercommunion deliberately accepted as the way by which, while we are still divided, we may be made into one. This is a new factor in the debate since 1933, and, although as whole denominations we may not yet have reached this stage, it should clearly be taken into account in any fresh resolutions. Moreover, there may well be local situations in which it is already relevant, where for instance a group of congregations reaches the point of desiring to move beyond mere co-operation to an organically constituted team-ministry of the whole church of God to its local area.

4. There has been a notable increase of foreign travel. This may be a non-theological factor, but when combined with the greater frequency of Communion raises some very real new problems. Thirty years ago only a small section of the people of England regularly travelled abroad, and they resorted on the whole to places where they expected to find English chaplaincies. A sod of England, with its God, was transported for them, and even if they missed Communion for a week or two it was probably no more than they did at home.

But now the situation is very different. Thousands of our communicants go to the Continent every year, men and women, boys and girls, who have been taught that their first duty on the Lord's Day is to meet at the Lord's Table. The English chaplaincies are fewer, and in any case these people do not keep to the well-worn tracks. What are they to do and what guidance are their parish priests to give them? The Bishops in 1933 may properly have judged that the provision (in Resolution 42 of the 1930 Lambeth Conference) for Anglicans to receive communion at the hands of non-Anglican ministers 'has no application in this Province, inasmuch as the conditions contemplated in it do not exist within the Province'. But no reference was made to Christians of the Province who might travel beyond it. One Bishop in the debate raised the question of Anglicans who found themselves cut off from their own ministrations in the remoter parts of Scotland. Archbishop Lang's reply, 'That is a matter which must be reserved to each

Bishop to interpret as he likes', may have sufficed for the exceptional situation there envisaged. It is certainly not adequate today, and, with the Common Market round the corner, it will become increasingly less so.

What then, as a result of these four changes is now required?

It will be simplest to start with the fourth and least theological change – the notable increase in travel, particularly to the Continent. For the question of intercommunion with foreign churches raises separate and somewhat less complicated issues.

The late Dr Norman Sykes showed that there was a clear tradition in the sixteenth and seventeenth centuries whereby visiting members of the Church of England regularly received Communion at the hands of the Continental Protestant churches.[4] This practice was seen to rest on a different basis from intercommunion with the dissenters at home. In the latter case it meant communicating with Christians in direct and open schism with the Church of England. In the former case it was sharing the hospitality of a sister national church, which might order its life on different, and in Anglican eyes deficient, principles, but which was nevertheless not in schism or competition with the Church of England. In the Preface to the Prayer Book 'On Ceremonies' it was expressly stated : 'In these our doings we condemn no other nations, nor prescribe anything, but to our own people only.' The Confirmation rubric was not framed to act as a barrier to Continental Protestants receiving communion in England, nor were reciprocal acts of fellowship debarred.

In this case, then as now, the question of schism or reunion was not directly involved in intercommunion. Sister churches may not be in full communion, in the sense that they accept one another's ministers and laity to the full privileges and responsibilities of membership. But they can offer the courtesies and hospitalities of Christian fellowship without their faith or order being impugned. No theological principle is involved beyond the acceptance by each side of the others as fellow members of Christ. Nor is anything prejudged with regard to their eventual relationship of full communion.

I would urge that the Church of England frankly and officially

[4] *The Church of England and Non-episcopal Churches in the Sixteenth and Seventeenth Centuries.*

endorses a return to its classical practice in this matter. It has never forbidden its members to accept the hospitality of foreign churches where they are welcome : it has left the matter to the individual's conscience. But it has thereby placed a burden on the individual which it is not fair that he should be asked to bear. And over the years it has shifted on to him the onus to communicate only if he feels he must. By having to take the responsibility himself he is inevitably given the sense that by communicating he will be committing an act of individual indiscipline. Of course, liberty of individual conscience must be respected, and no one should be put under any pressure to communicate. But it would relieve much hidden guilt and put the responsibility back squarely where it belongs, if the church said unequivocally that Anglicans *may* communicate at other altars when cut off from their own. Resolution 42 of the 1930 Lambeth Conference in fact conceded the principle, but threw the onus upon the individual bishop :

> The Bishops of the Anglican Communion will not question the action of any Bishop who may, in his discretion . . . sanction an exception to the general rule ['that members of the Anglican Churches should receive the Holy Communion only from Ministers of their own Church'] in special areas, where the ministrations of an Anglican Church are not available for long periods of time or without travelling great distances.

In the first instance, naturally, Anglicans should be encouraged to worship with churches in full communion with themselves; but, where these are not available, then with other bodies, with whom it might well be desirable to enter into some reciprocal agreement in this matter,[5] which stated what was and was not implied for faith and order. But the freedom should not be made to wait or to depend on such a statement.

When we pass from the situation abroad to that at home there is a real difference. Here the ultimate relationship is not full communion with another branch of the catholic church, but the

---

[5] Resolutions of Convocation have already been passed (Canterbury, May 1954; York, October 1954) welcoming to Holy Communion in the Church of England visiting members of the non-episcopal churches of Norway, Denmark and Iceland. But no sanction was given for any reciprocity.

reintegration of schismatic churches in complete organic union. Indeed no state of intercommunion, however full, can ever be the proper or normative relationship between two churches ministering *in the same place.* Perhaps I may repeat some words I wrote earlier[6] in this connection:

> Full communion without union with a distant church, as in South India, or even in Scotland, may be a highly desirable step – so that when a member or minister moves from one to the other there is no break. But for disunited and competing churches *in the same parish* to claim to be in full communion with each other is to invite the world, not to believe in our unity, but to question our integrity.

Intercommunion between two churches in schism who have no intention to unite is a fearful thing. For steady insistence upon this the ecumenical movement may indeed be grateful to the (often apparently obscurantist) Anglican attitude, which was clearly formulated in the Lambeth Conference Report of 1930:[7]

> The general rule of our Church must therefore be held to exclude indiscriminate intercommunion, or any such intercommunion as expresses acquiescence in the continuance of separately organized Churches.

There are signs that this insistence is now being shared by the leadership of the Free Churches, who are becoming embarrassingly conscious that centuries of open communion have not brought them any nearer to union. Indeed, as Bishop Newbigin says, 'Intercommunion apart from any such passion [for union] merely slackens the tension of desire.'[8] The Bishops in 1933 were quite right to relate any possibility of intercommunion to 'efforts definitely intended to promote visible unity of the Church of Christ', even if they may have been led to define these too narrowly.

I therefore find the recent editorial suggestion of *The Church*

[6] 'Episcopacy and Intercommunion', *On Being the Church in the World* (Pelican ed.), p. 125.
[7] Pp. 116f.
[8] 'Anglicans and Christian Reunion', *Theology*, June 1958, p. 225.

Times of 'an invitation to all baptized and communicant Christians of good standing in their own churches to come, *when they so desire*, to receive the Holy Communion in their parish church'[9] rather shocking. I am not often more rigorist than *The Church Times*. But I believe this proposal reveals a much lower doctrine of the church than that of the Open Letter. It also discloses in a particularly instructive way the Anglican tendency to assume that as long as there is an episcopally ordained celebrant no other theological issue matters very much.

Let us try and set out as objectively as possible the situation in which we find ourselves. It is a thoroughly anomalous situation; and indeed one can say that any solution in these circumstances which is comfortable and clear-cut is certain to be wrong. We are in schism, yet it is schism within the church (rather than from the church); and it is, in greater or less degree, penitent schism. We admit the reality and efficacy of each others' ministries and sacraments, but question their validity. We have not got union; yet it would be a sin against the Holy Ghost to deny that at some points at least there is very deep unity. We are on the road to union, or at any rate, if we are not, we shall find ourselves having to do some pretty drastic back pedalling. For there is a momentum and a movement of the Spirit which we cannot ultimately deny. Where, if at all, should intercommunion come into this tragic yet forward-looking situation? And, if it should, what form ought it most honestly to take?

I believe, as I suggested in an earlier article,[10] that the spiritual and theological conditions of intercommunion can properly be stated only by holding *together* the two great Pauline principles that, on the one hand, if we eat and drink with no sense of the body we eat and drink judgement to ourselves (I Cor. 11.29) and, on the other, that it is *because* of the one loaf that we who are many are one body (I Cor. 10.17). For what we are taking to ourselves in Communion is the perfect unity of the one new man in Christ Jesus. None of us can bear that unity, and, if we have no will to let it break down our divisions, then we cannot but receive it to our own

[9] 12 January 1962. Italics mine.
[10] 'Intercommunion and Concelebration', *On Being the Church in the World*, pp. 117–22.

damnation. That is why casual intercommunion, like the casual communion, is so dangerous a thing. And yet in Communion is offered us the one thing that can heal as well as condemn our divisions. The one loaf and the common cup of the Lord have the power to recreate us, by union with our Head, as the one Body we so miserably fail to be. The Eucharist is constitutive of the church, locally and ecumenically. There comes a point of penitence when mercy can rejoice over judgement, when for all our failure we can be justified by faith, as individuals and as groups.

The Anglican witness has concentrated so heavily on the first truth, and the Free Church witness has related the grace of inter-communion so inadequately to union, that it is necessary to empha-size the implications of St Paul's second great truth. It has indeed been hidden from English eyes very largely by the sad failure at this point of the Authorized Version, which renders scarcely comprehensibly : 'For we being many are one bread, and one body.' (What, on inspection, does it really mean to say that we *are* one bread?) The Revised Standard Version and the New English Bible, however, bring out quite clearly the causal relationship – that it is *because* of the one loaf that we are one body – which St Paul goes on to underline in the second half of the verse : 'For we all partake of the one loaf.'

But the truth of this does not rest upon a single text. It has been confirmed for me beyond dispute by the experience of having seen it happen in a situation – in a Cambridge college chapel – where under the 1933 Resolutions we were indeed able to break one bread together and to know its power. It was the Communion which made of us, as nothing else could, a single ecumenical community. I have written more fully of that experience elsewhere;[11] but I should be false to my own vision of the truth if I did not testify to it. Nothing will persuade me that there at any rate intercommunion was not laid upon us as a saving necessity. In that situation it would have been a greater judgement to have broken bread separately than to have done it together.

And this, thank God, is coming to be the situation within the life of the church in a growing number of places. The point where

[11] *Liturgy Coming to Life.*

mercy rejoices over judgement may still have been reached in tragically few areas of the church's work and witness. But there *are* those places, and a great and dull frustration is sensed when the ceiling of co-operation is reached. As a result of our quickened sense of the centrality and power of the Eucharist that point is now being reached earlier. Nothing should be done to encourage intercommunion before that breaking-point of penitence. But at that point, when there really is one community capable of sharing one bread without hypocrisy, then in fear and trembling I believe we must go forward – and, equally importantly, we must draw back if, as may happen, the conditions that justified it cease to exist. Because this is an assessment which depends essentially on the spiritual realities of the local situation – and cannot be determined merely by the state of play between denominations as a whole – I would think it most important that it should continue to be a matter of, properly co-ordinated, episcopal discretion.

Fresh resolutions, giving recognition to these needs, would require to be drafted, and there is no reason why they should not follow fundamentally the same principles as those of 1933. But there is one further nettle which I am sure must be grasped, and that is the question of reciprocity.

In a school or college community where there is but a single altar, and that an Anglican one, the question of reciprocity does not arise; and in the occasional and discontinuous gatherings for reunion envisaged in 1933 it can be waived in the interests of Christian charity. But where there is continuous co-operation on a wide and deep level between two or more local congregations the question is quickly inevitable: 'Why must we always come to you? What is wrong with our sacraments?' I do not believe we can burke this question, because it contains the sting of the whole matter. If we are honest, a major part of Anglican reluctance, and often intransigence, over intercommunion has *not* sprung from a passionate desire to avoid obscuring the sin of disunity. It has sprung from a deep-seated and often disingenuous ambivalence over the status of Free Church sacraments. It was this, rather than bishops, that really caused the Presbyterian worm to turn in the Anglo-Scottish negotiations, and which earned us the reputation, whether rightly or wrongly, of perfidious Anglicans. We have so often said in print that we gladly acknowledge Free Church ministries as real and efficacious ministries of Christ's word and sacraments, and then appear to go back on that by retricting open celebrations to Anglican altars and by insisting that the Free Churches should 'take episcopacy into their system' *not merely as the price of union but as the condition for intercommunion.*

The situation is in fact somewhat ironical. In order to contrive the form of limited intercommunion blessed in 1933 recourse has had to be had to a device which has never had in Anglican tradition any serious theological principle behind it. For the Free Churches 'open communion' is a rule of faith; for the Church of England (except in definite Evangelical circles) it is a breach of order. Moreover, while careful restrictions have been laid down for the admission of Free Churchmen to Anglican altars, nothing has ever been said officially to restrict Anglicans sharing in (these supposedly dubious) Free Church sacraments. It has been left entirely to the individual's conscience, and there is no specific ruling of the church to prevent a group of Anglicans communicating at a Nonconformist celebration. Nevertheless, the onus is placed so heavily on the individual that most would feel it an act of disloyalty or indiscipline to do so.

Once again, the church as a whole should try to clear its mind on this issue – and not evade it merely by saying nothing, as in 1933.

Let us set down certain things that would seem to be agreed.

1. The Free Churches do not possess, and do not claim to possess, ministries which Anglicans can acknowledge as valid according to the criteria required by the preface to the Ordinal (namely, episcopal ordination and consecration). To ask Anglicans to recognize them as equally valid (or, in other words, to say that episcopacy makes no difference) would be to ask them to renounce the necessity of episcopacy where it can be had. I do not believe the ecumenically minded leaders of the Free Churches really want Anglicans to do this. For, as in South India, they want episcopacy as the future ministry of the coming great church.

2. The Free Church ministries are visibly blessed by the Holy Spirit as real means of grace. They do mediate the life of Christ to the believers: they show the marks expected of 'a congregation in which the Word of God is faithfully preached and the sacraments

duly administered' (Article XIX). To say that they are not real sacraments of the body and blood of Christ is to fly in the face of the spiritual evidence.

What is to be concluded from these two apparently contrary sets of statements? To ask Anglicans to say that efficacy *equals* validity, and that therefore Free Church ministries are, as it were, justified by their works, is again to ask them to renounce convictions conscientiously held. To say, on the other hand, that validity is all is to risk being found fighting against the Holy Ghost. Let us admit that full validity for all our ministries is only the fruit of union, and must wait upon it. But meanwhile let us acknowledge the relevance here, as Bishop Newbigin pleads,[12] of the principle of justification, not by works, but by faith – faith in the one Spirit who is even now at work through us all and who wills to bring us into unity not by our merits but by the sheer grace of God. When we are prepared to accept each other as Christ accepted us, not on the basis of what as denominations we have to contribute but for what he has the power to make of us, then, as in South India, mercy can triumph over judgement, and all things, validity and whatever else is necessary, can be added to us.

In fact one must, I think, say that if, and at the point at which, intercommunion is ever justified short of union, reciprocal intercommunion is also justified. If we are regarding ourselves and each other as self-sufficient coexistent denominations, content to continue living and working side by side, then intercommunion merely deepens our guilt. But if we are seeking to live by the unity which we know we do not possess but which we believe Christ has the power to make of us, then our *locus standi* is utterly different. Intercommunion is then the great sacrament of justification by faith, the pledge of our new being in Christ, and all that is required for it is the trust that grace indeed does meet through each of our sacraments however defective. And that the Church of England has long since confessed, most notably in the words of the 1923 *Memorandum on the Status of Existing Free Church Ministry*, and since constantly re-affirmed, that we 'do not call in question for a moment the spiritual reality of these ministries . . . but thankfully acknowledge that [they] have been manifestly blessed and owned

[12] *The Reunion of the Church*, especially chapter 6.

by the Holy Spirit as effective means of grace'.[13] It may be time
that we sought to receive this grace instead of merely conceding
it. For to decline it is to appear in practice to deny it. But above
all it is to put ourselves in the false position of trying to live by
works. To say that reunion can come through intercommunion at
Anglican altars only is to undercut the sole basis on which intercommunion short of union can theologically be justified. If we seek
to justify it on the basis that we at any rate have valid orders
(preserving a dignified, or a shifty, silence on the status of others),
then we are back at commending ourselves. We are not taking our
stand, *sola fide,* on the unity of Christ which condemns and heals
us all.

If and where we judge reciprocal intercommunion to be right
(and I would wish to stress again the spiritual and theological
conditions in which alone it makes sense), then *how* we communicate is a secondary, though still important question. It may be, as
Bishop Newbigin would argue, that the simple acceptance of each
others' ministries as they stand witnesses most unequivocally to the
principle of justification by faith. It may be, as I have argued,[14]
that concelebration is the most appropriate procedure. This, I
would suggest, is in any case the proper practice even when two or
more *Anglican* congregations meet together with their priests or
bishop. (I recently concelebrated with the priests of six parishes
which had joined for a single Confirmation and first communion.)
For it means that each priest or minister is performing that part
in the liturgy for which he was ordained by his church and is leading his flock in a *joint* celebration of the whole people of God rather
than at one in which one congregation is the host and the others
merely visitors. Ecumenically, too, concelebration has the advantage of making it easier for those with scruples to accept a celebration which is fully Anglican *at the same time* as it is fully non-

[13] Cited in G. K. A. Bell, *Documents on Christian Unity*, Series I & II
(1955 ed.), p. 55. This weighty memorandum was signed by the two Archbishops (Davidson and Lang) together with the Bishops of London (Win-
nington-Ingram), Winchester (Talbot), Ely (Chase), Lichfield (Kempthorne),
Peterborough (Woods), Chelmsford (Watts-Ditchfield), Hereford (Linton-
Smith), Ripon (Strong), Salisbury (Donaldson), Gloucester (Headlam), Bishop
Gibson and W. H. Frere.
[14] In the two previous articles on intercommunion referred to above.

non-Anglican (for no non-episcopal minister presumably has the power to detract from the fullness of Anglican orders!). But I would not wish to see any condition laid down, since to insist on con-celebration could be the cover for disingenuous thinking about the basis on which the Free Church sacrament is being accepted. (It is not justification by faith if in fact the consecration is 'made all right' by the presence of an Anglican priest at the table.)

But, in whatever form, I believe that the Church of England should declare itself, over against a situation which (God grant) will yearly become more pressing as the growing prayer for unity takes effect and we are forced closer together by co-operation and con-versation. It should lay the strain (and let us not suppose any solution short of union can be anything but a strain) unequivocally upon *itself*, rather than upon its individual members – though it must not, of course, compel the conscience of any. It should define carefully but simply the spiritual and theological conditions in which intercommunion can be right. And then I believe it should have the courage and the faith to recommend that in these circum-stances it should also be reciprocal. A clear lead along these lines at this time could have an immediate and far-reaching effect in unblocking the log-jam into which we are in danger of drifting.

15

Let the Liturgy be free!

'The Gospel is about planned obsolescence – a making of all things new.' So Brian Frost in a review of the liturgical scene in Britain today.[1] And never has the liturgical scene been as fluid since the first molten moment of early Christian history. There is ferment everywhere, not least within the area where until yesterday things were most fixed – the Church of Rome. After two successive Roman Catholic masses I attended recently in widely separated parts of the world, I asked the question, 'What liturgy was that he was using?', and received the casual answer, 'Oh, he was making it up himself.' I don't in fact believe it, but at least it was credible, whereas until the other day it would have been totally incredible.

At all times one of the glories of the Christian Eucharist has been its marvellous adaptability to every conceivable human occasion. In a now classic description Dom Gregory Dix writes, in a masterly passage of English prose[2]:

Was ever another command so obeyed? For century after century, spreading slowly to every continent and country and among every race on earth, this action has been done, in every conceivable human circumstance, for every conceivable human need from infancy and before it to extreme old age and after it, from the pinnacles of earthly greatness to the refuge of fugitives in the caves and dens of the earth. Men have found no better thing than this to do for kings at their crowning and for criminals going to the scaffold; for armies in triumph or for a bride and bridegroom in a little country church;

[1] 'Prayer, Praise and Protest' in *Risk* (Youth Department, the World Council of Churches) 5, 1 (1969), p. 14.
[2] *The Shape of the Liturgy*, p. 744.

for the proclamation of a dogma or for a good crop of wheat; for the wisdom of the Parliament of a mighty nation or for a sick old woman afraid to die; for schoolboy sitting an examination or for Columbus setting out to discover America; for the famine of whole provinces or for the soul of a dead lover; in thankfulness because my father did not die of pneumonia; for a village head-man much tempted to return to fetich because the yams had failed; because the Turk was at the gates of Vienna; for the repentance of Margaret; for the settlement of a strike; for a son for a barren woman; for Captain so-and-so, wounded and prisoner of war; while the lions roared in the nearby amphitheatre; on the beach at Dunkirk; while the hiss of scythes in the thick June grass came faintly through the windows of the church; tremulously, by an old monk on the fiftieth anniversary of his vows; furtively, by an exiled bishop who had hewn timber all day in a prison camp near Murmansk; gorgeously, for the canonization of St Joan of Arc – one could fill many pages with the reasons why men have done this, and not tell a hundredth part of them. And best of all, week by week and month by month, on a hundred thousand successive Sundays, faithfully, unfailingly, across all the parishes of christendom, the pastors have done this just to *make* the *plebs sancta Dei* – the holy common people of God.

On the face of it one would never expect that it should be done in the same way in such a rich variety of cirumstance. Certainly this would be true of no other human meal. Yet throughout the main traditions of Christendom there has operated a sort of 'steady state theory'. The assumption has reigned that wherever one went, in every age, one should ideally be able to find the Eucharist the same. This, of course, has found its most explicit expression in the fixed canon and universal language of the Latin mass. But *de facto* it has operated in the static liturgical tradition of the eastern Orthodox Church. And within the Anglican Church, in so many ways the least uniform in Christendom, the Book of Common Prayer is still theoretically grounded in the Act of Uniformity – which actually made non-conformity a penal offence.

The only recognized variation has been in the recurring cycle of the Christian year, though this has been marked by a very limited and repetitive lectionary, and even the familiar change of collect, epistle and gospel is unknown to eastern Orthodoxy. All recent ecumenical work in this field[3] has emphasized the need for much greater scope and flexibility.

But there is a growing awareness that liturgy must reflect other changes as well. Among these are those of:

1. *Time*. There has been an assumption that liturgies should last for centuries, if not for ever. Historically liturgy has been one of the most conservative elements in society, and in a rapidly changing world many hanker after it as something at any rate that is timeless and stable. The resentment at liturgical innovation goes psychologically very deep. But precisely the same was true (and still is true) of changes in 'the Bible' – the so-called Authorized Version (which was never in fact authorized[4]) having had about the same run in the English-speaking world as the Book of Common Prayer. The instructions given to the translators of the New English Bible never presupposed that it would be read in church – that was simply not 'on'. Yet within the decade spent on the New Testament section the situation had entirely altered – largely thanks to the breakthrough achieved by J. B. Phillips' version. Moreover, experience as a translator of the New English Bible brought home to me how rapidly the English language is changing. The various age-groups represented on the panel often had subtly different ideas of what was contemporary English, and as the youngest member of it I was acutely conscious that there was a whole generation below me which thought very differently again.

Liturgically, the current Series II experimental Communion Service of the Church of England may be said to correspond to the Revised Standard Version of the Bible. It is a vast improvement on the old and eliminates obvious archaisms, but it cannot claim (as the American translators of the RSV were rash enough to claim at the time) to be in contemporary English. The Liturgical Com-

---

[3] E.g., the Lectionary of the Church of South India, *The Calendar and Lessons for the Christian Year* of the Church of England Liturgical Commission, and *The Daily Office* produced by the Joint Liturgical Group in Britain.

[4] Ironically in fact it has on its title page simply 'Appointed to be read in churches', whereas the Bishops' Bible before it had 'Authorized and appointed to be read in churches'.

mission's more recent offerings in *Modern Liturgical Texts* merely
tend to show how far there is still to go.[5] But at least the need for new
language is officially acknowledged.

Yet liturgy to be effective must not simply reflect the immediate
present generation. Somehow, it must combine the contemporary
with the classical, the 'now' with the 'then', the momentary with
the ages of ages. It cannot just be *ex tempore* without losing its
eternal dimension. For it has to make present the Christ who is the
same yesterday, today and for ever and yet who because he is the
contemporary of every generation is a profoundly different Christ
today from the Christ of the fifth century or the fifteenth or the
nineteenth.

I would still wish to point, for a remarkable successful shot at
this difficult art, to the liturgy of St Mark's in the Bowery, New
York, which I wrote up in my earlier book *But That I Can't
Believe!*[6]. More recently, from the other side of America, comes 'The
Freedom Meal' as celebrated by the Free Church of Berkeley, California. This is very different and combines a quite untransferable
here and now with an even more deliberate echo of the Christian
centuries. The liturgy (as prepared for Easter 1969) is reproduced
at the end of this chapter,[7] but the treatment of the Reproaches
in the Good Friday service strikingly illustrates the fusion of the
contemporary and the classical. After the traditional suffrages
beginning

Minister   O my people, what have I done to you, or how have
                 I wearied you? Testify against me. Because I
                 brought you up out of the land of oppression, you
                 prepared a cross for your liberator.
Congregation   Holy God, Holy Mighty, Holy Immortal, have
                 mercy upon us.

---

[5] Thus, in the central prayer for the Spirit in the Confirmation Service
(a prayer which I believe will eventually have to be scrapped and started
again), 'the spirit of counsel' is still astonishingly perpetuated.
[6] Chapter 22, 'Local Liturgy'.
[7] The material will be published (after revision) in *A Prayer-Book from the
Free Church of Berkeley* by Morehouse-Barlow Co., New York. These extracts
are used by permission.

Minister	Because I led you through the desert forty years, and gave you manna to eat, and brought you into a land flowing milk and honey, you prepared a cross for your liberator.
Congregation	Holy God, Holy Mighty, Holy Immortal, have mercy upon us,

comes the calculated shock of the *ad hoc* and the *ad hominem*:

Minister	Because I brought you across the great ocean, out of the house of bondage, and set you in the broad and fair land of America; you have exterminated the red man, you have brought the black man into a new bondage, and kept him out of your pleasant homes.
Congregation	Holy God, Holy Mighty, Holy Immortal, have mercy upon us.
Minister	Because I brought you into the land of my great Spirit, a land of many waters and deep forests; you have cut down the forests with your chainsaws, and put poisons of your own invention in the waters that my creatures drink, in the air they breathe, and in the soil out of which I made you.
Congregation	O my people, what have I done unto you, or how have I wearied you? Testify against me.
Minister	Because I liberated you from the oppressor overseas, and led you safely through a civil war; you have dropped fire from the sky upon Japan and Viet Nam, and locked up in your prisons the young men and women who spoke the words of my judgement upon you.
Congregation	Holy God, Holy Mighty, Holy Immortal, have mercy upon us. O my people, what have I done unto you, or how have I wearied you? Testify against me.

2. *Place.* This leads into the second change which liturgy must reflect, that of locality. Originally, of course, it did. The Christian

community in each area had its own liturgical tradition, and it was a sad moment in the history of the church when uniformity finally squeezed this out. For if liturgy is to be real it must, like anything else, be local. It must represent the offering and celebration of that community's own life and not someone else's. And as society becomes more pluriform the number of identifiable groupings within 'one place' (the classical designation of local catholicism) becomes greater and more complex. To quote from an article to which I shall be referring later, 'We live in our own space and time, and so we must develop many liturgical "spaces" – schools, homes, neighbourhoods, professional and student groups, friends of a weekend or a lifetime.'[8] And, to offset the increasing standardization of our commercial culture from Tokyo to Timbuktoo, a genuine sense of place ('Truly the Lord is in this place') is surely something to be reverenced and recalled.

Yet again, if liturgy must reflect locality, it can never simply become parochial (in the debased modern sense) without ceasing to be itself. Liturgy is of its very essence catholic, belonging to that which links Christians *kath' holēs*, throughout the whole inhabited world. It is this that lies behind the proper instinct that wherever a baptized person goes he should be able to find himself at home in the Christian Eucharist. The mistake has lain in supposing this to be ensured by insisting on a universal set of unchanging words. This has purchased catholicity at the price both of locality and contemporeity. For language divides. But action unites. And we are all indebted to Dom Gregory Dix for the reminder that the shape of the liturgy is primarily a pattern not of talking but of doing – set by the fourfold action of Jesus at the Last Supper, when he took and he blessed and he broke and he gave. Essentially, it can be done in mime. And, as one knows from experience in a foreign country (especially now that in all our traditions the skeletal action has been allowed to stand forth much more clearly from the verbiage that has clothed it), one can enter into the action without being able to follow a word. Moreover, the more truly local and indigenous the expression which it does receive, the more whole and catholic the

[8] Thomas F. O'Meara, 'Liturgy Hot and Cool', *Worship*, 42:4 (April 1968), p. 220.

total effect. In neither place nor time is the unique the enemy of the eternal.

3. *Level*. This I believe to be even more important than the other two. In ordinary meals there are many variations both of century and of country, but even within a single person's experience there are still greater differences occasioned by levels of formality. So used are we to adapting to these that we scarcely notice them. But consider the vast differences between a state banquet, a club dinner, eating out in a restaurant (in itself a matter of wide range), a celebration party, 'Sunday dinner', an ordinary meal round the family table, a picnic, fish and chips out of a newspaper, etc., etc. Each has its appropriate style – of dress, formality and manners.

And the same should be true of our experience of the Lord's table. Yet it remains a great impoverishment that the vast majority of Christians have only known the eucharist at one level – that of the parish church (at which at most there are two styles of 'high' and 'low' mass). This, however, represents a highly formalized best-behaviour occasion for which elevated speech and public ritual are appropriate. It is a face-to-back assembly, with seating in rows, rather than face-to-face meeting of 'com-panions', in the original sense of men who share bread together. It is significant that amid the variety of human occasions that Dix listed as native to the Eucharist the one he omits to mention at all is that of the regular group of friends meeting to form the basic unit of Christian exist-ence, the gathering of two or three together in Christ's name.

Having personally been much involved with the recovery of the house-church, I may perhaps quote from an address I gave back in 1949 that was destined to give considerable impetus to the move-ment.

We should clearly be missing something vital if the only meal we ever knew was a boiled-shirt dinner party or a Lord Mayor's banquet.

What will happen if the Eucharist is really lived back into the everyday soil-stained world only the Holy Spirit can say. I should be surprised, however, if we do not see its reintegration with the *Agape* meal, so that once more the Eucharistic elements become something taken off the table 'as they were eating'. The special vestments, the special vessels, will either disappear at this level or be radically modified. (Incidentally, if the chalice and paten become the best 'piece' that the household possesses, it may make people realize how unworthy so much modern crockery is of the Lord's table, which is what every Christian table should be – and that goes also for the whole setting and manners of the meal.)[9]

It all sounds very tame now. But I can feel the shock waves still. The very thought of the body and blood of Christ coming into contact with ordinary cups and saucers! It was the same later when at the college chapel for which I was responsible[10] we first introduced an ordinary loaf and bottle of wine – despite the Prayer Book rubric that the bread should be 'the best and purest wheat bread' 'such as is usual to be eaten' (a combination in these packaged days not readily available!) There was still more horror when what was not set apart and consecrated of the loaf was taken into breakfast and smeared with butter and marmalade (again, despite the Prayer Book rubric regarding both the bread and wine left over that 'the curate shall have it to his own use'). For all this shatters the glass-case of the sanctuary in which liturgy has its life – its own life, insulated from the world. 'Desecration' was the word that came instinctively to the lips of those who had never experienced a house-celebration. It was the argument employed against priest-workers less than forty years ago by that much loved Bishop of London, Dr Winnington Ingram, that no one would want to have to do business on Monday with someone from whom he had received the Sacrament on Sunday! The late-Jewish concept of holiness, in which the holy was the opposite of the common and the holy of holies was to be entered only by the high priest once a year, could hardly be expressed more starkly. But all that was declared obsolete with the rending of the Temple veil. The meaning of the Incarnation is precisely the making holy of the common and the communalization of the holy. And it is this *koinōnia hagiōn*,

[9] 'The House Church and the Parish Church', reprinted on *On Being the Church in the World* (Pelican ed., 1969), p. 110.
[10] See further, *Liturgy Coming to Life.*

which means both the communion of saints and the common sharing of holy things, that is epitomized in *the* Holy Communion.

All this is fundamental to any contemporary spirituality. 'In our era, the road to holiness necessarily passes through the road of action' (Dag Hammarskjöld).[11] 'You may see the disc of Divinity quite clearly through the smoked glass of humanity, but not otherwise' (Coventry Patmore).[12] As I have sought to bring out elsewhere,[13] the fundamental aim of modern theology, spirituality and liturgy is not to reduce (to excise the dimension of the transcendent) but to locate – to set 'the beyond' 'in the midst', the sacred in the secular, the holy in the common. Hence the recovery in our day of liturgy, like theatre, in the round, and of all that goes with that.

Hence, too, the growing concern for centres rather than edges. The Christian religion has been obsessively preoccupied with drawing lines, with defining who is in and who is out, what is orthodox and what is not – so much so that it has frequently appeared to the outsider more of the excommunicating than of the accepting community. And nowhere has this been more marked than in the fencing of its altars. But, without any loss of the distinctive centre from which its life is lived, I believe that in future the edges and the ends will have to be much more open – so that the frontiers are free for exploration and dialogue, cross-fertilization and common action, with those of other religions and of none. Constant concern for drawing lines is a mark of insecurity and uncertainty, of fear that we shall lose our centre if we do not guard our borders.

In the remaining half of this chapter I should like to suggest, in the area of liturgy, some of the dividing walls whose crumbling, I believe, must be welcomed.

1. *Between secular and sacred.* Liturgy, as has often been remarked, is a word with a secular origin. It had nothing in the first instance to do with church, but with the world of public works – with the town hall rather than the temple. And I suspect we are nearing the end of 'separate development' in this field. How long we shall go on

[11] *Markings*, p. 108.
[12] *The Rod, the Root, and the Flower*, p. 45.
[13] *Exploration into God*, especially in this connection in chapter 6, 'The Journey Inwards'.

consecrating buildings to be 'set apart for ever from all secular and profane uses' I do not know.[14] But at least we are discovering – or rather rediscovering – what Professor J. G. Davies of Birmingham has splendidly documented in his study *The Secular Use of Church Buildings*. And we are learning the meaning of the multi-purpose church – which is very different from the old unsatisfactory dual-purpose church, where the sanctuary area was rather uncomfortably screened off during the week from the all-purpose nave. Rather, the whole house of God exists for opportunities and functions in which any hard line between sacred and secular dissolves.

Similarly, from the other end, I am convinced that the *normal* setting for liturgy, except on special days when Christians want to 'go to town', will increasingly be ordinary rooms in ordinary clothes and ordinary language, and will be integrally connected, as in the early church, with the other things, serious and light-hearted, for which they naturally come together. Certainly wherever I have glimpsed in parochial, and even more in para-parochial, settings something of what the church might look like in 1980 it has been in such a context.[15] The marks of the liturgy in future are likely to be informality, flexibility, and continuity with ordinary life-style, so that there is no forced sense of stepping out of one world into another, no compulsory cultural circumcision as one 'enters church'.

2. *Between clergy and laity.* As the declericalization of the Eucharist progresses, the question increasingly recurs: 'Why can't a layman celebrate?' I always want to begin by insisting that *every* celebration of the Eucharist is a lay celebration. The celebrant is the whole *laos* or people of God. The only question concerns what the early church was careful to call not the celebrant but the president. And he is there, not vicariously to do what the others cannot do,

---

[14] Thanks to a last-minute amendment, in which I had some part, to the Pastoral Measure of 1968 the Church of England no longer requires a parish to have a consecrated church. The bishop can designate *any* building as the parish centre of worship. This I regard as a great liberty.

[15] I would specially draw attention in this connection to John V. Taylor's pamphlet *Breaking Down The Parish*, reprinted from the CMS *News-Letter* (October-December 1967) obtainable from the Church Missionary Society, 157 Waterloo Road, London, SE1.

but representatively to do in the name of the whole Body what all are doing. And it is his representative position that from the earliest days made him the focus of unity not simply of the local community but between the local community and the wider church. The concept of apostolic succession, later degraded by the 'pipe-line' theory to emphasize the continuity of the clergy over against the laity, originated to safeguard the solidarity of the local congregation with the bishop's Eucharist. And schism at the table, which authorization of the local president by the representative of the Body as a whole was intended to forestall, is certainly not a danger that can now be ignored. Indeed, the recovered awareness of a genuinely local catholicism makes its corollary more rather than less important. There are, alas, sad lessons to be learnt from church history at this point.

Yet when all this has been said, the clergy line, by which the ministry both of the word and sacrament has been kept within the hands of a professional caste, must go. There will have to be increasing diversification of ministry, as in the early church, according to what the Spirit demands. The qualifications needed for that member of the *laos* chosen and accredited for presiding at the table will not be essentially different from those of every other ministering Christian. Nor will it be normal for him to be *paid* to be ordained. And increasingly the gifts required of him will not be to do it all himself but to *enable participation – leading* the breaking and sharing of the Word as of the Sacrament. For *sermo* means 'conversation'; and it was not for nothing that Jesus *sat* to teach – on the level. The entire conduct of liturgy demands preparedness (rather than formal preparation), and a ministerial leader able to shape and be shaped by it. 'Let the president give thanks as he is able' is one of the earliest recorded Christian rubrics. There is an essential open-endedness to an assembly whose central expectation remains the *maranatha* cry of the earliest Christians: 'Come, Lord Jesus.' Yet such preparedness demands great gifts, great care, and great prayer. 'Good arrangement for liturgy should not mean control, but rather planning for every occurrence, and spontaneity sometimes takes more organization than an agenda of prayers.'[16] The requirements for the breaker of bread do not grow any less. The breaking down of the clergy line does not

[16] *Risk,* 5.1, editorial.

mean that ordination is to be treated casually – only less hieratically.

3. *Between denominations.* 'I believe that within twenty-five years most acts of worship will be on a weekday, will not take place in a church building, and will not be Anglican but ecumenical.' So the Provost of Southwark, Ernest Southcott, has predicted.[17] I should like to think he has merely overestimated the time. For I detect, unless I am mistaken, a rapid quickening of the pace in the matter of inter-communion. Paradoxically it has been hastened rather than retarded by the failure of the Anglican-Methodist negotiations to achieve the first stage of full communion. I have never been one who has seen the logic of deliberately dividing (by setting up a parallel Methodist episcopate) the commended focus of visible unity in order to achieve full communion.[18] But if Stage I of the scheme were the unavoidable preliminary to union, then I was content to vote for it to get it behind us. But this having failed, I am all for pressing on to the goal of organic union itself by reciprocal intercommunion, using, where appropriate, joint celebration,[19] rather than by the Methodists' 'taking episcopacy into their system'[20] (though, to make the eventual integration of ministries easier, certainly let us meanwhile use the agreed new Ordinal with mutual participation in each other's ordinations). For increasingly the recognition is dawning that it is '*because of* the one loaf' that 'we who are many are one body' (I Cor. 10.17).[21] In other words, the Eucharist is the most potent means towards unity *as well as* the seal of its achievement. Of course, if the one loaf does not correspond to a spiritual reality, if we have no intention of being the one body we take to ourselves – then it is

[17] *Cathedral and Mission*, Report on Southwark Cathedral (1969) by the Birmingham University Institute for the Study of Worship and Religious Architecture, p. 86.

[18] See my article 'Episcopacy and Intercommunion' written in 1959 after the first Interim Report and reprinted in *On Being the Church in the World*, pp. 123–32.

[19] For a careful definition of these terms see the Report *Intercommunion Today*.

[20] Frankly, I fear what they might do to episcopacy through bureaucracy more than I fear what Anglicans may do to it through prelacy!

[21] The mistranslation of the Authorized Version, 'For we being many are one bread, one body' is still unhappily perpetuated in the Series II Communion Service.

much better that we should not break the bread together. But it is increasingly being recognized, by Roman Catholics as well as others, that this is the *only* serious theological criterion, and that it must be spiritually discerned according to the local circumstance, not juridically imposed from above. And if we have not a mutually recognized ministry, there is no excuse for letting this act as a veto: we must celebrate if necessary through our separated ministries together.

The other insight that is increasingly gaining recognition, especially among the young, is that (to use New Testament terms) the context of the Eucharist is not simply the church but the Kingdom. It was instituted as a pledge and a foretaste not only of a new church fellowship but of a new world order (Mark 14.25 and parallels) and in St John's gospel (6.51) Jesus insists that the bread that he gives is for the life of *the world*. To treat the Eucharist simply as an ecclesiastical ordinance (and it has been right to stress its ecclesial character against both Protestant and Catholic individualism) is to be in danger of 'shutting the kingdom of heaven against men'. And this is the final condemnation of the church. To highlight the matter by illustration, to have refused the sacrament of solidarity on the road to Selma with Martin Luther King because you were an Episcopalian and he was a Baptist would appear to growing numbers inside the church – as well as out of it – to be trifling with the Word of God. And it is this sort of context – a worldly context – in which the Eucharist must increasingly be celebrated, and that by an ecumenical community or not at all.

4. *Between liturgy and life.* This last discussion has already introduced what is ultimately the most decisive breaking down of all – of the line that separates liturgy from life itself. The distance we have travelled in ten years is perhaps indicated in the difference between the title of my book *Liturgy Coming to Life* (which was deliberately intended to combine both senses of that ambiguous phrase) and that of the number of *Risk* I cited earlier, *Living: Liturgical Style.* At first I misread this, as doubtless did others, not observing the colon. But 'living' is the noun, 'liturgical style' the adjectival phrase. For 'liturgy' and 'life' are not parallel realms that have to come together. The one is but the focusing, the celebration, the lift-

ing into true relation, of the other. For liturgy is life lived up to its proper divine potential, to the level at which it becomes truly joyous, loving, peaceful, heavenly – all that is meant by 'new in the kingdom of God'. The matter of liturgy is simply life – bread, wine, people. Worship is the shaping of its true, eternal worth. And for that nothing can be excluded as a means of expression. 'Let the liturgy be splendid!' said Abbé Michonneau in his *Revolution in a City Parish* back in the forties. 'Let the liturgy be free!' is perhaps today's way of saying 'Give it all you've got'. To quote Brian Frost again,[22] 'Above all let there be with prayer and praise – protest, satire and doubt, mocking and laughter, anger and hate, aggression and sexuality. For we are beings made in the divine image with fire in our hearts and bodies, finesse even in our follies, and our lives are touched and fashioned not only by acceptance but with finery: the finery of Christ, the new man.'

Perhaps the question of the future could be posed by asking: 'What of liturgy at the end of the age of literacy?' Liturgies have always been associated with *service books*. In fact the word has come to be used simply to designate the text – e.g. the Liturgy of St John Chrysostom. But this is like equating ballet with the choreography. Today the dominance of the printed word is fast disappearing. (Already in our society as much is now spent on records as on books.) This, of course, is the message of Marshall McLuhan. And amid the exciting new material that is constantly being thrown up,[23] I would end by referring to an article from the American Roman Catholic journal *Worship*[24] which seeks to apply his insights to this field, 'Liturgy Hot and Cool' by Fr Thomas F. O'Meara.

For McLuhan, a hot medium is one in which the maximum amount of information is given, and little is left to be filled in. It is high on definition, low on personal involvement. In a cool medium, on the other hand, the minimum is given and the maximum participation

---

[22] *Risk*, 5.1, p. 14.

[23] See the bibliography in *Risk* 5.1, pp. 66–9. I would draw attention in this context to Sister Corita's *Footnotes and Headlines: A Play-Pray Book*, published jointly by the United Church Press and Herder & Herder. Loose-leaf examples of her imaginative use of advertising media are included in *Sister Corita*, published by the Pilgrim Press, Philadelphia.

[24] *Worship* 42, 4 (April 1968), pp. 215–22.

is required if one is to get anything out of it. O'Meara quotes in illustration McLuhan's *Understanding Media*: [25]

> A photograph is, visually, 'high definition'. A cartoon is 'low definition', simply because very little visual information is provided. Telephone is a cool medium, or one of low definition, because the ear is given a meagre amount of information. And speech is a cool medium of low definition, because so little is given and so much has to be filled in by the listener. On the other hand, hot media do not leave so much to be filled in. . . . Naturally, therefore, a hot medium like radio has very different effects on the user from a cool medium like the telephone. . . . Any hot medium allows of less participation than a cool one, as a lecture makes for less participation than a seminar, and a book for less than dialogue.

We live – so the thesis goes – in a cool generation. Youth wants direct involvement but neither needs nor wants high content. The production of *Hair*, for instance, is extremely low on definition, but high on participation. And the same applies to the current experiments in the so-called 'Living Theatre'. Indeed, many productions, such as *US* (with its deliberately ambivalent title to stress *our* involvement with the U.S. in Vietnam), would seem to demand to be understood not as theatre but as secular liturgy.[26]

Hot media today 'turn off' rather than 'turn on'. 'Involvement,' says O'Meara, 'through dogma, system, ideology, establishment is out.' And the traditional liturgy of the church, he argues, has precisely the same effect:

> What is our present liturgy – a liturgy we are reforming but not recreating? It was and is a 'hot' liturgy. It contains a great deal of content, of information; it is low on personal involvement; it repeats itself over and over; it keeps the same structure, filling it out with different blocks of detailed information about God and the saints; it dictates our responses. The form and content of the liturgy introduces us to this particular day, singled out of the

---

[25] Pp. 36f.
[26] Cf. my article 'The Aldwych Liturgy', *The Guardian*, 3 November 1966; also *The Empty Space* by Peter Brook, the producer of *US*, where almost all he says about the theatre could be transposed directly into terms of liturgy.

year by its 'liturgical' or festival differentiation; the milieu is not fashioned by the needs and situation of the worshippers.[27]

'For our cool culture,' he concludes,[28] 'an "over-data-ed", content-filled, preachy, complex liturgy is too hot.' For the 'mutual exchange of creativity' that is required in its place he proposes (among many fascinating suggestions) two pre-conditions:

> First of all . . . it cannot happen in large groups. Real communities, smaller groups celebrating their lives and their community, are necessary. Secondly, Christian liturgy is not the addition of a second, supra-natural world-order to our daily life, but rather the consecration and sublimation of the secular. . . . *After all, our life, our society, our man-ness is blessed, not covered up, in liturgy.*[29]

If one might add in that last sentence, as I am sure he would be willing to do, 'broken' to 'blessed' (for our celebration is the celebration of the Cross), his words could serve as a summary of that breaking down of the final barrier between liturgy and life which is anticipated in every making holy of the common in the eschatological fellowship of the Spirit.

Appendix

THE FREEDOM MEAL

According to the use of the Free Church of Berkeley, Easter 1969

1. *As the Ministers enter the church a psalm or hymn may be sung*

2. *The Minister may begin by saying*

> Minister   God alone is our peace.
> People   None but Jesus is our Liberator.
> Minister   We affirm the spirit of love.
> People   We offer it to the world.
> Minister   This is the bread of life.
> People   Here is the cup of freedom.

[27] *Op. cit.*, p. 217.   [28] *Op. cit.*, p. 222.
[29] *Op. cit.*, pp. 218f. Italics mine.

3. *The Minister, either privately or openly, says the* Prayer attributed to St Francis

> Jesus, make me an instrument of your peace. Where there is hatred, let me sow love; where there is injury, pardon; where there is doubt, faith; where there is despair, hope; where there is darkness, light; and where there is sadness, joy. Our Leader, make me not so much want to be comforted as to comfort, to be loved as to love. For it is in giving that we receive, in pardoning that we are pardoned, in dying that we are born to the life of the Age to come.

4. The Litany of the Saints *is then said, if convenient in procession*

> Bridegroom of poverty, our brother Francis of Assisi, follower of Jesus and drop-out, friend of the creation : *Stand here beside us.*
>
> Confessors in flames, Norman Morrison, Roger LaPorte, Jan Palach, Thich Quang Duc and all their companions, immolated for the cause of peace :
>
> Confessor in Russia, Boris Pasternak, poet of reconciliation :
>
> Confessor in Denmark, Søren Kierkegaard, diver in the sea of his own soul :
>
> Confessors in America, Henry David Thoreau and Thomas Merton, hermits and resisters :
>
> Good Pope John, friend of the poor, who longed for the unity of mankind :
>
> Apostle of non-violence, Gandhi the Mahatma, reproach to the churches :
>
> Mask of the Christ, Gautama the Buddha, fountain of compassion :
>
> Peacemaker in America, A. J. Muste, father of activists :
>
> Peacemaker in the world, Dag Hammarskjöld, denier of himself :
>
> Priest and panhandler, Benedict Joseph Labre, fool for Christ :
>
> Madman in America, Johnny Appleseed, planter of Eden :
>
> Witness in England, John Wesley, street minister :
>
> Faithful harlot, Mary Magdalen, first witness of new life :
>
> Inductee of Africa, Simon of Cyrene, who carried the cross of your liberator :

Reformers and preachers, George Fox and Menno Simons, who founded communities of peace:

Visionary and poet, William Blake, on trip by power of imagination:

Visionary and apostle, John the Evangelist, resister to the power of the Beast:

Patrons of healing, Luke the beloved, Louis Pasteur, and Florence Nightingale:

Priest and scientist, Pierre Teilhard de Chardin, voyager in the past and in the future:

Those who speak the soul's language, Bach, Mozart, Beethoven and their brothers:

Peter Maurin, Catholic worker:

Harriet Tubman, black liberator:

Martin Luther, reformer and leader of protest:

Martyrs of Africa: Perpetua, mother; Felicity, slave; and your companions:

Martyrs and Confessors, Polycarp, Ignatius and Justin, who refused the incense to Caesar:

Martyr in Prague, Jan Hus, reformer:

Holy Innocents of Birmingham, in your undeserved deaths:

Victims of lynching, known and unknown, brothers of Stephen the martyr:

Victims of Hiroshima and Nagasaki, pierced by needles of flame:

Victims of Coventry, Dresden and Tokyo, caught up in a storm of fire:

Victims of Auschwitz and all concentration camps, in your despair and death:

Children of Viet Nam, mutilated to preserve a way of life:

Martyrs in the streets of the South, Jonathan Daniels, James Reeb, Medgar Evers, Michael Schwermer, and all your companions:

Martyrs to the State, Maximilianus and Franz Jägerstatter, draft resisters:

Martyr in Bolivia, Camillo Torres, priest and revolutionary:

Martyr in Germany, Dietrich Bonhoeffer, confessor and revolutionary:

Martyr in America, Martin Luther King, organizer for peace
and justice:

Unwed mother, blessed Mary, wellspring of our liberation:

Our hero and leader, Jesus the manual labourer, root of our
dignity:

Our hero and leader, Jesus the prophet, who resisted the
Establishment:

Our hero and leader, Jesus the Liberator, a king because first
a servant:

Our hero and leader, Jesus the poet, who laid down a new
form of speech:

Our hero and leader, Jesus the son of God, bright cornerstone
of our unity in a new Spirit: *Stand here beside us.*

5. The Rule of the Free Church

Deacon   Love your enemies, do good to those who hate you,
bless those who curse you, pray for those who persecute you.
Whoever strikes you on the right cheek, turn to him the
other also; and whoever takes away your coat, give him your
shirt also. Give to everyone that asks, and from him who takes
away what is yours do not ask it back. And as you would
like people to do to you, do the same to them. Your reward
will be great, and you will be sons of the Most High; for he
raises his sun on the evil and the good, and he rains on the
just and the unjust. You shall therefore be merciful, as your
Father is merciful.

6. Statement of complicity, *repeated by the people after the Minister*
   (*This and the Absolution may be omitted on festivals*)

We confess that we are accomplices
  with the demonic powers of violence
We grow rich on oppression
We sleep in white beds of racism
We speak well of love
  and we curse our enemy
We take pride in freedom
  and invent new slavery

We say that our goal is peace
    and prepare new instruments of war
We cry out against exploitation
    and we exploit ourselves and each other
And so we are accomplices
    in the crime of burnt bodies
                burnt villages
                burnt ghettos
                burnt freedom
We are accomplices
        by our violence
        by our violence
        by our most grievous violence
           of turning our face away
           and of doing nothing.

7. **The Absolution**

Minister The Power of history, to whom all things are possible, who puts down kings and raises up the poor, can also do away with our twisted and broken existences, and make all things new for us. If anyone is in Jesus our Liberator, he is a new being; the old has passed away and the new has come. And as he was made known to his followers after his death, so he is to his gathered people today in the breaking of bread. Therefore I, a sinner, no better than any of you, say in his name that, for all who wish to make a fresh start, their guilt for the past has been done away with; the door of our freedom opens by itself for all who knock.

8. **The Canticle,** *from among those in the Supplement*

9. **The Prayer of the Day;** *or the following, if none is appointed*

Minister Father of all benefits, lead us after the example of your Son always to meet violence with love; set our feet in reparation where your Liberated Zone is continually breaking into the world, among the victims of force and neglect on every continent; restore to perfection every defect brought by our folly into the fabric of your universe; give the society of nations peace even while their mind is set on war : and in the end, O Power of nature and history, lead the remnant of your loyal people out to the marriage-feast where our alienation will find its quiet, in the spirit of the one who through doubt and temptation remained consistent, Jesus our holy Hero and Liberator. *So may it be.*

10. *Here the Lector reads the* Old Testament Prophecy *and/or the* Epistle

11. A Psalm *or* Canticle *may then be sung or said*

12. *Here the Deacon reads the* Gospel

13. *Announcements and Sermon*

14. The Litany of Intercession, *led by the Deacon*

For the reconciliation of mankind through the revolution of non-violent love: *We call on the Spirit.*

For the established churches, that they may be humbled, reformed and united:

For the global movement of peace and liberation, the church of Jesus incognito:

For all poor and hungry, migrant workers and hobos, outcast and unemployed:

For the people of the streets and ghettos, for children unwanted in their homes:

For the wounded, for prisoners and exiles, all those persecuted for conscience or resistance:

For victims of discrimination, harassment and brutality:

For the sick and suffering in mind and body, for those freaked out on drugs or fear:

For all oppressors, exploiters and imperialists, that they may be confused and disarmed by love:

For the masters of war, N. N. and N., that they be given a new transplant in place of their heart of stone:

For uptight authorities, police and officials, especially N. and N., that they may all listen to the voice of the humble and meek:

For all whom we fear, resent, or cannot love; for the unlovable:

For the liberation of our twisted lives, for the opening of closed doors:

For those who are dying and have died, whether in bitterness or tranquillity:

For doctors, nurses, and social workers, for ministers to the poor:

For organizers, students and writers, all who raise the cry for justice:

For all who are close to us, here and in every place:

That all couples may realize their union with the universal flow of love:

That our tables may be spread with the natural fruits of the earth:

That every person in his work may express the child's vision:

That our grandchildren may inherit a restored planet:

That we may have desire to study the books of ancient wisdom:

That people's revolution everywhere may become humanized and democratic:

That each one who enters our house may receive the hospitality due the Christ whom he bears:

That with compassion and fidelity we may work for renewal to our life's end:

In thanksgiving for all who have turned away from exploitation, especially N:

In thanksgiving for all who have been freed from the prisons of this world, especially N: *We call on the Spirit.*

Here the Minister shall ask for free intercessions from the people. When they are finished, the Deacon shall conclude

We call on the Spirit to bind us in solidarity with all who are using their lives to resist evil and affirm community: *We call on the Spirit.*

15. The Free Church Affirmation, *led by one of the People*

God is not dead
God is bread
The bread is rising
Bread means revolution
God means revolution

Murder is no revolution
Revolution is love
Win with love
The radical Jesus is winning
The world is coming to a beginning
The whole world is watching
Organize for a new world
Wash off your brother's blood
Burn out the mark of the Beast
Join the freedom meal
Plant the peace garden
The asphalt church is marching
The guerrilla church is recruiting
The people's church is striking
The submarine church is surfacing
The war is over
The war is over
The war is over
The Liberated Zone is at hand.

16. The Kiss of Peace, *introduced by the Deacon*

> If you are bringing your present to the altar,
>> And remember there that your brother has something
>> against you;
> Leave your present there before the altar,
>> Go first and be reconciled to your brother.

17. The Offering and Preparation of the meal, *while the Minister says*

Now that we have been brought together as brothers and sisters in love, let us offer to our Liberator our united service of celebration and radical action.

18. The Thanksgiving

> *Minister* Peace be with you.
> *People* And with you.
> *Minister* Lift up your hearts.
> *People* We lift them up to our Liberator.
> *Minister* Let us give thanks to the Power of creation.

People   It is right for us to do so.

Minister It is right for us at all times and places to affirm our union with the Fountain of nature and history. As our doors of perception open they testify to a universe of glory outside ourselves: the touch of fabric, rocks, skin; the smell of redwood, fish, flowers, our neighbour's sweat, the smoke of incense; the taste of grain and the blood of the vine; the sound of bird-song and animals, waves and wind, voice and music; the light of our sun and the farthest galaxies. In our consciousness that the cosmos is everywhere ready to blossom into a love not of our devising, we rise to a sphere of liberation beyond space and time; we hear words passing human speech, as our brother Isaiah once did in the Temple; standing beside angelic Energies with head bowed, we confidently sing to you, O Father of splendours:

People   Holy, Holy, Holy is the Power beyond all hosts,
            The fullness of the whole world is his glory.
            Blessed is the one who comes in his name;
            May he be given many good successes.

Minister Still by our own fault we have abandoned the Fountain of waters and built broken reservoirs which hold no water. But the chain of complicity linking our twisted lives to past guilt has been snapped, through no power of our own; and though living in occupied territory, we walk in hope. We lay hold on a golden thread leading back to the foundation of space and time: the history of our liberation from the powers of darkness, the succession of saints in the community of love (*and especially of* N.) who looked to you, O Jesus, as their Morningstar. (*Here is inserted the Proper Preface, if any.*) Like us you were denounced and beaten, you forgave your exploiters and proclaimed the blessedness of the poor. Today we recall how at your last Freedom Meal with your friends you took the loaf as we do, said thanks over it and broke it, and gave it to them, saying: 'Take, eat: this is my body broken for you: do this for my remembering.' Also after the meal you took the cup, said thanks and gave it to them, saying:

'Drink this, all of you; for this cup is the unending Constitution of a new society in my blood, poured out for liberation from your guilt. Do this whenever you drink it, for my remembering.'

People   Your death we recall,
Your resurrection we announce,
Your coming we await.

Minister   That constitution is his new way of non-violent reconciliation, of which this meal is our permanent reminder. He put himself so completely in others that nothing of him could die; therefore in the Liberated Zone of his spirit we are made whole and given new life. And we call on you, O Spirit of Jesus our Brother, to put his death and life into this bread and wine, so that through them the barriers may be broken down between rich and poor, black and white, man and woman, old and young, East and West; beat our swords into ploughshares, plant the garden of this planet; gather humankind together and restore us as true sons and daughters of those first parents created after God's likeness in the Paradise of Eden; and strengthen us as servants of the poor and messengers of that peace brought in by our Liberator, through whom (in the community of love) nature and history move towards their desired Goal.

People   So may it be, here and everywhere, now and always. Come quickly, Jesus!

19. The Lord's Prayer

Minister   And now we take heart and say in the words our Liberator has taught us:

Minister and People   Father:
Holy is your being,
At hand is your ruling,
Done is your desiring.
Our bread provide us,
Our debt forgive us,
From trials free us.

20. *Then the Minister breaks the bread, saying*

    Minister   The bread of justice which we break,
                Is it not unity in the body of the Liberator?
    People   We who are many are one body,
                For we share the one loaf.

21. *Then the persons appointed distribute the bread and wine, while there is said*

    Jesus the lamb of liberation is sacrificed,
       Therefore we shall keep the feast.
          Holy things for the people of God!
    Jesus is risen from the dead.
       See, he makes all things new,
          A new earth under a new sky!

22. *After all have finished, the Minister says the* Blessing

    Blessed are you poor, for yours is the Liberated Zone.
    Blessed are you meek, for you inherit the earth.
    Blessed are you who mourn, for you are comforted.
    Blessed are you hungry and thirsty, for you are filled.
    Blessed are you merciful, for you receive mercy.
    Blessed are you pure in heart, for you see God.
    Blessed are you peacemakers, for you are called children of God.
    Blessed are you persecuted, for yours is the Liberated Zone.

23. The Dismissal

    Deacon   Go in peace and love,
              Serve God with joy.
        Keep the faith, baby,
           You are the Liberated Zone.

16

A Church Truly Free

1. A Centre of Christian Freedom[1]

'Christ set us free, to be free men' (Gal. 5.1).

'Live as free men; not, however, as though your freedom were there to provide a screen for wrong-doing' (I Peter 2.16).

The church has been remarkably fearful of freedom – and not the church only; but the church should know better.

Freedom of thought you would suppose to be central to the Christian style of life – for did not Jesus promise that the truth would make us free? Yet 'free thought' has been suspect – and espoused by those seeking liberation from the Christian dogma. 'The Free Thinker' is the name not of a Christian journal but of an atheist magazine.

Again, 'free love' has been proclaimed as a protest against the Christian moral standard – though what goes under that name is usually neither love nor free. Yet, truly understood, what could be nearer to the heart of the Christian than

> ... of that free love
> The breadth, depth, length and height to prove?

In the same way, a 'free church' immediately suggests to an Englishman the opposite of the Church of England. It has been an ideal conceived largely in negative terms of freedom from; and in these days the reality is not, alas, particularly liberating. Yet

[1] The substance of a sermon preached at the Institution of the Revd Paul Oestreicher to the Church of the Ascension, Blackheath, London, 26 November 1968.

the free church is a notion absolutely central to St Paul's argument in the Epistle to the Galatians from which my first text is taken. He contrasts the old church of Israel, the established Jerusalem, who is in slavery with her children, with the Jerusalem who is free – and 'she is our mother'.

This vision of a church which is truly free – free for God and free for men – is one that we all sigh for within the bondage of institutional religion. The marvellous song of Sydney Carter's which has just been sung, 'Bird of Heaven'[2] exactly captures (if that is the right word) the elusive spirit of that freedom. I have told him that if he will write it out, I will have it framed to be hung in this church. For I should like to think that this church might be, more than anything else, a centre of Christian freedom.

I went, last year, with a party from this diocese to the French Protestant community at Taizé, which many of you may know. And what one caught there was precisely this sense of freedom – a freedom, in loyalty, to question so much in the established churches which makes burdened men of us all. '*La provisoire*' was the watchword – all structures are provisional, expendable: this is what they felt, as a twentieth-century monastic community, they had most to say to the churches today.

Some time ago I jotted down some notes for an article I have never written on 'the new non-conformity'. Heaven forbid that this should take the form of another dissenting denomination. Yet I believe that in each area there is a call – cutting across all our denominations (and, dare one hope, supported by them?) – for what I would style

[2] Catch the bird of heaven,
  Lock him in a cage of gold.
Look again tomorrow
  And he will be gone.
  Ah, the bird of heaven!
  Follow where the bird has gone.
  If you want to find him,
  Keep on travelling on.

Lock him in religion,
  Gold and frankincense and myrrh
Carry to his prison,
  But he will be gone.
  Ah, the bird of heaven! . . .

Temple made of marble,
  Beak and feather made of gol'
Bell and book and candle!
  But he will be gone.
  Ah, the bird of heaven! . . .

Bell and book and candle
  Cannot hold him any more.
Still the bird is flying,
  As he did before.
  Ah, the bird of heaven! . . .

a parochial monasticism, a community of freedom whose particular
vocation within the whole body of Christ is to exist for those who,
as Charles Davis put it, are 'blocked' by the institutional church.
From time to time in different places I believe the health of the
church demands Christian communities who can sit much more
loosely to the things that oppress us. Ideally every church should be
able to do this. But if we are realistic we know the severe limits imposed by plant, by legalities, and above all by the religious in-group
and by the conservatism in each one of us that loves to have it so.

But from time to time an opportunity opens. I believe that it has
in the case of this church, which enjoyed in origin the freedom of a
private chapel. With the extraordinarily trustful support of the
Patron, the Churchwardens, and members of the Parochial Church
Council with whom I met, we decided to stick our necks out. So almost uniquely in the Church of England, though it is the obvious
procedure in any other field, we put the job of vicar up to public
advertisement. And now you see what you have got! As it was he
came in at the eleventh hour after the applications were closed.
Indeed, I should never have dreamt of approaching Paul Oestreicher,
whom I did not think to be free. In fact he wasn't, and he could have
continued his important work at the British Council of Churches
for several more years. But free man he is, and he responded to
the vision we saw for this place, with its openness to all that is
going on in the secular and cultural life around.

A genuinely free church is free *for all men.* It is not an eclectic
community catering for those who are attracted by it. Let us not
forget that we have at the foot of the hill, stretching down into
Deptford, one of the most completely de-Christianized areas of the
whole diocese, from which the vicar of the next door parish says
that not a single person comes to his church. Part of that area (in
this parish) is now being torn down and rebuilt. Let it be a reminder that any Christian freedom must have its feet firmly grounded
in the lowly service of the one who took a towel and girded himself.

Yet I hope this church *will* attract from other parishes (and I
trust none will resent it if they do), because, as I know, there are
plenty of unchurched people all over the Blackheath area. They
are people who are blocked and clogged by what they think (often
rightly) organized religion stands for. I want windows to be

opened, and all kinds of things tried out – in the church building and beyond. Let this place be a centre of experiment and exploration and meeting for many around.

'Live as free men – but not (if St Peter will forgive a free translation) as a cover for bolshiness or bloody-mindedness.' There are churches enough that do that – one not far from here signals its freedom in Christ by refusing on principle to pay its quota to the diocese! Use your freedom responsibly and creatively; but above all use it. And if you are doing your job there are bound to be tensions. Do something which we must have the humility to see that we cannot all do. Risk envy, risk rocking the boat. It is asking quite a lot for an establishment (of church or indeed of state, as our Marxist visitors tonight know only too well) not only to tolerate genuine freedom, but to encourage and abet it. But that is what I should like to see happening here above everything else.[3]

2. *Freedom for Ministry*[4]

As he said this, many put their faith in him. Turning to the Jews who had believed him, Jesus said: 'If you dwell within the revelation I have brought, you are indeed my disciples; you shall know the truth, and the truth will set you free.' They replied. 'We are Abraham's descendants; we have never been in slavery to any man. What do you mean by saying, "You will become free men"?' 'In very truth I tell you,' said Jesus, 'that everyone who commits sin is a slave. The slave has no permanent standing in the household, but the son belongs to it for ever. If then the Son sets you free, you will indeed be free' (John 8.30-36).

This passage comes from the great controversial section at the heart of St John's gospel, which revolves around the true meaning of such fundamental themes as authority and status, security and freedom. Where are roots to be found? And at this particular juncture Jesus

---

[3] It was a first-fruits of my vision for this church that it should have been the setting for my 'swan song' as Bishop of Woolwich on 28 September 1969, which included the first performance of the setting to music by Donald Swann of Cecil Day-Lewis's *Requiem for the Living*.

[4] Sermon preached for the Trinity Ordination, 1968, Southwark Cathedral, London. Reprinted in *New Christian*, 11 July 1968.

is addressing 'the Jews who believed in him', that is to say, people already deeply grounded in religious tradition who had come to put their trust in him. They knew where they stood – or thought they did. With incredulity they asked, 'What do you mean by saying "You will *become* free men"?'

It is in some such similar context that I suggest Christ addresses us here today. Ordination revolves around the same themes of authority and status, security and freedom. There is an inescapable solemnity and grandeur about it and we are conscious at this moment of standing within a long and rich religious heritage. Nowhere perhaps is the Church of England more subtly rooted in tradition than on Trinity Sunday in a cathedral city. And as one who was himself born on Trinity Sunday in a cathedral city, at the very heart of the ecclesiastical establishment, I know well the address to 'the Jews who believed'. And it is easy on such an occasion to fall back upon certainties that seem proof against change and decay. Indeed, I could discourse on them with a genuine resonance. For there have traditionally been a number of dykes and buttresses by which the ordained ministry has been surrounded that have afforded real authority and status, security and freedom. No one is saying they are wrong, any more than Jesus was decrying descent from Abraham. Yet there comes a moment – and in Christ there has to come a moment – when we must face the truth that we cannot rest upon them. And today many of the traditional confidences are in fact dissolving that previously threw an invisible aura of protection around 'the sacred ministry' of the Church. Let me simply mention three.

1. There has been the clergy line, which has subtly but firmly divided what a mediaeval lawyer called the 'two sorts of Christians' – not good Christians and bad Christians, but clergy and laity. In the Church of England this line has been drawn below the diaconate, despite the fact that in function deacons and readers have almost everything in common except membership of the clerical club whose directory is Crockford's. The most newly ordained deacon at twenty-three arrives to sit at the parish table, as it were, above the salt – from the other side of the line. This is a line within the diversity of ministry shared by the whole Spirit-filled community of which the New Testament knows nothing. It was imported into the church

from the provincial government and class-structure of the Roman Empire. It is now mercifully being blurred, not by obliterating real distinctions of ministerial function within the church but by liberating them from the stranglehold of what we have been pleased to fix as 'the threefold ministry'. But this has broken the mystical ring-fence marking off the so-called 'sacred' ministry of the church – from what? The profane ministry? In most cases, alas, from no ministry at all – for the laity (rather than, as it should have been, the world) has primarily been there to be ministered *to*. This line, as I said, is fast disappearing – and with it the sanctity and the security of ordination as different in kind and not only in degree from any other commissioning within the church of God. This is threatening to many clergy and makes them question their distinctive role.

2. Dissolving, too, is the security that has been afforded by holy orders as a profession. Not for nothing has the point of 'arrival' in the whole career-structure of the Anglican church been called a 'living'. In every other job you make a living: in this you have a living, and the security is more or less complete. But quite apart from the parson's freehold, whose actual effect can, I believe, be exaggerated, ordination has meant a job for life. Concealed up the sleeve of the Bishop's hands will be an invisible cheque averaging over the years more than £1,000 a year for life. It may not mean much these days and in fact is palpably inadequate. But ordination has implied a commitment by the church to place a man on its pay-roll for the rest of his days. I believe that it should – and under economic pressure will – imply no such thing. Ordination, as its name indicates, means enrolment in an order, the order of those within the body of Christ authorized to minister the word and sacraments. If I had my way – which fortunately for you I haven't! – you would receive with your licence a letter stating that this act guarantees you, and commits the church to, nothing more. Of course there must be proper security and freedom for those whom the church *does* put on its pay-roll, with clear contracts and terms of employment. And if it doesn't promise a career-structure then it mustn't ordain any men without other qualifications for earning their living, and it must make responsible provision for the retraining and rehousing of those whose paid services it ceases to require. Let it show the way to

industrial firms in this matter. But all this is, and should be, quite independent of its high and solemn commission to a man to do what the ordination service lays upon him and which Cranmer's charge, that you will shortly hear, so magnificently expounds. Nothing of spiritual value or authority is diminished, but one of the most visible supports is going – if that is what we are relying on.

3. Thirdly, and much more intangible, is the magic circle, that spiritual 'ring of confidence', that has been thrown round holy orders since the Middle Ages. Like the 'divinity that doth hedge a king', or the mystical sense of 'degree' on which Shakespeare also dilated, or the metaphysical indissolubility of marriage, the mystique of the indelibility of orders has given marvellous protection to the clerical caste. But it has done this to the detriment of other ministries in the church, and one of the more forthright of recent reports to Church Assembly contained the pungent sentence: 'Many would receive fresh encouragement to be better people in their own spheres if the too-prevalent attitude towards the clergy as the recipients of some semi-magical status could be clearly and forcibly disclaimed, discouraged and discarded.' But like much else in the mediaeval view of life it is in any case rapidly dissolving in the acids of modernity. It is as strange to the contemporary scientific consciousness as it is to the New Testament. Most young people today are unashamedly pragmatic. Writing out of experience of interviewing many for work overseas, John Taylor of the Church Missionary Society has spoken of 'the preference for getting on with the immediate technical job – building a dam, discovering a vaccine, teaching a class – without offering any religious or ideological reasons for doing so'. 'This *ad hoc* response,' he says, 'is the only kind of obedience which rings true to many of the liveliest young Christians today. They will give themselves to meet a need without reserve but also without pretensions. They will serve but without a label. A call makes sense to them but not a vocation. The only response they can make with integrity is in such terms as: "I will go now. . . . How can I tell what the opening will be after that?".' This does not in the least mean, as he insists, that life-long commitment is no longer required. But the forms of that commitment may change freely. We have been too fundamentalist about ordination, as if it fixes a man for life. And this can set up real guilt-complexes. I was recently counselling

an incumbent (not from this diocese) who is trying to decide whether to leave the parish ministry, for the best of reasons. I suspect that in this case he very probably shouldn't; but the whole issue was distorted from the beginning by his wife's response (learnt, as she thought, from the church): 'If you break this vow, how do I know that you won't leave me too?' Without questioning the need, and the desire, for unconditional commitment to ministry for Christ, I believe the church should be as concerned to enable a man to change from, as to change to, this particular ministry – with genuine freedom, spiritual, psychological and economic. At the moment many feel trapped, guilty and unfree.

I have spoken of three securities by which in the past the ordained ministry has been defined and protected – the line between those in the clergy and those not, the line marking off this profession from 'worldly' occupations, and the line which puts it the other side of ordinary job-changes. All these have served a real purpose, and most people in the church would say like St Paul of the Law that they were 'holy, righteous and good'. And they will ask, like the Jews of Jesus, 'What do you mean by saying "You will *become* free men"?'

Yet we dare not *rest* on these securities, any more than on Abrahamic pedigree or circumcision. You are entering the ordained ministry at a time when its future is more in the melting than at any time since the Constantinian settlement. This is something I believe we should welcome. But it means that true freedom, as opposed to indeterminacy or bolshiness, is a desperately valuable commodity. How in this situation are we to *become* free men?

First, we must recognize the need for it. And this for those of us who are in the position of 'Jews who believe' is almost the most difficult thing of all. Indeed, as one sits in gatherings like Convocation listening to debates on any issue that touches clerical freedom one wonders if the need will ever be seen till it is too late.

Secondly, we must really believe that it is *the truth* that sets us free. I don't find, again, that most people in the church act as if they believed this. They appear to fear truth. If you seek to lay bare what is happening to the church or the ministry, you are quickly accused of aiding and abetting despondency. But I believe passionately that only an honest facing of the truth will ever make us free.

But, thirdly, is is not just a facing of common human facts of

which Jesus speaks. Rather, he says, 'If you dwell within the revelation I have brought . . . you shall know the truth, and the truth
will set you free. . . . If then the *Son* sets you free, you will indeed
be free.' Real, deep freedom is the freedom of sons, of men come of
age – in contrast with the relationship either of slaves or of minors.
And we shall know this freedom only if we are prepared to rest our
ministry in no other security than that of our being-in-Christ. This
is what St Paul's battle for justification by faith was about. And this
is what the gospel is always about. And it is to bring ourselves and
others back to *this* that we must be prepared to sit light to any other
foundation – and when other foundations are being shaken not to
worry overmuch or cling to them. Let them go if necessary – even if
they are genuinely precious. For if the Son sets us free, then, like St
Paul, we shall be free to reckon anything else as dung. My hope for
the church is that in all our denominations we shall at this juncture
be ordaining a supply, however small, of truly free men, who rely
on no adventitious supports, hate nothing but evil, fear no one
but God, and have the love of Christ in their hearts. For with them,
as John Wesley said, we *can* change the world.

3. A Ministry from among Men[5]

Every . . . priest is taken from among men and
appointed their representative before God (Heb. 5.1).

If there is a text that expresses the peculiar emphasis of the Southwark Ordination Course it might be this. Every priest is 'taken from
among men'. But our ordination course stresses the fact that the
ordained ministry must *continue* to be rooted in the on-going life
of secular humanity. Priests do not come from God out of the blue –
they come from among their brother men. And they are appointed
'their *representatives* before God'. They are indeed called to be men
of God, but in no way that cuts them off from men. And the
author to the Hebrews goes on to draw out the pastoral necessity

[5] Sermon preached at the annual service in Southwark Cathedral of the
Southwark Ordination Course, 10 December 1967. This is a course which
enables men to train for the ordained ministry of the church without
leaving their secular work, whether they wish subsequently to continue in
it as priest-workers or to serve full-time in a parish.

of retaining this solidarity: the priest 'is able to bear patiently with the ignorant and erring, since he too is beset with weakness'. The priest remains 'one of us', part of the stuff of our common humanity. Yet his entire life is also a response to another dimension. It is not just 'of man, of the will of man'. 'Nobody,' says the writer, 'arrogates the honour to himself; he is called by God.' And it is only in response to this call that he can speak to men of God.

Then our author goes on: 'So it is with Christ.' And he boldly makes the point that Jesus, too, as it were, came up from among his brother men, being perfected in the school of suffering, in response to the claim 'Thou art my Son' that set the seal upon his call to the priestly ministry. Only thus could he be genuinely representative and become the 'source of eternal salvation' to men. Simply as Son of God, coming from 'the other side', he could have said or done nothing for them.

This is a theme that I should like to explore with you tonight. It is, I believe, fundamental to the Christmas gospel and crucial to the understanding of our ministry and message. For so much thinking both about the gospel and about the ministry in practice reverses it. It says in effect that something can only be of God if it does *not* come from among men, and that if it does come *from among men* it is merely *of man*. This is a deeply ingrained assumption, and you will find it operating the more powerfully the closer you get to the core of the church in-group. Yet I believe it is profoundly heretical; and it is not the only way in which the supposedly most orthodox are in fact the most heretical.

It is those who take the highest view of the ministry – as indeed, if we are true to the New Testament, we should – who tend to see the priest or man of God as one who comes to them not from among themselves but from the other side. He is not one of us but belongs to a caste apart. And this applies not only to the sacerdotalist but to the most reformed. It was a German Lutheran I remember making the remark to me that 'our minister is like God: we do not see him during the week and we do not understand him on Sundays'.

For this, note, is *also* men's idea of God, even in Christ. Christ is essentially a heavenly figure who comes to them from the other side to speak the things of God. To suggest that he came *from among men* is to be thought to question the divine initiative. And so we get the interpretation put on the Virgin Birth which sees it as there to safeguard the fact that Jesus is precisely *not* one of us, making his response to God like anyone else out of the solidarities of heredity and environment. But any interpretation of the Virgin Birth stands self-condemned that sets it *against* the genealogies to which the Evangelists append it – quite apart from the fact that it cuts at the very root of the good news by suggesting that Christ was not a normal man. The infancy stories, like the prologue to the fourth Gospel, were told not to question the fact that Jesus was a genuine man 'taken from among men', but to assert *by whom* he was taken, to affirm that his whole life, from conception to the grave and beyond, was of God, lived in response to God, and was not founded simply upon the will of the flesh or of man. If the story of the divine conception (which is where the New Testament writers place the emphasis, rather than on the virgin birth) in fact for you denies his humanity (as it does for so many moderns) rather than draws out the meaning of his humanity (as it did for the men of the first century), then it is much better that you *shouldn't* believe it. For it is there to answer the question 'Who is this man, taken from among men?', not to throw doubt on his complete and utter humanity.

But, since this is Bible Sunday rather than Christmas Day, I should like to draw out how this view of Christ and of the ministry is reflected in our attitude to the message we have to preach. Of the sacrament of the Word the pulpit is the outward and visible sign, and the higher our doctrine of the Word the loftier our pulpits tend to be. I remember going into a Baptist Church in Texas where a brand new million-dollar pile had just been erected apparently to say one thing from the massive minister's dais that dominated all : 'The message comes to you from on high, not merely six feet above contradiction but from another world (in which, of course, its minister lives).' But in our more humble way have we not all, laity and clergy alike, got caught up in a way of thinking that supposes that a real sermon does not start from among men at all but is a message from the other side, if not out of the blue, at any rate direct from the Bible viewed as the Word of God? It is, in fact, almost impossible to state this view, let alone question it, without *appearing* to deny both God and the Bible and to wish to substitute a message that is merely of man. Such is the mess into which we have got. To start from man (as I believe we must) is to seem to deny God, to start from relationships is to deny revelation, to start from immanence to deny transcendence. But we must somehow get out of this box – or we shall either preach a gospel that cannot be 'a source of eternal salvation' because it simply does not begin from where men are or we shall speak a pure humanism that makes nonsense of our appointment as 'representatives before God'. How do we get out of it?

Let me start from a book which I have just read. It is called *Partners in Preaching* by Reuel Howe, Director of the Institute for Advanced Pastoral Studies, near Detroit (that's just American for clergy refresher courses). His theme is that preaching is essentially dialogue not monologue, even though it may be by the mouth of one man. This is a ministry in which the laity are involved as much as the clergy and it has to start from the world as much as from God. It must begin from listening to the man-questions – to which he says frankly 'our present grasp of the God-answer is not adequate'. 'Contemporary meanings,' he writes, 'have for both the preacher and his listeners more importance today than ever before because man's contemporary search for meaning confronts so much new data that has never been properly related to the traditional source of meaning. The preacher, therefore, faces a different kind of congregation from one he would have fifty years ago, but, because of the situation we are discussing, he has one of history's greatest opportunities to preach the gospel. He must learn to look for the values in what people value, and help them to affirm their truth, power and need so that with it they may move into greater truth.'

'He must learn to look for the values in what people value.' Like the prophet Ezekiel he must begin by 'sitting where they sit'. And the values in what people value will not usually be Christian. The theme of this sermon in fact came to me through conversation with a French Communist, Roger Garaudy, whose book *From Anathema to Dialogue* I commend as a starting point for doing theology today. When the humanist Edmund Leach says in the Reith lectures that men have become gods, 'look for the values in what people value' before you jump to condemn. I wonder how many of you read the *Daily Mirror*. If you do you will have seen the brilliant pieces of reporting recently called 'The Cool Four Million' – built up of interviews with young people in this country between sixteen and twenty. The articles on sex, on drugs, and on religion revealed views about as far away as you could get from those of the average churchgoer. Yet there were values in what they valued which I believe take one very far, and are often nearer to the heart of the man-questions than 'our present grasp of the God-answer'. Do not misunderstand me. These things are not the source of the gospel; yet they are the material of the Gospel. We are not called to preach these things; but we are called to preach from them. And that, not in the sense of taking off from them in order to refute them, but like Jesus in the parables, in order to speak of God through them (and some of the parables start from equally doubtful values of men of his day).

More than ever today I believe that we have got to start from man-language. Indeed for vast numbers of people God-language that cannot be translated into man-language is meaningless. But surely the very meaning of Christ is simply that God-language *can* be translated into man-language – in this case without remainder. Equally – in this case without remainder – man-language can be translated into God-language. (What Edmund Leach is saying of man come of age is after all not so far from what Christianity has always said of the full-grown Man – which in the Epistle to the Ephesians is Humanity, not just Jesus.) The truth in the 'death of God' theology is that God-language that cannot be translated into man-language, that remains disincarnate, is dead, that any transcendence that is not also immanent, any 'beyond' that cannot be met 'in the midst', is out. But that is *not* pure humanism. It is incarnationism. Bonhoeffer's question 'How do we speak of God in a worldly fashion?' has already received an answer in Christ's parables (which, unlike the Evangelists' interpretative additions, usually do not speak of 'God' at all), and indeed in Christ himself, whose whole life was a sign and a parable. He is the one in whom God-language is interchangeable with man-language. Indeed, one might venture to replace the classical formula, which spoke of two natures in one person (which today inevitably suggests a hybrid, a bag of flesh with two natures inside it), by speaking of one nature (our nature, the only nature we know) of which one can and must use two languages. Confronted by Christ, we have to say 'This is what we mean by

man', but also 'This is what we mean by God'. Here are two complementary sets of translation, which in this instance coincide. As the
Gospel for Christmas Day puts it, 'What God was the Word was'.
The two ways of stating it are not identical, so that one can be
reduced to the other (God to man or man to God). There is not an
equation, but there is an equivalence.

And in this lies the trust behind all Christian preaching, that
whichever way in we go we shall in Christ arrive at the same place.
The answer to the question 'Where may I find the gracious God?'
and to the question 'Where may I find the gracious neighbour?' is
for a Christian the same. But which way in we start from is, I
believe, coming to matter more than it did. I am not saying that we
cannot move from transcendence to immanence, from the Son of
God to the Son of man (which has been the church's traditional
order) – though I suspect it is a journey fewer and fewer of our
contemporaries can make. What I am saying is that the journey
home by the 'other way' is not just 'of man' – leading to a self-
sufficient humanism – but 'of God'. It is the way trodden for us by
the one who was himself 'taken from among men and appointed
their representative before God'. And it is the way opened up, as
this ordination course seeks to insist, for 'every priest', and indeed
for every member of the priestly people. It is the way of Bethlehem,
the way into worship by the stable door of our common humanity.

4. *Leadership as Letting Be*[6]

I was invited last winter by the London Newman Circle (a Roman
Catholic graduate society) to speak to the title: 'The role of a bishop
in transforming the world.' (I can only think that I was asked because
their own hierarchy was at the time somewhat otherwise preoccupied!) It was a pretentious title. But it was nice at least that anyone
should suppose we had any role in transforming the world – as
opposed to maintaining the church.

As I thought about it, I realized that almost any influence we might
have (we have little power) was not in pushing people around, but
in *letting be*: allowing freedom to others to do *their* work, hinder-

[6] Article for *The Times*, 27 September 1969, to mark the end of my time
as Bishop of Woolwich.

ing hindrances, trying here a little there a little to remove the clogging restrictions and exhausting frustrations of law and money and plant – in other words, simply enabling people to be themselves, to grow and to fruit.

Now bishops and archdeacons and popes are not most notable for letting be. They are more associated with binding than with loosing. Despite the complete reversal of the world's idea of leadership of which Jesus spoke, the church, almost as much as the world, has learnt to live with the notion of leadership as something imposed from the top – authoritarian, paternalistic, however benevolent. Particularly in inner-city areas or housing estates it has been taken for granted that leadership, in ecclesiastical life as in civic, comes from above and is imported from outside – with a consequent ingrained feeling, respectful but resentful, of 'them' over against 'us'.

The world's idea of a leader is of a man who gets things done. Jesus' idea of a leader is of a man who is there above all to serve, to put himself out, to enable others to lead *their* community and to renew it, not from above or outside, but from within. And this fundamentally is what the church exists for – to be an agent for liberating individuals and communities to discover *in themselves* the transforming power of God. And those who chiefly serve the church are those who *allow* it to be that.

In the world the boss is at the top: the office boy is there to serve him. In Christ's order (though not always in the church) the deacon does not exist to serve the bishop. Rather, the bishop is there to serve, to make possible, the work of the deacon. That is why the word used for the Christian ministry as a whole is *diakonia*, deaconing. For this is the real work of the church being the church at the ground level. The 'higher' supposedly one gets in the church's hierarchy, the more one is involved not in this being but with letting be – creating the conditions and allowing the freedom for others to be.

The vicar is more involved in this than the curate, the bishop than the vicar, and the title of the Pope above all is 'the servant of the servants of God'. He exists for the lowest – which was the vision men glimpsed and responded to in John XXIII. And Professor John Macquarrie has argued that for speaking of God himself the most fundamental category – more basic even than that of 'pure being' in which he has traditionally been described – is that of 'letting be'. 'And God said, Let there be . . .'. He is supremely the creator and sustainer of other beings' freedom, the servant of his people. That is why he can most faithfully be revealed in the man for others who took a towel and girded himself.

I would end by applying this to the realm of thought. Bishops are by tradition guardians of orthodoxy, defenders of the faith. But how is this to be done today? By asserting from above what must be believed? I think not – despite the present Pope. The bishop's role rather is to lead in setting men free. And that means allowing them, for a start, really to see that *the church has a greater invest-ment in integrity than in orthodoxy*. Not without reason, men find this hard to believe. But to attempt this very elemental liberation is something for which I believe it has been worth trying to use the modest opportunities that a bishopric still provides in the modern world.

17

Staying In or Getting Out[1]

'Involvement with organized religion is a Christian vocation.' I
quoted that from Peter Berger's book *The Noise of Solemn Assemblies*
in a footnote to *Honest to God* as a 'percipient but dangerous proposition'. But I have not seen it taken up or thought through as I think
it deserves. Meanwhile, for clergy and laity alike, the vocation becomes yearly more problematic. Some are oppressed by it; some have
voted with their feet, and made their quietus; others soldier on for
fear of having to think about it, or simply because they know they
are trapped.

Charles Davis has done us all a service by making it an issue of
courageous theological freedom. Yet his particular solution, of leaving the religious organization without (he would claim) leaving the
church, is not the only one open. To follow it if it is not genuinely
one's own is merely to compound confusion and to bury guilt. Hence
these reflections on what I believe to be an increasingly typical
dilemma – the dilemma of the Christian who believes profoundly
in the church, who knows it is impossible to be a Christian without
what the Acts and Epistles are talking about, and who yet finds it
very difficult to believe in the institutionalized religious organization
as a credible body of its resurrection.

I am not here concerned with those – and they are the great
majority – who believe in both or who believe in neither. Among
the former are the mass of those whom the Roman Catholic hierarchy cosily call 'the faithful', who may have their problems with
the institutional church (to the extent from time to time of lapsing
from it or of switching denominations) but for whom nothing

[1] *New Christian*, 8 February 1968; *The Christian Century*, 22 May 1968.

radically different has seriously entered their reckoning. In the latter camp are the millions for whom the church is no problem because what faith they have is simply not related to it. They include, and are likely increasingly to include, many highly sensitive people. Indeed, I myself find myself responding very strongly to the kind of incognito secular mysticism which Henry P. van Dusen has exposed in his biography of Dag Hammarskjöld. Yet, as he brings out, 'the church holds no place whatever in Hammarskjöld's recognition'; and he adds: 'It is quite possible that had Dag Hammarskjöld maintained even a minimal formal association with conventional ecclesiastical practice, we would never have had *Markings* – and the remarkable faith there declared.'

That poses a problem in its own right. But in this article I want to confine myself to the question presented to those who, like Charles Davis, believe that the church is an essential part of the gospel and who yet find the 'vocation' to 'involvement with organized religion' perplexing often unto despair.

I have cited the recent biography of Dag Hammarskjöld. Three other biographies that have also appeared within the past quarter may serve to clothe with flesh and blood differing responses to this problem with which I believe we have all got to reckon.

1. The first is that of George Bell by Canon Ronald Jasper. A remark of Bishop Bell's *not* quoted in that luminous but cautious life is recounted (and doubtless improved) by John Collins in his autobiography *Faith Under Fire*: 'The Church of England as an organization is not approaching a precipice, it is already over it. But my job as a bishop is to stay in the creaking machine and do what I can to keep it going till it crashes.' Whether or not that conversational retort reflects a balanced judgement, it shows that over twenty years ago Bell recognized a tension which is far more acute today. Yet he knew his vocation was an endlessly painstaking 'yes' to the organization he prophesied within and against.

This is the first and in some ways the most burdensome calling. Yet it is also likely to be that of the numerical majority. Most of those genuinely concerned for the life of the church will go on accepting office, whether as laymen, priests or bishops. For to make the break requires an ability to stand against the stream for which few have the psychological, the spiritual, or indeed the economic resources. (Most of the clergy are trained for nothing else.) But there are also deep-seated reasons for this response, which make it for many the most honourable and least escapist. To leave to wither on the vine so many things – and above all so many people – for which one has by one's baptism or ordination accepted care is a fearful decision. One cannot after all lightly leave to die the church that has been one's mother or wash one's hands of the things she has loved to have about her.

But there is also the theological conviction in this position that the body of resurrection, for the church as for the Christian, is to be built up day by day within the structures of the old. As St Paul recognized (II Cor. 4.16–5.5), we do not want to be found naked. Our desire is for the new body to be put on over the old, by the transformation which is even now at work through the power of the Spirit. Hence we gladly carry the burden of buildings and dilapidations, of church councils and assemblies, of endless commissions and interminable conversations, knowing that 'in the Lord' not even this labour is vain (I Cor. 15.58). That there can be creative affiliation as well as creative disaffiliation to the religious organization hardly perhaps needs to be said. Yet I believe it does need to be said, especially as several other things also need to be said – within the same community and perhaps even within the same person. For it is the complementarity of seemingly opposite vocations that makes the situation so bewildering.

2. If the first answer to be heard is a clear, however reluctant, 'yes', the second is a clear but equally agonizing 'no'. This is the position indicated with great cogency and responsibility in Charles Davis's autobiography already referred to, *A Question of Conscience*. Indeed it is the cogency of his case for 'creative disaffiliation' that set me thinking on this article. For the liberation, if one is able to make the break, is undoubtedly tremendous. It is the freedom, to live *or* to die, which shines through St Paul's other words about death, in Phil. 1.23: 'To depart and be with Christ is far better.' For there is a burden about this body: and the lightness of step of those who have learnt indifference to it is an essential element in the Easter proclamation. In relation to the forms of the instititutional church this has been the classic witness that has constantly found rebirth in fresh springs of the monastic movement, affirming

the provisionality of all structures, of all bodies (without harbouring the illusion that there can ever be no structure, no body). Non-involvement in organized religion is indeed a Christian vocation, perhaps in the same way as absolute pacifism is a Christian voca-tion. While not renouncing the power-political world of ecclesiastical institutionalism as evil, it yet points to another way of living without which the church can scarcely escape going down to judge-ment with the world.

For most of us the choice will not be focused in the black or white terms in which it formulated itself for Charles Davis. It comes, as often as not, in the shape of a decision whether we will take *more* responsibility for the religious organization. Can we face this without losing ourselves in the process? It was the need to 'take possession' of himself by a radical decision that brought Charles Davis to the point of 'rending': 'Had I let things slide, balked the issue and refused to act decisively, with the vague hope that all my difficulties would eventually resolve themselves, I should have destroyed my real self and lapsed by default into a diminished existence.' One shares the heart-searchings of laity and clergy con-fronted by the feeling of having come to the point at which they can *only* be for the church by being against it. We are not many of us the equivalent of absolute pacifists. Yet, as with the Vietnam war, one may reach the point of saying, 'This is so evil', or, with the ecclesiastical set-up, 'This is so irrelevant', that there is nothing to be done but come out. For most of us, most of the time, that point is not reached. Yet for any of us at any time, more insistently now perhaps than ever before, we have to be open to the call of this second vocation.

Yet there are also other possibilities.

3. Besides those who, however qualifiedly, say 'yes' and those who, however regretfully, say 'no', there are those who manage in some degree not to have to say 'yes' or 'no'. This is the position of the layman who avoids ecclesiastical involvement by immersing himself in his secular priorities, of the priest who opts out of the parochial system for teaching, of the bishop who steps sideways into some non-episcopal, though usually still ecclesiastical, post. It is a position that can be chosen, or compelled, for numerous reasons, sometimes sterile and uncreative, but often valid and liberating.

The biography which epitomizes this position is that of Teilhard de Chardin by Robert Speaight. Teilhard, of course, was quite untypical of most in this class, and the reasons which confined him to it were not of his choosing. No one could have had a higher doctrine of the church and its place in the cosmic drama. But direct confrontation with the religious organization was avoided by siphoning off his enormous creativity into palaeontology in China. He is untypical also in that no one now would stand for what the religious organization forced upon his obedience. (The contrast, within the religious orders, in the response of Robert Adolfs, the Dutch Augustinian prior, to attempts to suppress his book *The Grave of God* shows how much water has since passed under the bridge.)

But this position, freely chosen, from whatever motives, is one which more and more people within the church today are seeking. It can be dishonourable, but it can also reflect the conviction that the battle with the organizational church is not the one most worth fighting. To keep this front quiescent, to be able to get on with a valuable job, without provoking the constant tensions and frictions of rubbing up against the 'religious club', seems to many a freedom worth a side-step or even a compromise. And, as a positive witness, this position is testimony to the fact that the gospel is bound up neither with 'circumcision' nor with 'uncircumcision'. One can get over-preoccupied with its relation to either.

Nevertheless, any position which involves saying neither 'yes' nor 'no' is inevitably less creative than one which takes its stand on one or the other. (Teilhard was certainly drained and diminished by it.) It solves nothing. It leaves the problem to others. It may represent a necessary holding operation and be the only available option for many – especially for the many who are not able emotionally or economically to go out and who yet cannot stay in. It can be a real vocation and a valid point of departure for exploring other ways that are not at the moment open. Yet I am convinced that there is, or ought to be, a further alternative.

4. This fourth position is more difficult to define, and indeed to follow. There is, as far as I know, no biography yet that embodies it. It involves saying both 'yes' and 'no'. It means accepting responsibility for the religious organization and yet constantly finding

oneself having to work against it. It means having one foot as firmly outside it as one has the other firmly inside. It is the position, in clerical terms, of the genuine priest-worker, who lives his life *from* the world but also *for* the church; who does not go out, and yet at the same time will not stay in in such a way as simply to be 'of' the religious organization. His very existence is an irritant, and he will constantly be told, organizationally, doctrinally, and in many other ways, 'Why don't you either go out or come in?' Though he may be paid wholly or partly by the world, he refuses to let the church decline responsibility for him or to continue on its way as if he did not exist. His witness is from within – yet as a 'resident alien' (the *paroikos*, seen in I Peter 2.11 as the norm of all Christian existence and subsequently domesticated into the 'parochial' system).

His position, needless to say, is an extraordinarily difficult one to maintain, and, if he is a priest, it depends both on the world being prepared to employ him and the church being prepared to 'wear' him – even to pay him – and to give him responsibility. It can, of course, be adopted as irresponsibly or from as mixed motives as any of the other positions. It could represent nothing more than ecclesiastical jay-walking, with a desire to keep a foot in both camps and get the best of both worlds. Yet I am also persuaded that it could represent an increasingly needed vocation, both among the laity and the clergy, and I am still looking for the episcopal version of it!

Such men will be rooted but not bound (perhaps as close a designation of a radical as one can get). They will be regarded as reliable by neither camp. They will sit loose to the party – in the name of the party. They will press the church for time and money for things that bring no visible return to the religious organization. Yet the church's capacity to transcend itself as the religious organization may depend on its acknowledgement, and indeed its encouragement, of such people. It may also be the condition of its getting kingdom-men rather than church-men, questions-men rather than answers-men, willing to give their lives to it.

I have explored four options – and doubtless there are other variations upon them – open to those confronted in some form or other with the issue I have raised. The health of the church depends, I believe, on its being able to accept that *each* is a valid and complementary vocation. If so the tension will be creative. Otherwise it will be destructive and the church will die through disintegration or blood-letting.

The kind of mutual respect which each ought to have for the other has not been better expressed than by Harvey Cox in his latest book, *On Not Leaving It To The Snake*:

> The forces of renewal in the church would be irresponsible if they were to abandon all hope for the reformation of its present structures. No one can tell whether a given institutional expression of church life can be renewed or not. This often takes a long time to determine. Those who have chosen to work outside existing institutional structures, however, need not feel guilty that they are not spending their lives renewing church institutions. In short, this is a matter of vocation. The church of the future will emerge at the edges of the existing church. It will include many who are within in and many who now are not. It will exhibit certain transfigured structures of today's church as well as completely novel forms of church life which we have not yet even imagined.[2]

He goes on to say that those who have made 'the hard choice' to work within the present structures deserve support and encouragement. 'However, it is important to ask them in love and in concern whether their hope for the renewal of the church can really be realized within their present commitment. Equally, from the other side, those who have made the choice to leave the existing institutional forms of the church 'should be asked occasionally whether their decision to pull out of the church is still a valid one, and whether their zeal for renewal might help influence changes in the larger structure itself'.

Is the church capable of such mutual understanding and forbearance? If so, the percipient but dangerous proposition from which I started would be welcomed in every local and central church body. I can only say that I hope that it would be!

[2] *Op. cit.*, pp. 145f.

18

Not Radical Enough?[1]

This was the title chosen for the Dutch version of *The Honest to God Debate*. It referred back to the closing sentences of the preface to *Honest to God*: 'What I have tried to say, in a tentative and exploratory way, may seem to be radical, and doubtless to many heretical. The one thing of which I am fairly sure is that, in retrospect, it will be seen to have erred in not being nearly radical enough.' How does that prophecy look now at the end of the decade?

Before trying to answer that I would go back before 1963 to the beginning of the decade. Inevitably *Honest to God* was a watershed, but for me it was not a divide. The notion that before that I was a moderately conservative biblical theologian, liturgist and church-man but that after it I was a wild extremist is an absurd assessment. True, as Dr Vidler has since confirmed in his *Twentieth Century Defenders of the Faith*, I was not approached to join his *Soundings* group at Cambridge because I appeared to be too traditionalist. But then I have always maintained that a radical must be a man of tradition, of roots – and of deep ones at that. Without these he is unlikely to have the security required to question to the depths.

I can, I think, claim to have been the source of the term 'radical' in the current theological debate. And if there has to be a name I prefer that to 'the new theology' popularized by the press in England. But in America 'radical theology' has now become so associated with the 'death of God' school that it is even a matter of debate whether I should be included in it at all.[2] It will perhaps therefore be useful to define how I was using what David Jenkins has since called 'the cant term "radical"'.[3]

[1] For *The Christian Century* series 'How My Mind Has Changed'. Reprinted by permission from the issue of 12 November 1969.
[2] The best survey I know is *Radical Christianity: The New Theologies in Perspective*, by Lonnie D. Kliever and John H. Hayes.
[3] 'Taking Jesus Seriously Today', *New Christian*, 24 July 1969.

It gained its currency from David Edwards's introductory essay to *The Honest to God Debate*, where he quoted at some length from a broadcast I had given, 'On Being a Radical'.[4] In it I sought to distinguish between three attitudes or responses, those of the reformist, the radical and the revolutionary. The reformist holds to the tradition but seeks to update it; the revolutionary, regarding the tradition as irreformable, places himself outside it; the radical goes to the root of his tradition and asks fundamentally what it is for.

Clearly, then, for me the radical stance was not intended to be extreme or iconoclastic. Indeed, I have said that 'fundamentalist' and 'radical' are two metaphors for the same thing. Both are concerned to go to the essentials. The difference is that the fundamentalist sees these, in inorganic terms, as foundations, the radical, in organic terms, as roots. And digging around foundations and digging around roots can have very different consequences. Disturb the former and the whole building may collapse. That is why the security of the fundamentalist is notoriously brittle. He dare not question too much, or everything may slip. The courage of the radical has a much more supple strength.

As I look to my roots I am grateful too for my Anglican heritage. The Anglican has never put his trust in an infallible man or an infallible book. His conception of authority is not single-stranded but the three-fold cord, not easily broken, of scripture and tradition and reason.[5] And because I am so steeped in the Anglican ethos I am by nature a man of continuities rather than discontinuities, of evolution rather than revolution, of both-and rather than either-or.

This has affected how my mind has changed. There have not been sudden breaks. There is practically nothing that I would wish violently to disavow. Thus, when recently I came to re-read, for a new edition, the first book I ever wrote, *In the End God*, I found that in one sense I could say it all still. In another, the whole scene had shifted, and I could never say it like that today. But it was more the questions that had altered in the interval than the answers.

In the same way, I am one who believes that the truth is more

[4] Chapter 1 above.
[5] For a beautifully succinct statement of this see A. R. Vidler's note to J. N. Sanders's essay in *Soundings*, pp. 142–5.

likely to lie in a tension than a choice of opposites. This has helped me in my pastoral work, combining being a bishop and a radical theologian. For, without dishonesty, I find I can be bilingual. I can talk the old language and the new, and I think I know how both language-groups feel. I have not been associated with one school of theological or ecclesiastical thought, but with seeking to hold together the complementary insights of each. I have said that probably the most original thing about *Honest to God* was its bringing together, without denying the very real differences, of Tillich and Bonhoeffer and Bultmann, who are now spoken of in one breath but before were not. Equally, in *Exploration into God*, which I regard as my most mature book to date, it is the combination of the two strongest but seemingly divergent streams of modern theology, the secular and the mystical, which I should like to think might prove its distinctive contribution.

Yet, having said all this, and underlined the continuities, I should wish also to stress the movement, the metabolism without which any organic structure dies. (Incidentally I have never regarded structure as the enemy of freedom – as long as it remains organic and is not, as so often in the church, inorganic.) I am essentially a man of movement, of exploration. I am usually thinking of my next book before I have finished the last, and their subjects have been closely related to the growing edges of Christian theology over the past twenty years – eschatology, biblical theology, the doctrine of the church, the liturgical movement, the God-debate, socialization and secularization. I am seldom happy except on a frontier; and I have a sense of constantly pushing out, or rather being pushed – drawn from ahead, yet held from behind, by a power that will not let me go. The centre remains the same but the edges and the ends are open and expanding. This gives one the courage to go on not knowing where one is going, and to find doubt extending rather than bewildering. This, as Tillich insisted, is an essential meaning today of justification by faith – to know oneself accepted *simul justus et dubitator*. And my deepest wish for the church is that it should be an *affirming structure* of that trust. That the Church of England has been that for me over the past decade I can only gratefully acknowledge. I do not think I should have been so free in any other organization, ecclesiastical or secular. That is why, despite all its failings, I believe in it and refuse to leave it, for my own sake as well as others'.

But now let me look at the question of my title in relation to some of my basic areas of concern over the past ten years.

1. *God.* There are certainly many here who would say that *Honest to God* has not proved radical enough. Indeed, it was hardly out before Paul van Buren's *Secular Meaning of the Gospel* had independently gone a good deal further, and that has since been followed by Hamilton and Altizer and 'the death of God'. As in race relations, the moderate scarcely satisfies anybody; and I have been accused either of failing to follow to the end the logic of my honesty or of selling out to humanism and secularism. I would dispute both of these conclusions. I regret the polarization that has taken place in American theology (as in race relations) and which temporarily at any rate has squeezed out the 'white liberal' and made 'reconciler' a dirty word. The trouble with the 'death of God' theologians is not that they went too far (as I suppose most people in England would think) but that they were pushed (and almost gleefully allowed themselves to be pushed) into a position of isolation by the conservatives, liberal as well as fundamentalist. The result has been, as I feared, that the genuine questions they were raising seem to have fizzled out, rather than been fed into the wider debate. Whereas two years ago I should have said that the USA was unquestionably the growth-point of new theology, today I am not so certain. But neither can I point to any other – despite the signs of come-back from Germany (where they can still write as though the German-speaking world were the circumference of the theological circle: witness the footnotes in Gollwitzer, Moltmann and Pannenberg!).

I tried to sketch what I saw to be the next frontiers for theology and the church in a lecture at Princeton printed in *Theology Today* for July 1968.[6] I will not repeat what I said there except to say, very summarily, that 'speaking of God in a worldly fashion' has increasingly, I believe, to be complemented (*not* replaced) from the other end by speaking of the world in a godly fashion – locating the dimension of transcendence 'from below'. (For an exercise in this I recommend Peter Berger's latest book, A *Rumour*

[6] Chapter 12 above.

of *Angels*.) For the casing has disintegrated, which has enabled us to think of theology as primarily about *a* Being (God) who *has* a world. Rather, it is about the whole of Being, which must be explored simultaneously from the end of God-language and from that of man-language, in the confidence, grounded for the Christian in the person of Christ, that from whichever end one starts both sets of language must ultimately coincide (without either being reduced to the other). This is an enterprise that can engage the co-operation alike of theologians, whether they believe the word 'God' to be dead or alive, and of 'transhumanists' like Roger Garaudy or Julian Huxley.

2. *Christ*. This brings us to the area of Christology, which I predict will be the next focus of debate. From the time of my first response in *The Honest to God Debate* I said that this was what I wished to pursue next. But hitherto the size of the subject has forced me to give preference to other themes. However, the object of my return to Cambridge is in the first instance to allow myself time for the Hulsean Lectures of 1970. These I propose to devote to Christology, and I will not anticipate them here. Enough to say, that almost all the basic affirmations that Christians have wanted to make about Christ raise today quite radical questionings. How, for instance, do we now speak of his humanity, his divinity, his historicity, his sinlessness, his uniqueness, his finality, his 'full, perfect and sufficient sacrifice, oblation and satisfaction for the sins of the whole world'? And so one could go on. The heart of the matter, as I see it, is not how is one now to say different things about Christ, but how, supposing one wants to (and here too the ends must be genuinely open), does one say today the same things of him that the church has always intended. The reformulations will, I suspect, have to be much more radical than most church people imagine or are prepared for.

3. *The Church and the Kingdom*. I have bracketed these because I become increasingly convinced of their inseparability. One of the virtues of Fr Richard McBrien's book *The Church in the Thought of Bishop John Robinson* (which I commend as the best attempt to see my theology whole) was that he recognized the centrality of a formula which for me goes a long way back: 'Have as high a doctrine of the Ministry as you like, as long as your doctrine of

the Church is higher; and have as high a doctrine of the Church as you like, as long as your doctrine of the Kingdom is higher.' It has been a seriously distorting factor in Christian theology that the church has been seen as the centre of God's action, rather than the Kingdom. This is challenged in McBrien's subsequent book *Do we need the Church?*, in which he pleads for a Copernican revolution in this regard *and* for an Einsteinian one (refusing absoluteness to any ecclesial position) at the same time. Earlier he had noted a certain 'attrition' in my doctrine of the church over the past ten years. But it is nothing to the (very creative) 'attrition' that has occurred in his own thinking over the past three!

All of us today, I suspect, are less interested in the church *for its own sake*. Jürgen Schultz, the German lay-theologian, has even raised again the dead and almost heretical question 'Did Jesus really want the church?'[7] ' "*Ecclesiam habemus!*" he writes. Forty years ago Otto Dibelius ushered in the "century of the church" with this exclamation. But just as the thousand years of the Third Reich passed quite quickly, so "the violet century" (Karl Barth) lasted only a few decades. Now we speak more hesitatingly, more brokenly of the church.'

And we raise more existentially the question of 'Staying in or Getting out'. In my article of that title,[8] I suggested, again, that this was not a simple matter of either-or, but of trying to hold together in mutual tension and respect at least four main positions (of saying 'yes' to the religious organization, of saying 'no', of saying neither 'yes' nor 'no', and of saying both 'yes' and 'no'). For myself, without leaving the church, I find I wish increasingly to witness in the name of the church (and that by remaining actively a bishop, as I shall do) to the subordination of the church to God-in-the-world and to the-world-in-God, which is what the New Testament means by the Kingdom. In what ways the church has to die to the body in which it now lives (whether as a social institution, a religious organization, or even as a gathered fellowship) becomes less obsessing in the light of its complete disposability

---

[7] 'Hat Jesus die Kirche eigentlich gewollt?', in the *Festschrift* for *Heinz Flügel zum 60. Geburtstag.*

[8] Chapter 17 above.

for the kingdom of God. Certainly I would now freely speak of the death and resurrection of the church, rather than simply of its reformation and renewal, in a way that I regarded as irresponsible when I first became a bishop in 1959.

4. *Prayer and Liturgy.* If it was the chapter on Christology in *Honest to God* that on the whole fared best with the theological reviewers, it was the chapter on prayer that attracted most gratitude in the letters. It clearly brought a lot of release. 'The platoon of bantam booklets' to which George Macleod referred as the 'bankrupt corner' on most ministers' shelves now looks dustier still. Liturgy too has begun to burst the old wine-skins, in a way that makes the avant-garde of the fifties (reflected in my *Liturgy Coming to Life*) look very dated. The container is cracking, here and elsewhere, that made prayer and liturgy 'worlds' of their own. And this is thoroughly healthy. For 'the spiritual life' is not for the New Testament a department of life, but *the* new life in the Spirit. And the material of liturgy *is* life. Indeed, my starting point for a definition of liturgy today would be 'living it up' – living life up to the level of its true, divine, 'eternal' potential. This is what, in Christ, Christians are called to celebrate or, in a suggestive paraphrase from the Kirkridge retreat-centre, to 'make unforgettable'.

For how my mind has moved at this point I would refer, for lack of space here, to two recent pieces I have written. The first is the chapter in *Exploration into God*, 'The Journey Inwards', in which I plead for a *secular mysticism*, with both apparently contrary words given full force. The second, 'Let the Liturgy be Free!' (a title which I hope speaks for itself), is one of a forthcoming collection of essays[9] (parallel to *On Being the Church in the World* a decade ago) which I am calling *Christian Freedom in a Permissive Society*. And mention of this title introduces the final area of concern.

5. *Morals and Politics.* Here I believe that it is the climate of opinion which has changed more than my mind. I never imagined in any case I was saying anything new in my chapter on 'The New Morality' and much of the material in that and my subsequent *Christian Morals Today* I had earlier given in lectures at Cambridge without a flicker of controversy. However, the shake-

[9] Chapter 15 above.

up occasioned by the 'situation ethics' debate has been valuable, and many thought-barriers have been breached in the last few years, both in personal attitudes and in social legislation. Sydney Barr's recent study *The Christian New Morality* supplies an encouraging vindication from the New Testament point of view, and, more surprisingly, liberal Roman Catholic thought seems to have veered round almost completely. Above all, the hysteria of public opinion, which threatened the picketing of Liverpool cathedral for my lectures on Christian Morals, has well-nigh entirely abated. Having experienced the barrage that greeted my appearance for the defence of *Lady Chatterley's Lover* I can testify that the climate is almost unrecognizably different. After a recent article[10] in favour of the Report of the Arts Council of Great Britain recommending the repeal of all our obscenity laws the net bag was *one* letter – and that of appreciation from a senior Cabinet Minister!

But I am under no illusion that the permissive society is itself more Christian – nor have I any confidence that the church will not join the backlash against it. Defining – and refusing to retreat from – genuine Christian freedom in this situation seems to me a vital frontier for the gospel today.

I am increasingly convinced that in politics as in morals, the real danger comes from the right (and that includes the post-Stalinist establishment as well as Governor Reagan and Enoch Powell). In the course of ten years I have certainly become more radical politically. Indeed, it is on this front that I have most sympathy for the view that in many parts of the world, including the United States, only a revolutionary and not a radical solution is going to be adequate. In confirmation of my own American experience, I would cite, with permission, a recent letter from William Sloane Coffin, Jr.:

I am afraid we are gradually moving towards that situation where citizens will have to choose between options no citizens should have to confront – namely, between change forced by violence and the repression of violence forced by no change. To me this means that the marching order for the church should read: twice as non-violent, and twice as militant.

[10] An earlier and shorter version of 'Obscenity and Maturity' (chapter 4 above) in *New Christian*, 24 July 1969.

I am not optimistic. On almost all the fronts that matter – population, poverty, race, and war – we seem to be losing rather than gaining ground. *Nothing* that is politically possible looks likely to be radical enough. Yet I would end with the closing words of the same writer's notable interview for *Playboy* in August 1968 – itself a symbol of the communications breakthrough in theology over the past ten years:

I am not optimistic, but I *am* hopeful. . . . Realism demands pessimism. But hope demands that we take a dim view of the present because we hold a bright view of the future; and hope arouses, as nothing else can arouse, *a passion for the possible.*

In that last phrase I recognize the twin concerns for persons and for Christian eschatology, focused in the Man to whom all things have been subjected, which in this decade, as before, have marked the centre of my thought and engagement.

19

Farewell to the Sixties[1]

Just ten years ago I moved from academic life to become **Bishop of Woolwich** and now I move back – not to cease to be a bishop (for I shall remain an Assistant Bishop of Southwark) but to do my theology once more within a secular rather than an ecclesiastical framework.

The period has coincided with the sixties, a decade like the 1860s, of religious ferment and transition. By contrast, the 1950s seem in retrospect a temporary plateau of relative self-confidence. After the shaking of the foundations in the forties it was a time of reconstruction and renewal. At the end of his primacy, Dr Fisher could report that the Church of England was 'in good heart'. The assumption was still credible that by Tory reformist measures organized religion could be refurbished for a flourishing and relevant future. By 1960 *The Church of England Newspaper* was able to announce (and I remember the words because I quoted them in hope): 'A new Church of England is being born, a Church efficient, sophisticated and progressive, a Church with money enough to spare.' Indeed, I find that my first Confirmation sermon in 1959 contained the peroration: 'You are coming into active membership of the church at a time when great things are afoot. I believe that in England we may be at a turning of the tide. Indeed, in Cambridge, where I have recently come from, I am convinced that the tide has already turned.'

[1] *The Observer*, 28 September 1969. This article, written to say goodbye to the decade during which I was a Bishop of Woolwich, may serve as a summary of many of the themes of this book.

How wrong can one be? The tide was indeed imperceptibly on the turn. But 1960 was to represent the high-water mark not the low! From then on the vital statistics of organized religion in this country (and not only in this country) began to reveal a dramatic decline from which they show no signs yet of recovery.

Very summarily, the infant Baptism rate has dropped in ten years by 15 per cent (but by twice that in the London area). The Confirmation rate, after remaining surprisingly stable since the end of the first war, has fallen by nearly one-third in six years (over three times the national rate of decline for baptism) and in the Southwark diocese the actual figures have almost halved in the past seven. Ordinations, after recovering steadily since the last war, have plummeted by a quarter in the past five years and, more ominously for the future, those definitely recommended for training by nearly 60 per cent – virtually eight times the rate of baptismal decline.

I stress these figures not to be depressing or defeatist but as symptoms of a process which I believe to be of much wider significance, and on the whole exhilarating. Indeed, the only surprise is that the break has not come earlier. For the statistics are for a pattern of membership and ministry adapted to maintaining the church as a religious organization with an established place (whether or not legally entrenched) within a paternalistic society. In such a society participation can effectively be enjoyed only on somebody's say so, by joining or accepting accreditation from an institution that officially defines what is 'in' and what is 'out'.

The sixties have proved a climacteric in the transition from the paternalistic to the permissive society. This latter is chiefly to be recognized not (as the unhappy name suggests) by its superficial symptoms of licence but by the cracking of the containers within which power, influence and leadership in the community has hitherto been exercised. The various establishments which have been the arbiters of orthodoxy, discipline, and often of employment, in their particular spheres, are under attack. The church has functioned as one of these, and the influence of Christianity has been geared to its success as such. Hence the figures I have cited are interpreted as unmitigated failure, and those from within who draw attention to them are regarded as agents of alarm and despondency.

So let me make my point from three success stories of the past decade, which at least indicate what people respond to as opposed to what they don't. For it so happens that I have been associated in one way or another with three best-sellers.

The first in point of time was *Lady Chatterley's Lover*, for which I gave evidence at the Old Bailey, where, thanks to the Director of Public Prosecution's prodigious misjudgement, it received maximum publicity. I have no regrets whatever for my part in this crucial test case, and it was a body blow for what the recent Report of the Arts Council called 'Big Brother wigged and gowned on the judicial bench'. How long the anachronism of literary censorship will survive the exit of the Lord Chamberlain remains to be seen. But the Establishment has been visibly shaken and I believe freedom here as elsewhere to be worth its inevitable abuse and casualties.

Secondly, and very differently, there was *The New English Bible*, of which I was one of the translators. The effect of this and other new versions has been to loosen a stranglehold of 350 years. For until very recently, 'the Bible' for the Englishman meant one thing, significantly called 'the Authorized Version' – though in fact it has never been authorized. Similarly, the 1662 Book of Common Prayer, enforced by the Act of Uniformity, has almost literally disintegrated over the past few years in a plethora of experimental services. The established religion, summed up by the Catechism in the Creed, the Lord's Prayer (even that has been altered) and the Ten Commandments, has broken up or broken out – according to which way you look at it. It is now available loose rather than packaged.

Thirdly, there was my own little contribution in *Honest to God*. Its offence was to break open received dogmas and to by-pass the pulpit, the accepted platform of interpretation. Its quite unexpected reception lay in the fact that it evidently articulated a good deal of hidden questioning. For good or for ill, theology 'got out'. It has been more of an open and more of a secular subject ever since. I personally rejoice in this, though I recognize the loss of definition and old-style authority.

In all these ways the casing has been eroded. That is why I have written, hopefully, of 'the exploding church'. My fear is that under pressure it may prove to be the 'seizing-up church'. For then what does get out, whether of truth or of ministry (and the latter seepage is increasing), will have more of the qualities of spilt milk than of released energy.

What of the seventies? My hope is that the disintegration of the sixties will be seen positively. I believe the religious institution is dying – and that applies just as much to institutional ecumenism, which tries to reinforce the container by new alloys. But the institution is not all. Medicine does not die if the grip of the British Medical Association is weakened. In fact, if the BMA (and even more the American Medical Association) were related to medicine in as relaxed a way as the British Association is related to science, things would be healthier.

The pervasive influence of Christianity is not promised to the strength of a self-contained ecclesiastical organization, but to leaven and salt mixed and dissolved in the lump of the world's life. Movements and groupings there must be, clusters of action and sanctity and thinking, and these must be structured if they are to penetrate effectively. But basically the attractive power of love and hope, integrity and justice – and these are the signs of the Kingdom at work – do not depend on institutional orthodoxies and establishments. Ours is an age in which these things have ceased to carry their own authentication. But if the resources of man-power and money, sacrifice and devotion, locked in the various religious containers can be released to combine with the drives of secular yearnings at their best I see no reason for pessimism or for the diminishment of genuine faith.